INTERNATIONAL TAX

Bringing a unique voice to international taxation, this book argues against the conventional support of multilateral cooperation in favor of structured competition as a way to promote both justice and efficiency in international tax policy. Tsilly Dagan analyzes international taxation as a decentralized market, where governments have increasingly become strategic actors. Dagan argues that although many of the challenges of the current international tax regime derive from this decentralized competitive structure, curtailing competition through centralization is not necessarily the answer. Conversely, competition – if properly calibrated and notwithstanding its dubious reputation – is conducive, rather than detrimental, to both efficiency and global justice. *International Tax Policy* begins with the basic normative goals of income taxation, explaining how competition transforms them and analyzing the strategic game states play on the bilateral and multilateral levels. It then considers the costs and benefits of cooperation and competition in terms of efficiency and justice.

TSILLY DAGAN is Professor of Law at Bar-Ilan University, Israel. She is a leading tax theorist who has published extensively on a broad range of tax-related issues and distinctively combines tools from game theory and political philosophy to challenge the field's conventional wisdoms.

CAMBRIDGE TAX LAW SERIES

Tax law is a growing area of interest, as it is included as a subdivision in many areas of study and is a key consideration in business needs throughout the world. Books in this series will expose the theoretical underpinning behind the law to shed light on the taxation systems, so that the questions to be asked when addressing an issue become clear. These academic books, written by leading scholars, will be a central port of call for information on tax law. The content will be illustrated by case law and legislation. The books will be of interest for those studying law, business, economics, accounting, and finance courses.

Series Editor
Dr Peter Harris, Law Faculty, University of Cambridge,
Director of the Centre for Tax Law.

Dr Harris brings a wealth of experience to the series. He has taught and presented tax courses at a dozen different universities in nearly as many countries and has acted as an external tax consultant for the International Monetary Fund for more than a decade.

INTERNATIONAL TAX POLICY

Between Competition and Cooperation

TSILLY DAGAN

Bar-Ilan University, Israel

CAMBRIDGE
UNIVERSITY PRESS

CAMBRIDGE
UNIVERSITY PRESS

University Printing House, Cambridge CB2 8BS, United Kingdom

One Liberty Plaza, 20th Floor, New York, NY 10006, USA

477 Williamstown Road, Port Melbourne, VIC 3207, Australia

314-321, 3rd Floor, Plot 3, Splendor Forum, Jasola District Centre, New Delhi - 110025, India

79 Anson Road, #06-04/06, Singapore 079906

Cambridge University Press is part of the University of Cambridge.

It furthers the University's mission by disseminating knowledge in the pursuit of education, learning and research at the highest international levels of excellence.

www.cambridge.org
Information on this title: www.cambridge.org/9781107531031
DOI: 10.1017/9781316282496

First published 2018
First paperback edition 2018

A catalogue record for this publication is available from the British Library

ISBN 978-1-107-11210-0 Hardback
ISBN 978-1-107-53103-1 Paperback

In Memory of my Mother

CONTENTS

Acknowledgments   *page* ix

Introduction   1

1   Dilemmas of Tax Policy in a Globalized Economy   12
   1.1   Income Tax Policy in a Closed Economy   15
   1.2   Tax Competition   23
   1.3   How Tax Competition Reshapes National Tax Policy   31

2   Global Planners and Strategic Players   43
   2.1   The League of Nations Solution: Allocating Rights   44
   2.2   Solutions at the National Level: Attempted Neutrality   50
   2.3   Taxing Strategically   60

3   The Tax Treaties Myth   72
   3.1   The Conventional Story   73
   3.2   The Interaction between National Policies   80
   3.3   The Reality of Tax Treaties   98
   3.4   Winners and Losers   110
   3.5   Conclusion   118

4   Costs of Multilateral Cooperation   120
   4.1   The Costs of Tax Competition   121
   4.2   The Problems with Coordination   130
   4.3   Conclusion   139

5   Cooperation and Its Discontents   142
   5.1   A Brief History of International Tax Cooperation   146
   5.2   Why (Some) Actors Cooperate Against Their Better Interests   166
   5.3   Game-Makers and Game-Changers   180
   5.4   Conclusion   183

6   International Tax and Global Justice   185

    6.1   The Global Justice Debate in Political Philosophy   189

    6.2   The Lost State   193

    6.3   Where Are We Headed?   203

7   Perfecting the International Tax Market   213

    7.1   Market Failures   216

    7.2   Distributive Justice   221

    7.3   Undermining the Political Sphere   222

    7.4   A Possible Road Ahead?   223

    7.5   Two Possible Objections   225

    7.6   Perfecting Tax Competition   229

    7.7   Conclusion   244

Index   246

ACKNOWLEDGMENTS

This book has benefited from generous comments and discussions with numerous friends and colleagues who have read all or parts of it: Sivan Agon-Shlomo, Reuven Avi-Yonah, Eduardo Baistrocchi, Philip Baker, Yitzhak Benbaji, Jean-Pierre Benoit, Eyal Benvenisti, Pamela Bookman, Yariv Brauner, Kim Brooks, Allison Christians, Steven Dean, Ana Paula Dourado, Adi Ayal, Ron Davies, Yuval Feldman, Talia Fisher, David Gilo, Ofer Grosskopf, Assaf Hamdani, Werner Haslehner, Martin Hearson, Michael Heller, Mindy Herzfeld, Peter Hongler, Roy Kreitner, Tamar Kricheli-Katz, Adi Libson, Assaf Likhovski, Doreen Lustig, Tali Margalit, Yoram Margalioth, Ruth Mason, Ajay Mehrotra, Irma Mosquera, Jacob Nussim, Lisa Philipps, Pasquale Pistone, Katharina Pistor, Gabriel Rauterberg, Tali Regev, Diane Ring, Adam Rosenzweig, Ian Roxan, Steve Shay, Miranda Stewart, Max Stearns, Linda Sugin, Edoardo Traversa, as well as anonymous referees of Cambridge University Press and the Israeli Science Foundation. It also benefit from the discussions in a number of conferences: a Cornell–Tel Aviv conference on "Law, Economy and Inequality," a Brooklyn Law School symposium on "Reconsidering the Tax Treaty," a Humboldt University workshop on "Community Obligations in Contemporary International Law," a University of Lisbon workshop on "Tax and Development," a McGill University workshop on "Tracking Our Fiscal Footprint: Assessing the Impact of Conventional International Tax Standards on Low-Income Countries," an Institute of Advanced Studies, Jerusalem conference on "Sovereignty, Global Justice, and International Institutions," and an IBFD seminar on "The Brics and the Emergence of International Tax Coordination," and workshops at Bar-Ilan, Brooklyn, Fordham, European University Institute, IBFD, IDC, London School of Economics, Tel-Aviv, University of Connecticut, University of Florida, University of Lisbon, University of Maryland, University of Tokyo, and Vienna University of Economics and Business Administration. I am also grateful to Gal Ben Haim, Gaya Harari Heit, Dvir Hollender, Reut Israelshvili, Sapir Lancri and Rotem Spiegler for research assistance, to Dana Meshulam for exceptional editorial assistance, and to the Israel Science Foundation Book Grant for their generous support. Chapters 3 and 6 are revised and updated adaptations of essays that have appeared previously: The Tax Treaties Myth, 32 *NYU Journal of International Law and Politics* 939 (2000) and International Tax and Global Justice, 18 *Theoretical Inquiries in Law* 1 (2017).

~

Introduction

Rising inequality, within as well as between states, demands effective institutional solutions. Income taxation has traditionally been the textbook
policy tool for ameliorating such inequality. States' ability to promote their
normative goals through their tax systems has been seriously challenged,
however, by the decentralized structure of international taxation, which
has set states in competition for capital, residents, and tax revenues. Due
to this competition, states operating unilaterally are increasingly unable to
sustain their tax bases and fully pursue their normative goals, that is, to
collect sufficient taxes to finance their public goods in an efficient and just
way. This has presented policymakers and scholars of international tax
policy with a weighty task: to design international tax policies that will
support – to the greatest extent possible – the goals of justice and efficiency. In seeking such policies, much of the effort has been directed at
the supranational level, pursuing cooperative mechanisms that can regulate states' tax competition. A global regime that limits tax competition,
it has been asserted, would be praiseworthy from the perspectives of both
efficiency and justice. This book challenges this view. It makes the case for
more competition – or, rather, more efficient competition – which could,
I will claim, do a better job in promoting just and efficient international
taxation.

The driving argument made in this book is that international taxation
should be analyzed as a decentralized competitive market, whereby governments have increasingly become strategic players maximizing their
national interests. While many of the challenges of the current international tax regime derive from this decentralized competitive structure, curtailing competition through centralization is *not* necessarily the
answer, as I will show. As opposed to supporters of multilateral cooperation toward more centralization, the solutions I endorse here support
competition as a vehicle for promoting the normative goals of international taxation. Thus, rather than strive for a more comprehensive multilateral regime that curtails tax competition, I argue, a multilateral accord

should seek to improve – indeed, perfect – competition. Competition, if properly calibrated and notwithstanding its dubious reputation, is conducive, rather than detrimental, to global welfare as well as global justice.

International tax policy is making headlines these days. What started out as a mind-numbing highly technical area of public policy, appealing to only a select few, has become a topic that attracts the attention of not only the media but also political leaders, the business community, and public interest groups. The public has been riveted by revelations of bank account leaks from notorious tax havens and deals with informants; people follow closely such developments as EU institutional pressure on Ireland to collect high enough taxes from Multi-National Enterprises (MNEs) and agreements between countries to disclose information on taxpayers. Unilateral legislation abounds, bilateral treaties are now standard in all countries, and multilateral negotiations and accords are at a peak. The reason is clear: countries' tax policies are being severely challenged by international tax competition, tax planning, and tax avoidance. Countries are gradually losing their capacity to redistribute income and sustain their welfare systems, with greater proportions of the public funding falling on labor's shoulders. This has turned international taxation into a significant dimension of domestic income tax policy and, therefore, a political issue with serious ramifications not only for capital owners and multinational enterprises but for all of us.

At the same time, the international context is changing the way in which we generally think about income taxation. The traditional perspective envisions a state ruled by a sovereign that is entrusted with exclusive tax legislative powers, seeking (at least ideally) to maximize welfare (efficiency) and justly (re)distribute it, while reinforcing the underlying normative values shared by its constituents. From the current globalized perspective, however, the powerful sovereign is only one of approximately 200 sovereigns competing with one another for investments, residents, and tax revenues. Taxation is the currency of this competition, with states luring investments as well as residents to their jurisdiction with attractive taxing and spending "deals." Hence, in conditions of tax competition, tax policies almost inevitably become marketized, as countries attempt to tailor their taxation and benefits packages to the needs and requirements of their most valuable current and potential investors and residents. Mobile capital enjoys lower tax rates; foreign investors benefit from attractive exemptions; and sought-after MNEs enjoy favorable tax regimes (e.g., favorable regimes for R&D). As a result of this marketization, redistribution is increasingly falling by the wayside. State welfare systems are struggling to survive, while the wealth disparities within and between states grow wider. The challenges of income taxation in this globalized competitive setting are substantial, almost overwhelming, leading many to lament the demise of the welfare state and sending policymakers as well as scholars in search of a viable solution for sustaining the efficiency and justice goals of income taxation.

At its base, international taxation is decentralized: there is no central government that sets the rules and tax rates or allocates rights to tax. Despite the considerable recent efforts of cooperation, and notwithstanding views that a customary international law of taxation has emerged and that its rules limit states' choices, every country is still independently making its own tax policy and setting its own rules and tax rates. These national policies interact to create the international tax regime. The decentralized nature of international taxation has led to several inconsistencies between systems, producing barriers to cross-border economic activities as well as opportunities for tax avoidance. Decentralization makes the international tax regime not only market-competitive but also highly fragmentized. Sophisticated taxpayers are able to pick and choose among the components of the various tax systems using tax-planning instruments and thereby free-ride states' public goods and services. The fragmentation and marketization of international tax in these conditions of competition have eroded the ability of states both to collect taxes to finance their public fisc and to redistribute wealth. This, in turn, has seriously undermined the legitimacy of states' use of their coercive power to tax.

The starting point of the analysis in this book is the marketized and fragmentized structure of international taxation. Seeking to arrive at a nuanced understanding of how this regime operates, it frames international tax in market competition terms: understanding states as providing goods and services to their constituents and investors for a price – i.e., the taxes they pay. At the heart of the analysis, therefore, is the state, which is conceived of as a rational actor that interacts with peer state-actors as well as with its constituents and other taxpayers. The picture of international taxation drawn by this analysis is of a complex market where states strategize, cut deals, cooperate, or defect, all toward the goal of maximizing their national interests. But taxes, of course, are not ordinary prices, and state-supplied goods and services are not ordinary commodities. Nor is the interaction among states or with their constituents ordinary market relations. The roles, goals, and measures of success are (or at least should be) quite different. Thus, this book does not stop with the market analysis, but goes one step further, critically examining and normatively evaluating the results of this market interaction and emphasizing not only efficiency but also distributive justice and political participation.

The book uses the market analogy as well as game theory to understand the operation of the international tax regime as a strategic, competitive game played by market actors with market-like motivations and market strategies. In the tax market, countries design (or, if operating rationally, need to design) their international tax rules to best serve their national interests, while their choices interact and compete with the choices made by other countries. This strategic-market view of international tax sets the book's methodological framework. First, I explain how states could tax strategically on the *unilateral* level, anticipating or reacting to other states' strategies, to best advance their national interests. Second, I apply game theoretical analysis to consider whether explicit *bilateral* cooperation under tax treaties could prove superior to unilateral strategies. Third, I look at the *multilateral* level, comparing competitive and cooperative strategies, and using network theory to hypothesize about the costs and benefits of various multilateral cooperative accords. This market-based analysis exposes the interests – and the power struggles – that underlie the current regime and offers important insight on how to design future multilateral initiatives.

From a normative perspective, the book takes a critical look at the outcomes of the international tax regime in terms of distributive justice, efficiency, and political participation, arguing for more competition (or more efficient competition) as a better way than cooperation to advance a just and efficient international tax regime. In so doing, the book considers what goals international taxation *should* pursue, examines what it can pursue, and offers some tentative recommendations. This normative analysis stears away from the current scholarship as well as recent policy initiatives, which tend to condemn tax competition for the erosion of states' tax bases, taxing powers, and, in particular, redistributive capacity. These phenomena have led scholars and policymakers down different paths in search of a solution. Since competition is commonly blamed for the ills of the international tax regime, curbing it through cooperation has been assumed to be the most effective approach. The idea of cooperation has gained considerable influence and support and is taken to be unquestionably desirable; competition, in contrast, is commonly deemed unequivocally undesirable. This book takes an opposing view. It argues that conventional analysis – in sweepingly rejecting competition and endorsing cooperation – has been too quick to dismiss the benefits of competition and possible costs of cooperation. Unconstrained competition, where (even) the rules of the game are not set, could certainly generate market inefficiencies, increased distributive gaps, and a shift in power from political institutions to market institutions. Yet cooperation can also have serious costs. Cooperation that involves centralization of power gives rise to efficiency, distributive justice, and political participation costs, and competition plays an important role in counterbalancing this power. Thus, cooperation in itself is not inevitably good and should be viewed with caution, while competition is vital to offsetting its potential disadvantages. I do not, however, hold competition to be the antithesis of cooperation. Indeed, I contend that a certain extent of cooperation is crucial to facilitate more effective competition. Similarly, efficient competition is vital for securing the best outcomes under cooperation.

The three main contributions this book offers can be encapsulated as follows: First, it provides a brief overview of the developments in international taxation in theory and practice over the past century. It describes the transformation of states' sovereign taxing powers, emphasizing the marketization and fragmentation of those powers, and how states are increasingly becoming market actors. The book also describes the multilateral initiatives on the policy front, beginning with the efforts taken in the framework of the League of Nations and concluding with the recent BEPS accord. Second, the book's methodology integrates a strategic analysis of the competitive market of international taxation. This approach sheds new light on existing conventions as well as initiatives currently on the table and offers a clearer understanding of the winners and losers of the (often seemingly innocuous) mechanisms applied and endorsed in the international tax realm. Third, the book's normative evaluation provides a defense – on efficiency as well as distributive justice grounds – of a more (or improved) competitive regime that adopts unified standards and cooperative mechanisms that enforce efficient competition.

A Road Map

The book begins with a critique of traditional conceptions of international tax policy, which tend to focus on either the right to tax or different concepts of neutrality. In contrast, the reading here of international tax as a competitive game suggests that states need to pursue their national interests and set their international tax policies to reflect their comparative advantage so as to attract and retain mobile residents and factors of production. The market setting dramatically transforms the underlying foundations of tax policy. By allowing taxpayers viable alternatives, tax competition gradually turns the tax policy decision-making process on its head. In the tax context, the state is no longer solely engaged in making compulsory demands on its constituents in order to promote their collective goals. Rather, it is increasingly functioning as a recruiter of investments and residents across the globe.

Chapter 1 discusses the dilemmas tax policymakers face under competition. To be competitive, states must offer incentives that maximize the benefits reaped by their constituents from foreign and local investments and, crucially, tax policies that will attract desirable new residents. This double-layered competition for residents and investments alters the very basis to how states think about tax policy. This competition has made conditional and tentative such fundamental goals as efficiency and redistribution and has challenged traditional concepts of collective identity. Tax policy goals are no longer tailored to a set group of constituents. Rather, the group of taxpayers and the tax regime designed for that constituency are forged simultaneously. Perhaps surprisingly, this seemingly additional power of policymakers to shape their constituency actually undermines their ability to set tax policy that is consistent with the classic tax policy goals. The need to cater to the preferences of the more attractive and mobile among potential residents and investors forces policymakers to choose between their state's original constituents and potential, possibly more attractive constituents. It thus pushes them to restrict their state's redistribution functions. Moreover, policymakers are induced to trade democratic participation traditions of voice for exit-based practices and to prioritize mobility over loyalty as a relevant factor (though by no means the only one) in setting economic rights and benefits.

Chapter 2 reviews and criticizes the traditional views on international tax policy in the context of double taxation prevention. Since the 1920s, international taxation scholars and policymakers have focused on states' sovereign right to tax income. The classic literature on international taxation developed concepts of territorial taxation, economic allegiance, and inter-nation equity. The international tax canon subsequently shifted its attention to what was termed "neutrality," seeking to determine which international tax policy would best promote economic efficiency. Scholars debated the relative efficiency of different types of neutrality in a global economy (Capital Export Neutrality, Capital Import Neutrality, National Neutrality, and, more recently, Capital Ownership Neutrality). Chapter 2 criticizes both the traditional right-based approach and the neutrality debate, offering a third approach for designing international tax policy: It claims that in the absence of a global decision-making body, an individual state has no viable option but to think strategically and design its international tax policy according to its interests given other countries' anticipated responses. In applying this strategic approach Chapter 2 focuses on the unilateral options for alleviating double taxation, while the bilateral and multilateral cooperative options are explored in the ensuing chapters.

Next, in Chapters 3–5, the book makes the case against cooperation. It argues that cooperative initiatives on both the bilateral and multilateral level, although portrayed as benefiting all actors involved, are, in fact, instruments that serve the interest of strong and rich countries at the expense of developing countries.

Chapter 3 unravels the myth of tax treaties. The prevailing view on tax treaties takes their indispensability as a mechanism for alleviating double taxation as a given. It is commonly argued that by reducing the burden of double taxation, treaties facilitate the free movement of capital, goods, and services. The analysis in Chapter 3 demonstrates that these treaties do not necessarily prevent double taxation but, in fact, serve far less noble goals, such as easing bureaucratic hassles and coordinating tax terms between the contracting countries. Moreover, they can have much more contentious consequences, in particular the redistribution of tax revenues from the poorer signatory states to the richer signatories. Using game theory, the chapter examines the interactions between the unilateral policies of different types of countries and demonstrates how these interactions reduce taxation levels to as great an extent as treaties do. Without offering any significantly higher degree of stability, treaties often simply replicate the mechanism that countries use unilaterally to alleviate double taxation. However, there is one substantial difference between the unilateral solution and the treaty mechanism: whereas the equilibria of the interaction between unilateral strategies tend to allow host countries to benefit from collecting tax revenues, tax treaties usually allocate the revenues more to the benefit of residence countries. The revenue disparity is probably negligible where two developed countries are involved. But in treaties between developing and developed countries, reallocating tax revenues means regressive redistribution – to the benefit of the developed countries at the expense of the developing ones.

Chapter 4 moves from the bilateral to the multilateral level to consider the costs of multilateral cooperation. Policymakers and scholars troubled by the race to the bottom created by tax competition tend to espouse a cooperative multilateral solution that will enforce universal standards of taxation. This chapter suggests that despite its positive reputation, cooperation is not inherently good and its consequences not always desirable. I illustrate this using an extreme (and admittedly hypothetical) case of cooperation, namely worldwide harmonization of all tax systems, which, it has been widely asserted, would enable countries to collect enough taxes to sustain (or restore) the welfare state and simultaneously promote both domestic distributive justice and efficiency. My analysis raises doubts about the prospects of achieving such comprehensive cooperation but also queries its actual normative desirability. Considerable collective action problems, I claim, make a comprehensive cooperative regime unlikely, given the strategic considerations that make defection a preferable strategy for individual actors as well as the poor detection and enforcement capabilities of cooperating players. In addition, such sweeping multilateral cooperation, touted as a universally beneficial strategy, is not necessarily desirable because of its inefficiencies and potentially regressive effects both among and within states. Thus, although coordination is certainly likely to improve states' ability to collect taxes for public goods, tax competition (the nemesis of harmonization) promotes other important efficiency goals. These include the matching of public goods with individual preferences, decreased governmental waste, and the removal of political constraints that drive states to provide benefits exclusively to certain select groups in society.

Distributive considerations further question the desirability of harmonization. Although coordination allows states to tax capital even under capital mobility, thereby enabling them to redistribute income by shifting the tax burden back from less mobile labor to more mobile capital, curtailing tax competition may have some very troubling distributive effects for poor countries. The increased tax imposed by a multilateral regime on cross-border investments (and the tax wedge it creates) could reduce the demand for labor in poorer countries. Moreover, those countries might be unable to collect enough taxes to compensate labor for their lost wages. For all these reasons, I conclude that cooperation is not desirable per se. While it may be useful as a rhetorical tool that supports a certain contingent policy choice, at the same time it obscures other, equally important considerations and alternatives. Identifying the winners and losers of cooperative policies is vital for properly evaluating these policies.

Chapter 5 explains why existing multilateral cooperation initiatives often favor the interests of strong OECD countries over the interests of developing countries. For almost a century, the impressive multinational cooperative campaigns in the international tax arena have been led primarily by OECD countries, some more successfully than others. These countries have relentlessly advanced cooperative initiatives, in line with the premise (or at least proposition) that cooperation is beneficial to all participants. The support for cooperation is consistent with the classic collective action rationale that all stand to lose if all promote their own self-interests and reject cooperation. However, the pro-cooperation narrative misses the alternative: sometimes states cooperate *despite* its not being in their best interests. The chapter offers a review of the history of the key multilateral cooperative efforts in international taxation. It explains, however, that the presumably voluntary nature of the cooperation is not, in itself, proof that the regime benefits all of its participants, just as a single state's refusal to cooperate is not a sweeping indication that the regime is necessarily not in its best interests. I support this claim through a discussion of four key potential flaws of the path toward cooperation: strategic interactions that leave states with no viable alternatives; substantial asymmetries between countries that tilt the playing field in favor of strong actors (in particular, developed countries that are better able to cooperate among themselves to seize [collective] market power); the prevalence of network products in international taxation, with their inherent lock-in and cartelistic effects that give developed states first-mover advantage and the ability to impose externalities on others; and the problematics of agenda-setting that help certain actors manipulate the process to their benefit. In some circumstances, these mechanisms put states in a position where they willingly cooperate even though, ex ante, they would have preferred that the cooperative accord had never come into being. That is not to say, of course, that *any* cooperation is bad, but rather that instead of assuming that a country's cooperation proves that the initiative is beneficial to it, we must look more closely at the interests at stake.

The final chapters of the book, offer normative paths for international taxation in the present state of a decentralized governance. These chapters discuss the conditions under which a just and efficient international tax regime could be achieved, as well as the difficulties of attaining this due to the decentralized structure of international taxation. This final part of the book begins in Chapter 6 by analyzing the challenge globalization poses for distributive justice, exploring the competing philosophical theories of cosmopolitanism and statism and their implications for international tax policy. Whereas proponents of cosmopolitan justice argue that justice should prevail between individuals irrespective of their national affiliation, statists argue that justice is a duty that is a derivative of political institutions and focus on the state as the primary forum for justice. State competition, I argue, has reset the terms of this debate by undermining the ability of states (rich as well as poor) to maintain the domestic background conditions necessary to sustain their legitimacy and that make the state a uniquely appropriate institution for promoting justice. The fragmented and marketized nature of sovereignty under tax competition erodes states' monopoly over coercive powers as well as their ability to give expression to the collective will of their constituents. Thus, we can no longer assume that justice can be realized within the parameters of the state. This, in turn, undercuts the state's legitimacy. Thus, cooperation among states is more than a way for them to promote their goals through bargaining: it is a means of regaining their legitimacy by bolstering their ability to ensure the collective action of their citizens and to treat them with equal respect and concern.

The traditional discourse in international taxation seems to endorse a statist position, implicitly assuming that when states bargain for a multi-lateral deal, justice is completely mediated by the agreement of the states. In contrast, Chapter 6 argues that a multilateral regime aimed at providing the state with fundamental legitimacy requires independent justification. Contrary to the conventional statist position, I explain that cooperation alone is no guarantee of justice and that certain transfer payments between rich and poor countries might be required to ensure this. For domestic jus-tice to thrive without its costs falling on the shoulders of the poor in poor countries, supporters of justice should strive for such transfer payments between rich and poor nations.

Chapter 7 brings the book to a close with some provisional recom-mendations. Assuming redistribution in rich countries at the expense of the poor in poor countries to be unjust and transfer payments between these states to be utopian, this chapter explores a third option: to refine, rather than curtail, tax competition. For this to be achieved, coopera-tion among states (or groups of states) is crucial so as to correct market failures such as free riding, transaction costs, information asymmetries, and strategic behavior. In international taxation these classic inhibitors to competition translate into the phenomena of tax avoidance, tax eva-sion, and governmental cartels. Of course, the improved market regime for international taxation would not cure all the ills of international tax-ation, most significantly the problem of sustaining domestic redistribu-tions. Nor would it sufficiently safeguard the autonomy of the political sphere from marketization through global processes. And yet, I argue, refined competition is the most preferred second-best option, particularly relative to increased centralization of the international tax regime, which is commonly endorsed in international tax circles.

A detailed blueprint is beyond the scope of this book, and yet, providing some rough ideas regarding such an improved regime may be helpful. Thus, the final chapter of this book illustrates a few alternative mechanisms that could be pursued to overcome these market failures. These solutions range from quite experimental (and potentially unrealistic) components to elements that seem to already be in the process of being established. The most radical of these is the proposition to institute an interstate antitrust agency to counter anti-competitive strategies by states; the more realistic suggested feature is an information-sharing system to counter asymmetrical information. A third possible mechanism would seek solutions for the structural question of rule-divergence among regimes, in an effort to prevent free-riding and reduce transaction costs while, at the same time, preserving states' ability to offer a variety of taxing and spending regimes.

1

Dilemmas of Tax Policy in a Globalized Economy

On the domestic level, tax is a central sphere in which the sometimes conflicting normative goals underlying our collective lives in the state intersect. Tax decisions are known for their impact on the size and distribution of the national welfare pie. They are, furthermore, significant to the shaping of taxpayers' identities and the kinds of communities we live in, as well as innately linked to our sense of belonging to and solidarity with the state. The state, we would like to believe, designs tax rules that are compatible with the fundamental normative values shared by its constituents: seeking to maximize the welfare pie and distribute it justly while reinforcing citizens' identity, supporting their communities, and representing their democratically pronounced collective will. The reality of income taxation is far more complex, of course, with budget constraints, technical complexities, and interest groups' politics often dominating the normative discourse. Without underestimating the complexities of the domestic level, this chapter (indeed, this book as a whole) looks beyond that sphere to focus on the global level. This chapter concentrates on the single state and assesses how the global sphere and, in particular, international competition impact domestic tax policy. I ignore, for the time being, any potential bilateral or multilateral cooperation between states. I will address such options further on in the book.

The decentralized nature of international taxation puts states in competition for residents and investments. This chapter makes the argument that the intensifying competition between states transforms the very basis of states' tax policy. Competition – the inevitable result of the decentralized nature of international taxation – makes everything about tax policy contestable and contingent upon states' respective competitive positions: efficiency, redistribution, the concepts of community, and personal and collective identity. Absent competition, in the domestic tax policy realm, tax is a coercive tool used by the state to overcome collective action problems in financing public goods, regulating behavior, and contending with redistributive challenges. In conditions of competition, the state-citizen relationship is transformed in that states become, to a large degree, market actors competing for residents (individuals as well as businesses), factors of production, and tax revenues. The implicit traditional conception of states sees them as powerful sovereigns that operate in a closed economy with the capacity to make and enforce mandatory rules, impose taxes, and set redistribution. However, in many ways states have come to resemble actors in a competitive global market, where their ability to govern is increasingly shaped by the international supply and demand of resources and the elasticity of taxpayers' choices. Individuals and businesses now have at their disposal a broad range of taxing regimes, rules, and rates from which to pick and choose, while states – which are gradually losing their monopolistic taxation position – are pressured to offer competitive deals of desired public goods and services at a low price.

In the absence of competition, policymakers could design tax policies with at least one clear purpose in mind: serving their constituents, namely, the group of people whose interests they are supposed to promote. Once the relevant group of constituents has been identified, policymakers must set their goals (e.g., maximizing welfare, promoting distributive justice, or supporting desirable social institutions and communities) and determine the optimal strategies for their advancement. These goals often clash and require sophisticated balancing, which makes policymaking anything but trivial. Yet at least it is relatively clear whom the policy should serve and what means are available for achieving this.

Tax competition throws a rather dramatic dimension of complexity into the mix, for it provides some taxpayers with an alternative: to shift their capital, residency, tax base, and even citizenship to another jurisdiction. Hence, not only does domestic tax policy affect taxpayer behavior, it also determines the composition of the group of people whose interests will (indeed should) be served. Moreover, in the current decentralized international tax regime, taxpayers do not even have to fully commit to the taxing regime of any given state in its entirety. Competition often enables taxpayers to unbundle regimes and (for those who are able to effectively tax plan their income production) pick and choose from among the specifics of the taxing regimes of different states.

Tax competition is by no means perfect competition. There are barriers to shifting capital and residency from one state to another, and tax is certainly not the only consideration in residency, investment, and citizenship choices. Tax planning is similarly constrained, and states are often able to enforce restrictions with anti-tax-avoidance measures. Yet, on the whole, it seems generally plausible to assume that changing taxing jurisdictions is a viable enough option for marginal taxpayers to actually influence their pattern of investment, how they run their business, the location of their residency, or even their citizenship choices. Of course, not all taxpayers are able or interested in considering alternative jurisdictions. But in order to make a difference for tax-policy purposes, it is sufficient that there is a group of taxpayers, investors, and residents who are weighing such alternatives.

By providing taxpayers with practicable alternatives, then, tax competition turns the decision-making process on its head. The state no longer makes coercive demands on a set group of subjects in order to promote its collective goals but, rather, increasingly acts as a recruiter, soliciting investments as well as residents. And since the state's tax policy shapes (among other things) the incentives of both individuals and multinational enterprises to be (or become) residents and/or investors in its jurisdiction, that policy needs to be competitive. Thinking strategically, the state must provide incentives that not only maximize the benefits for its current constituency but also attract "the right kind" of residents, investors, and investments.

Different groups of potential taxpayers can offer different benefits in terms of efficiency, distribution, political power, and even collective identity. Thus, policymakers set not only the size of the welfare pie and its distribution but also the size and composition of the very group whose interests they are supposed to represent. Indeed, whether they like it or not, in the current reality of global tax competition, policymakers' decisions affect both the size and makeup of their constituents. Tax policy goals are no longer tailored to a set group of constituents, but rather, the group of taxpayers and the tax regime to which they are subject are shaped simultaneously. Surprisingly perhaps, policymakers' additional power to shape their constituent group undermines their ability to set policy in line with the classic goals of income tax.

The bottom line, then, is that tax competition seriously impacts classic tax-policy goals. As this chapter will explain, the incentive to cater to the preferences of the more attractive and mobile potential residents and investors drives policymakers to constrain the state's redistribution function. It forces states to choose between their existing constituents and other, perhaps more attractive, ones and to forego democratic participation traditions of voice for exit-based practices, as mobility becomes a dominant relevant factor in attaining economic rights and benefits.

Section 1.1 of this chapter reviews briefly the goals of domestic income-tax policy: efficiency and distributive justice as well as personal and collective identity. Section 1.2 then presents the marketization of state policies under competition and their fragmentation due to the ability of certain taxpayers to pick and choose from among the taxing mechanisms offered by different states. Finally, Section 1.3 explains how the competitive international arena calls into question each of the normative goals described in Section 1.1, and makes their proper balancing challenging for policymakers who are now forced to make hard choices and compromises in setting domestic tax policy.

1.1   Income Tax Policy in a Closed Economy

Income tax is traditionally regarded as a vehicle for allocating the costs of government in an equitable and efficient manner.[1] Under this canonical depiction, income taxation is intended to achieve the sometimes contradictory goals of maximizing social welfare and promoting distributive justice. These goals are often also referred to as equity, efficiency, and simplicity, based loosely on Adam Smith's maxim regarding a good tax.[2]

a.   Efficiency

Indeed, since Smith, there has been wide consensus that taxes should be as efficient as possible.[3] In traditional thought, efficiency was understood

---

[1] *See, e.g.*, ADAM SMITH, AN INQUIRY INTO THE NATURE AND CAUSES OF THE WEALTH OF NATIONS 310–11 (4th ed. 1925); LIAM MURPHY & THOMAS NAGEL, THE MYTH OF OWNERSHIP 12 (2002); MICHAEL J. GRAETZ & DEBORAH H. SCHENK, FEDERAL INCOME TAXATION: PRINCIPLES AND POLICIES 25–27 (4th ed. 2002); Reuven S. Avi-Yonah, *The Three Goals of Taxation*, 60 TAX L. REV. 1, 3 (2006–2007).

[2] ADAM SMITH, PRINCIPLES OF TAXATION (1776):

> I. The subjects of every state ought to contribute towards the support of the government, as nearly as possible, in proportion to their respective abilities. . . . II. The tax which each individual is bound to pay ought to be certain, and not arbitrary. . . . III. Every tax ought to be levied at the time, or in the manner, in which it is most likely to be convenient for the contributor to pay it. . . . IV. Every tax ought to be so contrived as both to take out and to keep out of the pockets of the people as little as possible over and above what it brings into the public treasury of the state.

[3] While the concept of efficiency can encompass a wide variety of normative goals, in current legal scholarship, efficiency analysis often goes hand in hand with a utilitarian vision of income taxation as maximizing the combined welfare of society at large (with utility often taken for granted as the material well-being of taxpayers). *See, e.g.*, Edward J. McCaffery, *Tax's Empire*, 85 GEO. L.J. 71, 75, 106 (1996) (describing the utilitarian tradition of tax scholarship and offering a political interpretive analysis to complement both utilitarianism and formalism in tax policy analysis); Reuven S. Avi-Yonah, *Why Tax the Rich? Efficiency, Equity, and Progressive Taxation* (review of JOEL SLEMROD (ed.), DOES ATLAS SHRUG? THE ECONOMIC CONSEQUENCES OF TAXING THE RICH, 2001), 111 YALE L.J. 1391, 1413–16 (2002) (calling for a new balance between equity and efficiency analysis in tax policy).

as preventing taxation from interfering with the free market – that is, as ensuring that the economy operates as it would in the absence of taxes.[4] Under this view, the free market maximizes the well-being of its participants. The "wedge" that taxes create between the price paid by the consumer and the price received by the producer undermines the efficiency of the free market.[5] An efficient tax raises revenues while minimizing "deadweight losses" (i.e., the costs of distorting economic decisions). When some activities are taxed more heavily than others, taxpayers are incentivized to avoid heavily taxed activities in favor of relatively untaxed ones that they would otherwise value less.[6] Thus, a central goal of tax reform is often neutrality: the avoidance of arbitrary differences in tax rates across different types of consumption and investment. This helps to reduce distortions of decisions about what to consume and how to produce it.

Neutrality, however, does not always promote economic efficiency. Other things being equal, it is desirable to tax more heavily those goods for which demand and supply are relatively price insensitive. Thus, in recent years, "optimal taxation" has been suggested as a way to design a more efficient tax system.[7] Focusing on minimizing the deadweight loss caused by taxation, optimal taxation recommends "an 'inverse elasticity rule' – that taxes should, all else being equal, be levied in inverse relation to a party's degree of commitment to a good or activity, with inelastically-demanded necessities bearing higher taxes than elastically-demanded luxuries,"[8] since taxing the former will alter behavior less for any given amount of revenue raised compared to taxing the latter. But despite the theoretical appeal of optimal taxation, it is not considered a particularly useful guide for tax policy in practice.[9] It employs differential tax rates

---

[4] *See, e.g.,* JOEL SLEMROD & JON BAKIJA, TAXING OURSELVES: A CITIZEN'S GUIDE TO THE DEBATE OVER TAXES 120 (4th ed. 2008).

[5] *Id.* at 120, "This outcome maximizes the well-being of participants in the market in the narrow sense of maximizing the amount by which total dollar-valued benefits exceed total dollar-valued costs, a situation economists describe as 'efficient.'"

[6] *Id.*

[7] Joseph Bankman & Thomas Griffith, *Social Welfare and the Rate Structure: A New Look at Progressive Taxation,* 75 CAL. L. REV. 1905, 1945 (1987); McCaffery, *supra* note 3, at 81; David A. Weisbach, *Line Drawing, Doctrine, and Efficiency in the Tax Law,* 84 CORNELL L. REV. 1627, 1655–56 (1999).

[8] McCaffery, *supra* note 3, at 81.

[9] Slemrod & Bakija, *supra* note 4, at 132 ("although the optimal tax principle is correct in theory, it runs into practical problems that make it not particularly useful as a guide to policy").

(with the highest rates imposed on necessities) and – given the uncertainty as to which goods have relatively price-elastic demand – is susceptible to pressure from special interest groups. This is why broad-based uniform taxation is considered a very good rule of thumb: it is likely to cause much less economic distortion and allow lower tax rates.[10]

b.   Distributive Justice

Distributive justice has always been (and no doubt should be) a key tax-policy consideration.[11] Identifying the precise prescriptions of justice in the context of income taxation entails normative political deliberation beyond our current discussion.[12] What is significant for the purposes of this book is the underlying assumption regarding the role of tax in regard to distributive justice within states. In the past, taxation was implicitly perceived to be a cost people pay for the public goods they consume,

---

[10] *Id.*

[11] *See, e.g.,* HENRY C. SIMONS, PERSONAL INCOME TAXATION 18–19 (1938) ("The case for drastic progression in taxation . . . must be rested on the case against inequality on the ethical or aesthetic judgment that the prevailing distribution of wealth and income reveals a degree (and/or kind) of inequality which is distinctly evil or unlovely"); Murphy & Nagel, *supra* note 1, at 12. For examples of the discussion of distributive justice in recent academic literature, see Linda Sugin, *Theories of Distributive Justice and Limitations on Taxation: What Rawls Demands from Tax Systems,* 72 FORDHAM L. REV. 1991 (2004); Brian Galle, *Tax Fairness,* 65 WASH. & LEE L. REV. 1323 (2008); Barbara H. Fried, *The Puzzling Case for Proportionate Taxation,* 2 CHAP. L. REV. 157, 195 (1999). For a review of the political history of taxing the rich, see Avi-Yonah, *supra* 3, at 1409; J.J. THORNDIKE & D.J. VENTRY, TAX JUSTICE: THE ONGOING DEBATE 30 (2002); for a review of the arguments supporting various schemes of distributive justice see David Duff, *Tax Policy and the Virtuous Sovereign: Dworkinian Equality and Redistributive Taxation, in* PHILOSOPHICAL FOUNDATIONS OF TAX LAW, 167 (Monica Bhandari, ed., 2017).

[12] This is an issue that is too broad to be comprehensively addressed here. As Murphy and Nagel, *supra* note 1, at 73, summarize it,

> The values that bear on the assessment of public policy are very diverse, so there is much to disagree about. First, there are questions about the legitimate ends of public policy – whether they should be defined by collective self-interest, or the general welfare, or some conception of fairness, including equal opportunity. . . . Second, there are questions about the limits on the authority of the state over the individual, and whether property rights have any part in defining those limits, or whether they are mere conventions designed for other purposes. Third, there are questions about the proper role of responsibility and desert in the determination of people's economic rewards – and about what individuals can and cannot be held responsible for. Fourth, there are questions about the importance of equality of opportunity, and its relation to inherited economic inequality – and the broader question of what social causes of distributive inequality should be regarded as offensively arbitrary. Finally, there are questions about the importance of freedom of choice in economic life.

and the rationale of benefit taxation was widely supported.[13] In modern times, however, it has been commonly acknowledged that tax should be unlinked from the benefits a person receives from the state.[14] Instead, most commentators agree today that taxation and entitlement to public goods should be based on some function of social justice.

Under the currently prevailing view, tax should be allocated among individuals according to their ability to pay,[15] an approach that is broadly based on material well-being.[16] Underlying this approach is the idea that the state has grown so distinct and meaningful that it is no longer feasible or, more importantly, relevant to base people's tax obligation on the benefits they receive from the state. The duty to pay taxes is thus not based on the benefits one gets from the state but rather on a sense of civic identity.[17]

[13] Hobbes famously supported paying taxes in proportion to what people "consume" in society: "But when the impositions are laid upon those things which men consume, every man payeth equally for what he useth." THOMAS HOBBES, II LEVIATHAN 295 (A.P. MARTINICH & BRIAN BATTISTE eds., revised ed. 2010). For prominent support of the benefit principle in modern times, see F.A. HAYEK, THE CONSTITUTION OF LIBERTY 315–16 (1960). Murphy & Nagel, *supra* note 1, at 16, note that "[m]any have thought that fairness in taxation requires that taxpayers contribute in proportion to the benefit they derive from government" and criticize the benefit principle as "inconsistent with every significant theory of social and economic justice," *id.* at 19.

[14] For a detailed account of the shift in the scholarship of American tax theorists such as Ely, Adams, and Seligman and their efforts to expose the anachronistic social theory that underpinned the benefit principle, *see* AJAY K. MEHROTRA, MAKING THE MODERN AMERICAN FISCAL STATE: LAW, POLITICS, AND THE RISE OF PROGRESSIVE TAXATION, 1877–1929, at 111–18 (2013).

[15] "The subjects of every state ought to contribute towards the support of the government, as nearly as possible in proportion to their respective abilities: that is, in proportion to the revenue which they respectively enjoy under the protection of the state." Smith, *supra* note 1, at 371. But *see* Murphy & Nagel, *supra* note 1, who argue that tax burdens should not be considered independently of the social system as a whole.

[16] *See, e.g.*, Richard A. Musgrave, *Ability to Pay*, THE ENCYCLOPEDIA OF TAXATION AND TAX POLICY 1 (2005). For an extensive review of the literature, see Stephen Utz, *Ability to Pay*, 23 WHITTIER L. REV. 867 (2001–02).

[17] Ajay Mehrotra, *supra* note 14, at 113, cites Edwin Seligman in particular as "condemning the political theory that buttressed the benefits principle." He argued that the benefits doctrine was based, at its core, on an outmoded conception of citizenship:

> It is now generally agreed that we pay taxes not because the state protects us, or because we get any benefits from the state, but simply because the state is a part of us. The duty of supporting and protecting it is born with us. In a civilized society the state is as necessary to the individual as the air he breathes; unless he reverts to stateless savagery and anarchy he cannot live beyond its confines. His every action is conditioned by the fact of its existence. He does not choose the state, but is born into it; it is interwoven with the very fibers of his being; nay, in the last resort, he gives to it his very life. To say that he supports the state only because it benefits him is a narrow and selfish doctrine. We pay taxes not because we get benefits from the state, but because it is as much our

Though the exact meaning of ability to pay is vague and debatable, all its variants reflect the basic notion that taxpayers should pay their fair share (Mill's "equal sacrifice"[18]) in financing the public fisc based on their being equal members of the political community. Both the tax base (distribution of what)[19] and the tax rates (how much distribution)[20] are debatable in terms of tax justice. However, there is no question that the state is a key venue for ensuring justice[21] and that income taxation is a key tool (the *optimal* tool, some even argue[22]) for promoting distributive justice.

duty to support the state as to support ourselves or our family; because, in short, the state is an integral part of us. [footnote omitted] With these striking words, Seligman articulated visions of a new and revitalized sense of civic identity, one that went well beyond traditional social contract rationales to capture a citizen's "ability to pay," or what Seligman referred to as their taxpaying "faculty."

[18] The idea of equal sacrifice is attributed to J.S. MILL, THE PRINCIPLES OF POLITICAL ECONOMY WITH SOME OF THEIR APPLICATIONS TO SOCIAL PHILOSOPHY 485 (1866) ("all are thought to have done their part fairly when each has contributed according to his means, that is has made an equal sacrifice for the common object"). But *see* Murphy & Nagel's, *supra* note 1, at 20–25, opposition to equal sacrifice, indeed to vertical equity, on the basis that justice of tax burdens cannot be separated from the justice of the pattern of government expenditure.

[19] There are numerous interpretations as to what constitutes equal distribution in this context. Material well-being is certainly part of one's ability; however, distribution does not and should not focus on material well-being alone. Attributes such as health, physical state, family status, gender, prestige, quality of living, and level of education do not necessarily translate into material differences, yet they certainly affect people's well-being. *See* AMARTYA SEN, INEQUALITY REEXAMINED 150 (1992); McCaffery, *supra* note 3, at 106 ("But modern tax systems go well beyond affecting the distribution of money. A consistent limitation of the utilitarian turn in tax theory, as we have seen above, has been to reduce questions of taxation to a single index of resources in a narrowly framed problem of distributive justice. But even if tax were only ever intended to be about such matters, all practical means of seeking distributive justice transcend the single index of wealth, to affect patterns of work, marriage, family, education, savings, investment, charity, and so on. Behaviors, lifestyles, family models, and various market actions are inevitably at stake."). *See* also Murphy & Nagel *supra* note 1, at 57 ("Apart from these very broad questions of social justice, which obviously bear on the way tax policy should relate to inequalities of wealth, disposable income, consumption, and earning power, the aim of avoiding arbitrary sources of inequality can have an influence on the more detailed design of public policy. In relation to taxes, it manifests itself in controversies over the fairness of differential tax treatment of persons with distinguishing characteristics who are in other ways economically comparable. The question arises with respect to savers and spenders, the married and the unmarried, people with children and people without, and so forth.").

[20] For the case for and against progressive taxation, *see* Avi-Yonah, *supra* note 3, at 1399–1410.

[21] As Thomas Nagel in *The Problem of Global Justice*, 33 PHIL. & PUB. AFF. 113, 130 (2005), puts it, "The state makes unique demands on the will of its members . . . and those exceptional demands bring with them exceptional obligations, the positive obligations of justice."

[22] *See, e.g.*, Louis Kaplow & Steven Shavell, *Why the Legal System Is Less Efficient than the Income Tax in Redistributing Income*, 23 J. LEGAL STUD. 667 (1994).

c. Identity

The importance of these two classic normative considerations in income tax policy cannot be overstated. They do not, however, exhaust the normative underpinnings of tax. Tax is also a powerful social instrument that plays a significant part in the construction of people's personal and collective identities.[23] It both reflects and shapes how people perceive themselves and others. It influences how people interact with others in various contexts, including within their families and communities, and it affects their sense of social solidarity and modes of participation in social institutions.[24] Income tax law reflects and simultaneously shapes a certain vision of the self. When, for example, income taxation acknowledges certain differences (e.g., one's ability to pay, marital status, or business-travel expenses) while disregarding others (e.g., one's disability, common-law status, or commuting and childcare expenses), it reinforces a certain conception of the taxpayer and undermines the alternatives. In so doing, it draws on an image of an archetypical individual taxpayer but, at the same time, shapes that image.[25] If we assume the archetypical taxpayer to be healthy, married, childless, or living near his or her workplace, for example, we exclude those who are disabled, single, have children, or live at a distance from their workplace. Moreover, it is not only the specific contents of tax's rules that affect identities but also the way in which tax operates. Tax inevitably compares people and their behavior on a monetary scale, equating them to market transactions. The infiltration of the market nexus into the sphere of human attributes and interactions commodifies them. They are valued through the narrow and reductive prism of the market valuation, affecting, in turn, their meanings.[26]

---

[23] *See, e.g.*, McCaffery, *supra* note 3, at 106 (1996). For a more detailed discussion of this argument, *see* Tsilly Dagan, *The Currency of Taxation*, 84 FORDHAM L. REV. 2537 (2016).

[24] McCaffery, *supra* note 3, at 85:

> The critical problem is that tax is not just about the distribution of resources. Real-world tax systems affect a wide range of behaviors and diverse patterns of work and lifestyle: taxes affect decisions to marry, to have children, to become one- or two-earner families, to pursue education, to support charities, to save for retirement, to make inter-generational gifts or bequests, and so on. These are or, at least can be matters of principle. We could readily adapt Rawls's words to tax, once we fully understand its reach: "[T]hese institutions can have decisive long-term social effects and importantly shape the character and aims of the members of society, the kinds of persons they are and want to be."

[25] See Tsilly Dagan, *Commuting*, 26 VA. TAX REV. 185 (2006).

[26] For a more detailed explanation of this claim, *see* Tsilly Dagan, *Itemizing Personhood*, 29 VA. TAX REV. 93 (2009).

Significantly, tax's impact goes beyond the expressive dimension, for its effect on taxpayers' incentives has real-life consequences. It can shape not only taxpayers' perceptions of themselves and of others but also their choices and modes of action (to live at a distance from work, to work outside of the home, or to be a homemaker). Assuming enough taxpayers alter their choices, social meanings can change as can social norms. As a result, tax can affect the ways in which taxpayers function within their families, communities, and workplaces. Moreover, the makeup, size, and nature of the communities formed by taxpayers and the social institutions they construct can transform as well. The changes in the functioning of individuals and the nature of their communities could, in turn, reinforce people's choices, social meanings, and norms.

The conversion of life into the explicit or implicit currency of taxation is neither a neutral nor technical process and involves a considerable amount of normative (often implicit) choices. In addition to tax's traditional efficiency and distributive criteria, policymakers must thus consider its possible effects on taxpayers' personal and collective identities. Accordingly, a comprehensive analysis of income taxation must take into account the less traditional notions of identity and community alongside the traditional goals of efficiency and distributive justice.

Finally, not only social communities but also political communities are affected by taxation. As being the state's chief source of funding as well as a key issue of concern for voters everywhere, tax is one of the most prominent manifestations of civic participation in democratic societies. As implied by the famous call for "no taxation without representation," there are strong links (at least perceived) between the duty to pay taxes and having a voice in the political process.[27] Being a member of the state

---

[27] *See* Ruth Mason, *Citizenship Taxation*, 89 S. Cal. L. Rev. 169, 189–92 (2015) (reviewing and criticizing the link between the right of non-resident U.S. citizens to vote in U.S. elections and their duty to pay taxes to the United States); Michael S. Kirsch, *Taxing Citizens in a Global Economy*, 82 N.Y.U. L. Rev. 443, 480–84 (2007) (supporting the taxation of citizens, even if residing abroad, by explaining their belongingness to the national community). For a comprehensive analysis of tax policy, democracy, accountability, and legitimacy in the international tax context, *see* Diane M. Ring, *What's at Stake in the Sovereignty Debate? International Tax and the Nation-State*, 49 Va. J. Int'l L. 155 (2008). For a discussion of the link between the duty to pay taxes and having a voice in the political process in the context of the EU after the 2008 crisis, *see* Ana Paula Dourado, "Chapter 10: No Taxation without Representation in the European Union: Democracy, Patriotism and Taxes" in Cécile Brokelind (ed.), "Principles of Law: Function, Status and Impact in EU Tax Law" (IBFD, 2014). For some examples of the intricate links between taxation and democratic participation, *see* Saul Levmore, *Taxes as Ballots*, 65 U. Chi. L. Rev. 387 (1998); Nancy

usually imposes a duty to pay its taxes,[28] and the duty to pay taxes is often an indication of taxpayers' membership in the national polity.[29] Because of the centrality of tax in facilitating state operations, taxpaying is, in the eyes of many, a pillar of compliance with one's civic duties[30] as well as a major arena for setting the relationship between the individual and the collectivity through the institution of the state.[31] Though there are certainly other ways to participate, taxpaying has come to symbolize civic participation.[32] Moreover, taxpaying can also be taken as an expression of social responsibility and solidarity among co-members of the political community. In particular, a tax system that seeks to reduce inequality endorses a conception of citizenship aimed at cultivating a moral bond with the community and a sense of obligation toward one's fellow citizens.[33]

In sum then, paying taxes is a signifier of belonging to one's political community in two important ways: first, in the taxpayer's compliance

---

Staudt, *Taxation Without Representation*, 55 N.Y.U. TAX L. REV. 554 (2002); Lisa Philipps & Mary Condon, *Connecting Economy, Gender, and Citizenship*, LAW AND CITIZENSHIP 176 (Law Comm'n Canada ed., 2006).

[28] *See, e.g.*, Mehrotra, *supra* note 14, at 114 (explaining that the new school economists (Ely, Adams, and Seligman) viewed taxation as something people pay because they are citizens – members of an organized society); Cook v. Tait, 265 U.S. 47, 56 (1924) (Justice McKenna) ("[T]he basis of the power to tax was not and cannot be made dependent upon the situs of the property in all cases, it being in or out of the United States, nor was not and cannot be made dependent upon the domicile of the citizen, that being in or out of the United States, but upon his relation as citizen to the United States and the relation of the latter to him as citizen.").

[29] Mason, *supra* note 27, at 190, describes payment of taxes by illegal immigrants as a prerequisite for gaining citizenship status through amnesty procedures. Staudt, *supra* note 27, at 599, for her part describes the many cases in which taxpayers are granted a unique position in democratic processes due to their perception as stakeholders in society, but criticizes this as contradicting the Twenty-Fourth Amendment.

[30] Ajay K. Mehrotra, *Reviving Fiscal Citizenship*, 113 MICH. L. REV. 943, 944 (215).

[31] See Murphy & Nagel, *supra* note 1, at 41 ("The framework for the entire discussion is the question of the appropriate relation of the individual to the collectivity, through the institutions of the state. A state has a near monopoly of force within its territory, and it has the authority to coerce individuals to comply with decisions arrived at by some nonunanimous collective choice procedure. What are the legitimate aims for which such power may be used, and what, if anything, limits the way it may legitimately be exercised over individuals? These are questions about what we may be said to owe to our fellow citizens, and what kind of sovereignty we should retain over ourselves, free from the authority of the state, even when we are members of it and subject to its control in certain respects. Those questions define the issue of political legitimacy.").

[32] *See, e.g.*, LAWRENCE ZELENAK, LEARNING TO LOVE FORM 1040: TWO CHEERS FOR THE RETURN BASED MASS INCOME TAX 4 (2013).

[33] MICHAEL J. SANDEL, WHAT MONEY CAN'T BUY: THE MORAL LIMITS OF MARKETS 119–20 (2012), discusses the problematic role played by inequality in damaging the sense of common life shared by members of a political community:

with the state-imposed duties that finance the public goods and services provided by the state; and second, in the sense of solidarity and mutual dependence generated among the state's constituents, which go beyond their duties to others (i.e., constituents of other states).

1.2 Tax Competition

The conception of states embedded in the conventional discourse on tax policy is of powerful sovereigns functioning in a closed economy that wield exclusive power to make and enforce mandatory rules, set and impose taxes, and balance the various goals of income taxation. In conditions of global competition, however, the relationship between the state and its constituents has changed from a compulsory regime, where the state imposes taxes on its subjects, to an increasingly elective marketplace, where states are often compelled to offer competitively priced deals on public goods and services. The taxes we pay are not only a mechanism for financing the public goods and services the state provides but are also increasingly becoming a price that the state charges for those goods and services. Moreover, the ability of some taxpayers to select the tax rules and jurisdictions of their choice both marketizes and fragmentizes the relationship between the state and its subjects by de-facto allowing certain individuals and businesses[34] to pick and choose from among the rules of different regimes. Thus, competition exists not only among states providing shrink-wrapped take-it-or-leave-it packages[35] but also to an increasing degree among the various tax rates, rules, allowances, and benefits, as well as public goods and services offered by different states.

> The republican tradition teaches that severe inequality undermines freedom by corrupting the character of both rich and poor and destroying the commonality necessary to self-government.... [T]he argument from corruption directs our attention to the civic consequences of the gap between rich and poor so pronounced in our time. From the standpoint of the republican conception of citizenship, the danger is that this: the new inequality does not simply prevent the poor from sharing in the fruits of consumption and choosing their ends for themselves; it also leads rich and poor to live increasingly separate ways for life.

[34] They would be those with the most available alternatives and that can afford to do this. Such competition is by no means perfect competition, as taxpayers' responses are not entirely elastic and are dependent on many non-tax issues. It is therefore difficult to know, and to measure, the extent of taxpayers' electivity. And yet it is fair to assume that – at the margins – the phenomenon endures.

[35] *Cf*, Rick Hills, *Shrinking-Wrapping NYC: How Neighborhood Activists Are Strangling a City*, PRAWFSBLAWG (Nov. 29, 2009, 1:47 PM), http://prawfsblawg.blogs.com/prawfsblawg/2009/11/shrinkingwrapping-nyc-how-neighborhood-activists-strangle-a-city.html

a. Marketization

As noted, states' monopolistic power over their constituents is under-going a significant transformation. Many taxpayers – whether individuals or businesses – are increasingly mobile and can therefore select from alternative jurisdictions to relocate their places of residence and business activities. For example, in recent years, many ultra-rich individuals have expatriated in order to avoid the high tax rates of their home countries, shifting not only their places of residence but also their citizenship to another jurisdiction.[36] States often encourage such mobility by offering desirable incoming residents certain privileges and incentives.[37] Residents-in-demand relocate to more appealing jurisdictions; states lure away foreign medical experts, Olympic athletes, potential investors, and young productive individuals to salvage their collapsing social security systems.[38] Multinational enterprises are also, of course, mobile. They can incorporate and sometimes re-incorporate in their jurisdiction of choice[39] and move their production, marketing, and R&D activities to more favorable locations.[40] In addition, host states strongly

---

[36] Kirsch, *supra* note 27, at 490; NINA E. OLSON, TAXPAYER ADVOCATE SERV., 2013 ANNUAL REPORT TO CONGRESS 206 (2013). https://taxpayeradvocate.irs.gov/2013-Annual-Report/. Since 1999, the number of U.S. citizens living abroad has increased 85 percent while the number of annual expatriations has skyrocketed nearly 500 percent. Perhaps because renouncing citizenship "may be easier than staying in compliance with U.S. tax laws that can be onerous for citizens of other countries," expatriations are expected to continue to increase, with an expected 2013 level at least 33 percent more than the previous high in 2011.

[37] *See, e.g.*, OECD, Taxation and Employment 138 (2011), http://www.oecd.org/ctp/taxation-and-employment-9789264120808-en.htm (describing tax concessions for high-skilled labor in selected OECD countries).

[38] Ayelet Shachar, *The Race for Talent: Highly Skilled Migrants and Competitive Immigration Regimes*, 81 N.Y.U. L. REV. 148 (2006); Ayelet Shachar, *Picking Winners: Olympic Citizenship and Global Race for Talent*, 120 YALE L.J. 2098 (2011).

[39] For an extensive discussion of the electivity of corporate residency under U.S. laws, *see* Daniel Shaviro, The *Rising Tax-Electivity of US Corporate Residence*, 64 TAX L. REV. 377, 403 (2010). ("In gauging the electivity of U.S. corporate residence, the key issue is whether its nontax advantages to those who would choose it if they were tax-indifferent are low enough that any significant associated tax cost would lead to opting out. Unfortunately, this is hard to measure directly."); Cathy Hwang, *The New Corporate Migration: Tax Diversion Through Inversion*, 80 BROOK. L. REV. 807 (2015); Tsilly Dagan, *The Future of Corporate Residency*, available at https://papers.ssrn.com/sol3/papers.cfm?abstract_id=3045134, and references there.

[40] *See, e.g.*, Michael P. Devereux & Rachel Griffith, *The Impact of Corporate Taxation on the Location of Capital: A Review*, 9 SWEDISH ECON. POL'Y REV. 79 (2002); IMF POLICY PAPER, SPILLOVERS IN INTERNATIONAL CORPORATE TAXATION 19 (May 19, 2014) ("Between 1997 and 2007 about 6 percent of all MNEs relocated their headquarters.").

encourage enterprises to incorporate or relocate to their jurisdictions. States compete for MNEs' production facilities (as they provide jobs and spillovers of know-how),[41] for their headquarters and R&D centers (out of the belief that they create positive externalities),[42] and even for their formal incorporation (for the registration fees and tax revenues, even if sometimes minimal).[43]

For the mobile, the applicable tax rules and tax rates are important considerations when weighing their residency options and where to locate their economic activities.[44] Hence, for states, tax rules and tax rates have

---

[41] *See, e.g.,* Holger Goerg, *Productivity Spillovers from Multinational Companies,* in PERSPECTIVES ON IRISH PRODUCTIVITY 240 (Ciarán Aylward & Ronnie O'Toole eds., 2007); Duardo Borensztein, Jose De Gregorio & Jong-Wha Lee, *How Does Foreign Direct Investment Affect Economic Growth?,* 45 J. INT'L ECON. 115 (1998). Yoram Margalioth, *Tax Competition, Foreign Direct Investments and Growth: Using the Tax System To Promote Developing Countries,* 23 VA. TAX REV. 161 (2003) (supporting the provision of tax incentives for FDI where it provides positive productivity spillovers).

[42] *See, e.g.,* Michael J. Graetz & Rachael Doud, *Technological Innovation, International Competition, and the Challenges of International Income Taxation,* 113 COLUM. L. REV. 347 (2013); Jan I. Haaland & Ian Wooton, *International Competition for Multinational Investment,* 101 SCANDINAVIAN J. ECON. 631 (1999).

[43] *See, e.g.,* RONEN PALAN, RICHARD MURPHY & CHRISTIAN CHAVAGNEUX, TAX HAVENS: HOW GLOBALIZATION REALLY WORKS (2010). *See also* Wolfgang Schon, *Playing Different Games? Regulatory Competition in Tax and Company Law Compared,* 42 COMMON MKT. L. REV. 331 (2005).

[44] Devereux & Griffith, *supra* note 40; IMF Policy Paper, *supra* note 40, at 18–19; Mihir A. Desai & Dhammika Dharmapala, *Do Strong Fences Make Strong Neighbors?,* 63 NAT'L TAX J. 723, 724–25 (2010) ("The evidence provided, while clearly preliminary, indicates a trend towards foreign incorporation by firms conducting IPOs in the U.S. stock market, towards foreign acquisition of U.S. target firms by exemption and haven domiciled companies, and increasing use of foreign portfolio investment by U.S. investors to circumvent U.S. worldwide taxation"). To what extent their decisions are actually affected by tax considerations is hard to measure empirically. Daniel Shaviro, *supra* note 39, at 429, recently concluded in the U.S. context:

> In an increasingly integrated global economy, with rising cross-border stock listing and share ownership, it is plausible that U.S. corporate residence for income tax purposes, with its reliance on one's place of incorporation, will become increasingly elective for taxpayers at low cost.... Rising electivity is not nearly as great a problem, however, for existing U.S. corporate equity, which to a considerable degree is trapped, as it is for new equity (whether in new or existing corporations). In the course of this project, I have gotten the sense that rising electivity is not quite as far along as I had thought at the start that it might be.

For a comprehensive analysis of corporate residence shopping in the tax and corporate charter contexts, *see* Mitchell A. Kane & Edward B. Rock, *Corporate Taxation and International Charter Competitions,* 106 MICH. L. REV. 1229 (2008). But *see* Eric J. Allen & Susan C. Morse, *Tax-Haven Incorporation for U.S.-Headquartered Firms: No Exodus Yet,* 66 NAT'L TAX J. 395 (2013) (arguing that corporations do not actually weigh tax considerations in deciding on the location of their headquarters).

become, to a large extent, the currency of competition.[45] This puts states in an unfamiliar position. No longer do they impose compulsory tax and regulatory requirements on their subjects solely to advance the collective goals of a given group. Rather, competition has gradually transformed the policymaking process so that states are increasingly operating as recruiters of investments and residents from across the globe. Competition requires them to act like market players, offering their goods and services to potential customers. Individuals and businesses, for their part, compare the costs (or gains) of maintaining their residency or economic activities in their current jurisdiction to the potential costs (or gains) of relocating to an alternative jurisdiction.[46] The lower the costs of shifting jurisdictions and the higher the costs in the current jurisdiction, the more likely they are to relocate.[47] As will be explained, this marketized and competitive framework influences how states consider questions of efficiency, redistribution, and national identities as well as democratic participation. But before we turn to these implications, it is important to realize that this marketization is only the tip of the iceberg in terms of how competition bears on states' considerations.

b. Fragmentation

The ability of individuals and businesses to tax plan their economic activities not only marketizes the relationship between states and their constituents, by enabling the latter to shop for their jurisdiction of choice, but also allows constituents to unbundle the packages of goods and services offered by states. Thus, in this market, individuals and businesses can buy à la carte fractions of taxing regimes and governmental services.[48]

In the market for tax rules and rates, individuals and businesses can detach the different components of their activities from one another. In some cases, this entails relocating actual resources, whereas in others, it

---

[45] John Douglas Wilson, *Theories of Tax Competition*, 52 NAT'L TAX J. 269 (1999); IMF POLICY PAPER, *supra* note 40.

[46] For a classic description of competition for public goods, see Charles Tiebout, *A Pure Theory of Local Expenditures*, 64 J. POL. ECON 416 (1956) (offering a competition-based theory for efficient provision of public goods in the local government context). *See also* Schon, *supra* note 43; Wallace E. Oates, *An Essay on Fiscal Federalism*, 37 J. ECON. LIT. 1120, 1126 (1999).

[47] Similarly, those on the receiving end of the redistribution will seek the location with the highest rewards. *See* Roderick M. Hills Jr., *Poverty, Residency, and Federalism: States' Duty of Impartiality Toward Newcomers*, 1999 SUP. CT. REV. 277.

[48] See generally, Tsilly Dagan, *The Global Market for Tax & Legal Rules*, 21 FLA. TAX REV. (forthcoming 2017).

is merely a matter of signing certain documents or doing the necessary paperwork.[49] Thus, capital can move separately from its owner; IP can shift separately from the technology it manufactures; production can be separated from sales; and corporations can be detached from their stakeholders. People no longer have to reside or even be physically present where they do business, and the corporate structure enables businesses to set up residency in any number of locations. Individuals can, therefore, own property and reside in one jurisdiction (and consume its police services, public parks, and clean air), open bank accounts and do business in another (and use its local court and banking systems), invest in an industrial plant in a third (and reap the benefits of its publicly educated workforce), register their IPs in a fourth (and benefit from the local IP regulation), and vote in a fifth. Where and how much taxes they will be required to pay is an entirely different question, however, which is determined by the details of the various taxation regimes in the relevant jurisdictions: the rules setting deductions and exemptions; the rules defining the different entities, transactions, and sources of income; the transfer pricing rules and so on. With the help of skillful tax planners, (certain) taxpayers – those who are well counseled and those whose resources are least connected to a specific location, particularly MNEs – can often design the tax regime of their choice.[50]

International tax laws are infamous for the assortment of conditions that determine their application in different countries. As the 2015 BEPS deliverables highlight, one of the key challenges for states today is their inability to enforce their tax bases, which have been eroded by tax planning.[51] Despite the considerable efforts made by some states to fight this phenomenon, the rules that determine tax liability are extensively bypassed by taxpayers.[52] Specifically, although residency and source of income are still the official criteria for tax liability, tax planners use a host

---

[49] Joel Slemrod, *Location, (Real) Location, (Tax) Location: An Essay on Mobility's Place in Optimal Taxation*, 63 NAT'L TAX J. 843, 844 (2010).

[50] For a short description of the "tools of the trade" in tax planning, *see, e.g.*, IMF, *supra* note 40, at 11(2014); OECD, Addressing Base Erosion and Profit Shifting (2013), http://dx.doi .org/10.1787/9789264192744-en [hereinafter BEPS Report].

[51] OECD, EXPLANATORY STATEMENT, OECD/G20 BASE EROSION AND PROFIT SHIFTING PROJECT (2015), https://www.oecd.org/ctp/beps-explanatory-statement-2015.pdf.

[52] Of course, states all too often played a part in designing the loopholes that later served tax planners in avoiding either their own or their peer countries' taxes. *See, e.g.*, Omri Marian, *supra* note 4. Available at SSRN: https://ssrn.com/abstract=2685642 (describing the rogue behavior of tax-haven countries in facilitating tax-planning opportunities and exemplifying it with the Luxemburg leaked ATAs).

of techniques to de facto opt out of a jurisdiction, and they manage to do so without actually relocating their client's residency or economic activities. Tax planners prominently incorporate subsidiaries in tax havens to defer the taxation of their income (such as worldwide royalties or service income) to when the profits are repatriated, if ever.[53] They siphon off income through beneficial tax treaties to and from low-tax jurisdictions, thereby avoiding taxation at source.[54] They use hybrid entities to take advantage of a deduction in a high-tax jurisdiction, while avoiding taxation in the jurisdiction where the income was produced,[55] or to

---

[53] Anecdotal data on investments through famous tax havens are telling:

> [B]y searching through the IMF Co-ordinated Direct Investment Survey (CDIS), it emerges that in 2010 Barbados, Bermuda and the British Virgin Islands received more FDIs (combined 5.11% of global FDIs) than Germany (4.77%) or Japan (3.76%). During the same year, these three jurisdictions made more investments into the world (combined 4.54%) than Germany (4.28%). On a country-by-country position, in 2010 the British Virgin Islands were the second largest investor into China (14%) after Hong Kong (45%) and before the United States (4%). For the same year, Bermuda appears as the third largest investor in Chile (10%). Similar data exists in relation to other countries, for example Mauritius is the top investor country into India (24%), while Cyprus (28%), the British Virgin Islands (12%), Bermuda (7%) and the Bahamas (6%) are among the top five investors into Russia.

> OECD, BEPS REPORT, *supra* note 50, at 17; Gabriel Zucman, *The Missing Wealth of Nations: Are Europe and the U.S. Net Debtors or Net Creditors?*, 128 Q.J. ECON. 1321 (2013), estimates that around 8% of the global financial wealth of households is in tax havens, three-quarters of which goes unrecorded.

[54] *See* Rebecca Kyser, *Interpreting Tax Treaties*, 101 IOWA L. REV. 1387, 1418–21(2016). This technique is explained in the BEPS REPORT, *supra* note 53, at 41:

> [T]he fact that the owner of the income-producing asset (*e.g.* funds or IP) is located in a low-tax jurisdiction means that in most cases where income is derived from other countries the taxing rights of the source State will not be limited by any double tax treaty. The interposition of a conduit company located in a State that has a treaty with the source State may allow the taxpayer to claim the benefits of the treaty, thus reducing or eliminating tax at source. Further, if the State of the conduit company applies no withholding tax on certain outbound payments under its domestic law or has itself a treaty with the State of the owner of the income-producing asset that provides for the elimination of withholding tax at source, the income can be repatriated to the owner of the income-producing asset without any tax at source. Taxation of the income from the funds or IP in the State of the conduit company does not take place, since the income will be offset by a corresponding deduction for the payments to the owner of the income-producing asset in the low-tax jurisdiction.

[55] If, for example, a subsidiary is considered transparent in Jurisdiction A but opaque in Jurisdiction B, payments (e.g., interest payments or royalties) from B to A will be deductible in A (thereby reducing taxable income and tax liability in A) but not considered income in B. States' regulation de facto facilitates this planning. Thus, for example, the U.S. "check-the-box" regulations allow U.S. entities to effectively design their opaque, versus flow-through, tax treatment.

take advantage of deductions twice.[56] They use transfer pricing to allocate revenues to low-tax jurisdictions, by setting transaction prices between related entities to increase taxable income in low-tax jurisdictions and increase deductions in high-tax jurisdictions. In addition, tax planners employ earning stripping to erode the tax base in the country where the income was produced[57] and construct creative derivatives that are treated as loans in one country and as equity investment in another.[58] Moreover, they often use a combination of these techniques and others[59] to reduce the total tax liability of individuals and businesses without any need for residency or prime business relocation.[60] The ability of individuals and

---

[56] This is done by attributing the deductions to an entity that could file joint return with two different entities in two different countries.

[57] This typically involves setting up a finance operation in a low-tax country to fund the activities of the other companies in the group. The result is that the payments are deducted against the taxable profits of the high-taxed operating companies while taxed favorably or not taxed at all at the level of the recipient, thereby allowing for a reduction in the total tax burden. See BEPS REPORT, *supra* note 50, at 40–41.

[58] If, for example, Country A classifies a transaction an equity investment (and, hence, the payments as dividend distributions) and Country B classifies the same transaction a loan (and the payments as interest), then payments from B to A will be considered interest (and, hence, deductible) in Country B and considered dividends in Country A. If Country A exempts dividend income or accords it preferential treatment, there is a tax gain. See BEPS REPORT, *supra* note 53, at 9–10.

[59] Google's "Double Irish Dutch Sandwich" is a good example of such a combined structure. Google's worldwide income is channeled to an Irish subsidiary, thus reducing Google's income in high-tax jurisdictions because the fees paid are deductible at source. The Irish subsidiary's income is then reduced by royalty payments to another subsidiary – Google BV, a Dutch corporation – thereby enabling Google to benefit from the exemption of withholding taxes within the EU. Google BV's income is stripped using almost identical royalty payments to a Bermuda company. The Netherlands imposes no withholding taxes, and Bermuda is famous for not taxing income. The result is a near-zero tax on Google's income from customers in Europe, the Middle East, and Africa. For a detailed description, see Edward Kleinbard, *Stateless Income*, 11 FLA. TAX REV. 699, 706 (2011).

[60] It is important to note that not all of these tax-planning techniques are available to all taxpayers. In particular, individuals (who are the key target of redistribution policies) must be distinguished from corporations, for the latter enjoy far broader leeway in their tax planning. That said, however, individuals on the very high end (i.e., those classified by Commissioner Shulman as high-wealth individuals, Douglas Shulman, Commissioner, Prepared Remarks before the 22nd Annual George Washington University International Tax Conference [Dec. 10, 2009], *available at* http://www.irs.gov/uac/Prepared-Remarks-of-Commissioner-Douglas-Shulman-before-the-22nd–Annual-George-Washington-University-International-Tax-Conference) can and do operate through corporations as well other entities (e.g., trusts); they hence may also benefit from the loopholes generally available to corporations. Mitt Romney's offshore corporations, for example, made headlines in 2012 during his presidential campaign. See, e.g., Mark Maremont, *Romney's Unorthodox IRA*, Wall St. J. (Jan. 19, 2012), http://www.wsj.com/articles/SB10001424052970204468004577168972507188592

businesses to tax plan varies across jurisdictions and is ultimately a matter of the loopholes in the local tax system and the extent of domestic enforcement of the tax laws.[61] Yet there is no doubt that combined, the often conflicting tax laws of all states have created this fragmented international tax landscape, where flexible and well-advised taxpayers often have the ability to assemble the tax regime of their choice.

Thus, in contrast to the classic mobility story discussed above, which revolves around the vision of a market of states that offer take-it-or-leave-it package deals of legal rules, services, and taxes, the fragmentation perspective highlights the electivity and flexibility of these packages.[62] Instead of looking at the ability of individuals and businesses to shift their choice of jurisdiction en bloc by moving their residency to a new jurisdiction, fragmentation stresses their ability to mix and match regimes. Because many individuals and businesses are not bound exclusively to a single state but, rather, interact simultaneously with many states on various planes, the state-constituent relationship cannot, and does not, necessarily bundle together all of the dimensions of the potential interaction between taxpayers and the state. This reality affects the strategies of both individuals and businesses as well as states. Absent such jurisdictional fragmentation, the strategies available to individuals and businesses are essentially either voice (using their political power to shape state policy) or exit (relocating to a jurisdiction that offers a more favorable package);[63] however; taxpayers now have another option: to slice up activities and shift the various components to the tax regimes that maximize their benefits.

States, in turn, compete for residents, as well as for their (fragmented) resources and activities, using their taxing and spending regimes as the currency of this competition. Even if competing only for the marginal residents and resources, I argue, this can affect their normative considerations in setting their tax policies. The next section will discuss how considerations of efficiency, distributive justice, and identity all undergo a transformation in conditions of tax competition.

---

[61] The ability of individuals to internationally tax plan varies across countries. In the United States, especially post-FATCA, it has been argued that the opportunities to tax avoid and evade seem to have become much costlier. See, e.g., Avi-Yonah, supra note 3. Opportunities are still available, however, for offshore tax planning. For a catalog of some of these available options, see Davis S. Miller, *Unintended Consequences: How U.S. Tax Law Encourages Investment in Offshore Tax Havens* (Oct. 4, 2010), available at http://ssrn.com/abstract=1684716orhttp://dx.doi.org/10.2139/ssrn.1684716.

[62] *But see* Schon, *supra* note 43, at 336 (describing tax competition as competition between bundled goods, whereas company law competition is over only one particular good).

[63] Albert O. Hirschman, Exit, Voice, and Loyalty: Responses to Decline in Firms, Organizations and States (1970).

1.3   How Tax Competition Reshapes National Tax Policy

To be competitive, states need to design policies that will attract the right mix and level of activities and investments into their jurisdiction. They should also aim to attract (and keep) "the right kind" of residents, individuals, and MNEs. Moreover, because of the ability of (some) taxpayers to pick and choose from among the tax rules of different regimes, states must offer competitive tax rules and rates for each component of their tax regime or else taxpayers might be able to replace them with the compatible rules and rates of a foreign regime. This multilayered competition for residents and investments has altered how states set tax policy; it creates ambivalence about everything from efficiency, to redistribution, to the very concepts of personal and collective identity. In what follows, I will discuss the implications of this competitive reality for tax policy in a global economy.

a.   Efficiency

From the modified perspective of tax competition, the role of the state has changed from a central regime seeking to impose the most efficient rules (which usually means the least distortive rules) on an existing group of taxpayers to a market player seeking to maximize its "profits" from the market. Those profits include not only tax revenues, of course, but also the benefits that certain residents and investors generate for the domestic economy. A competitively successful state will recruit (and keep) the "best" residents,[64] the most profitable investments, and the most beneficial businesses and corporations by designing the most attractive regime and, at the same time, relinquish as little as possible in tax revenues. Such a market player is interested, perhaps even eager, to tilt the market in its direction, and thus, its perspective changes. A competitive state focuses on the costs and benefits for "its" constituent group (even if this means imposing costs on other groups), as well as on leading the winning team.[65]

There are a number of strategies that states can adopt to compete in this market, which would not be as attractive absent the competition. First,

---

[64] Note, however, that while countries are increasingly competing for desirable residents, they are less likely to be able to push away unwanted (individual) residents. This is for a variety of reasons, including governments' sense of commitment to their original constituents and the disturbing fact that such residents are often unwanted by other countries and therefore unable to emigrate out of their home country.

[65] Chapters 2, 4, and 5 will explain why unilateral cooperation is not a plausible strategy for state actors.

states can (and should in order to maximize gains for their "team") reduce the tax rates on more mobile economic activities, such as capital investments (portfolio investments and foreign direct investments) of capital owners that have the option to invest elsewhere.[66] Countries notoriously compete for MNEs' business by offering attractive packages of tax and public goods and services (for example, host countries often offer "ring-fenced" benefits to foreign investors[67]). Competitive states can reduce taxes on (more mobile) capital and offer tax benefits to local businesses with high mobility potential (e.g., high-tech industries whose markets are foreign or those engaged in extensive research and development[68]) but choose not to reduce taxes on (less mobile) labor and on businesses that are closely tied to local resources (e.g., natural resources).[69]

---

[66] Although it might seem, at first glance, that a country's interest would be to collect as much tax revenue as possible from foreigners, economic analysis explains that the optimal policy for a small host country would actually be to eliminate all taxes other than benefit taxes imposed on foreign investors. *See, e.g.,* Joel Slemrod, *Tax Principles in an International Economy,* in WORLD TAX REFORM: CASE STUDIES OF DEVELOPED AND DEVELOPING COUNTRIES 11, 13 (Michael J. Boskin & Charles E. McLure, Jr., eds., 1990). The rationale is that if the international capital market is competitive, a small country (whose market power can have no effect on the worldwide rate of return) seeking to attract foreign investment must compete with investment opportunities offered elsewhere. *See* A. Lans Bovenberg et al., *Tax Incentives and International Capital Flows: The Case of the United States and Japan,* in TAXATION IN THE GLOBAL ECONOMY 283, 291–92 (Assaf Razin & Joel Slemrod eds., 1990).

[67] *See generally* IMF POLICY PAPER, *supra* note 40, at 13–14. Ring-fenced activities were one of the key concerns of the OECD 1998 harmful tax competition reports; *see, e.g.,* OECD, HARMFUL TAX COMPETITION: AN EMERGING GLOBAL ISSUE 26 (1998). The 2015 Action 5 Report of the BEPS Project, however, played down ring-fencing and focused instead on corporate-tax-rate reductions on particular types of income, such as income from the provision of intangibles. OECD, *Countering Harmful Tax Practices More Effectively, Taking into Account Transparency and Substance, Action 5 – 2015 Final Report,* OECD/G20 BASE EROSION AND PROFIT SHIFTING PROJECT 23 (2015). But see Margalioth, supra note 41, supporting certain tax incentives in developing countries.

[68] As the recent IP boxes phenomenon indicates. *See* Lisa Evers, Helen Miller & Christoph Spengel, *Intellectual Property Box Regimes: Effective Tax Rates and Tax Policy Considerations 1* (Centre for European Econ. Research Discussion Paper No. 13–070, 2013). For an extensive review of current IP regimes within the OECD Action 5, *see id.* at 63.

[69] *See* Peter Mullins, International Tax Issues for the Resources Sector, in The Taxation of Petroleum and Minerals: Principles, Problems and Practice 378, 379 (Philip Daniel, Michael Keen, & Charles McPherson eds., 2010), explaining that while resource rich countries may be less concerned with tax competition as the natural resources are location specific, they may have to compete for scarce managerial and technical skills in resources extraction, or for available finance for resource projects. *See also* Carlo Cottarelli, *Fiscal Regimes for Extractive Industries: Design and Implementation 14* (IMF Working Paper, Aug. 15, 2012).

Second, competition for high-demand residents creates incentives for states to reduce their taxes on certain individuals and corporations. States may seek to attract young, skilled residents (as opposed to sick, old, or poor ones) and residents most likely to have a positive spillover-effect, such as entrepreneurs, potential employers, and MNE headquarters, which may use local banking, legal, accounting, and even research services. When a state competes for residents, it can reduce not only the tax rates imposed on sought-after residents but also their tax bases by offering a territorial international tax regime, deferral, or generous credits, deductions, and exemptions. The tax revenues a recruiting state would lose in taking such measures would arguably be offset by the profits reaped by local factors of production.

Third, states could also adopt the competitive strategy of catering to the needs of the more mobile and more valuable potential taxpayers. That is to say, a state will not only reduce the prices they pay in taxes but will also provide them with the services they need the most. For example, a friendly legal system could attract investors; a solid public education system and lax labor laws could attract potential employers; and a thriving cultural environment could attract skilled workers. Different states have different comparative advantages (e.g., an attractive residential environment, a desirable corporate governance regime,[70] or thriving financial markets),[71] and those in high demand because of such advantages enjoy greater leeway to set higher tax rates.

States also need to adapt their strategies to the reality of electivity under fragmentation. They must internalize the fact that they (should) operate as competitive players in multiple markets and should rethink, accordingly, their optimal market strategies or pay a price in terms of how well they do in those markets. The competition occurs simultaneously in a number of parallel markets: the market for residents, the market for capital, the market for production sites, the market for jobs, the market for IP, etc. Thus, certain services, public goods, and even legal rules have to be individually priced or packaged strategically, featuring the state's attractive advantages. This fragmented market regime has completely altered the considerations

---

[70] See ERIC L. TALLEY, CORPORATE INVERSIONS AND THE UNBUNDLING OF REGULATORY COMPETITION 4 (2014) (arguing that the United States can charge relatively high corporate taxes since it has bundled its tax system with its corporate governance regime). See also Schon, supra note 43, at 336 (discussing the unbundled "price" of company laws).

[71] Thus, for example, the United States used the comparative advantages of its capital markets to successfully promote FATCA. See Joshua Blank & Ruth Mason, Exporting FATCA, 142 TAX NOTES 1245 (2014).

states weigh in deciding on the most effective taxing (and spending) regime. Rather than an internal maximization problem, this is now a matter of determining the optimal market strategy for a supplier of goods (the state) competing for clientele (residents as well as investors). Hence, states are contending with a whole new set of dilemmas under competition.

States can compete for high-demand residents and investors not only by reducing tax rates for all taxpayers) but also by price discriminating among potential taxpayers. This can be done by providing targeted benefits, such as benefits to foreign direct investors in rulings upon request,[72] preferential treatment to certain industries through generous allowable deductions,[73] particularized exemptions, and selective enforcement of GAAR rules.[74] Alternatively, a state could include loopholes in its taxation regime that allow residents with extensive investments overseas relative leeway in planning their taxes[75] and foreign investors and foreign residents to plan around their own states' tax rules.[76] Thus, to efficiently plan their international tax policy in conditions of tax competition, states must take into account not only residents' mobility and the elasticity of their investments' location but also the degree of their responsiveness to such sheltering options.

The upshot is that the state has been forced to relinquish much of its monopolistic sovereign power over a non-negligible portion of its taxpayers and to adapt its tax policy and system to the market forces. This

---

[72] *See* Marian, *supra* note 52. This is a practice that seems to have come under attack in the EU Commissioner's recent state aid decisions. *See* Mindy Hertzfeld, *News Analysis: State Aid Bureaucrats Run Amok*, 82 TAX NOTES INT'L 1127 (June 20, 2016) (criticizing the commission's investigations into whether U.S. multinationals pay too little tax in Europe and arguing that "it is...hard to see how [it]...advances the original intent of the prohibition on state aid – to prevent countries from granting benefits to domestic companies at the expense of others within the EU. With the current investigations – which are all about preventing countries from disadvantaging domestic companies at the expense of multinationals – the commission has flipped the original purpose of state aid law on its head.").

[73] See, for example, the generous interest deductions explained in detail in OECD, *Limiting Base Erosion Involving Interest Deductions and Other Financial Payments, Action 4 – 2015 Final Report* 15–17 (2015), http://www.keepeek.com/Digital-Asset-Management/oecd/taxation/limiting-base-erosion-involving-interest-deductions-and-other-financial-payments-action-4-2015-final-report_9789264241176-en#page17. Patent boxes are another example of how states create special regimes to attract high-tech industries. *See supra* note 68.

[74] Benjamin Alarie, *Price Discrimination in Income Taxation: Defending Half-Hearted Anti-Avoidance* (Mar. 26, 2011), http://ssrn.com/abstract=1796284. Brian J. Arnold, *The Long, Slow, Steady Demise of the General Anti-Avoidance Rule*, 52 CAN. TAX J. 488, 491 (2004).

[75] For example, a tax deferral for business income.

[76] Alarie, *supra* note 74, at 24.

inevitably means that in order to serve its efficiency goals, the state has to limit its tax collection (from its mobile taxpayers) and more carefully design the public goods and services they provide. It also means, however, that the criteria for the provision of such goods and services are determined by market rules of supply and demand and by the preferences of the more mobile actors on the market rather than through a internal maximization process.

b. Distributive Justice

The market competition for residents and resources significantly constrains states' redistributive capacity. Because of competition and the loss of the state's monopolistic power over its taxation system, redistribution has ceased to be a discretionary mechanism for promoting justice and equal participation in a democratic society and has increasingly become a price some states are able to charge from high-ability individuals and businesses. An additional cost has been added to the state's considerations for and against redistribution: the cost of taxpayers on the paying side of redistribution opting out of the system either by physically relocating or by shifting their tax base to another jurisdiction.[77]

The outcome of states' struggle to attract investments (by lowering their tax rates) and woo residents (individuals as well as multinational enterprises) with attractive taxing and spending deals is the infamous "race to the bottom." Residence and host countries are pushed to constantly reduce their tax rates – ultimately to the point of zero taxes, according to the theoretical prediction[78] – thereby undermining their ability to redistribute wealth. Although the empirical evidence does not unequivocally support the zero tax prediction[79] and even though there are certainly other

---

[77] Empirical data on the extent of the phenomenon are hard to collect and measure, especially as it is hard to distinguish the tax from the non-tax motivations in residents' decisions to relocate. For an elaborate discussion of the issue in the U.S. corporate sector, see Shaviro, *supra* note 39, at 429, reviewing the existing evidence and concluding that the problem of rising electivity of corporates' residency is "not nearly as great a problem, however, for existing U.S. corporate equity, which to a considerable degree is trapped, as it is for new equity (whether in new or existing corporations)."

[78] For comprehensive surveys of the research, see Wilson, *supra* note 45, at 52 NAT'L TAX J. 269 (1999); John D. Wilson & David E. Wildasin, *Capital Tax Competition: Bane or Boon?*, 88 J. PUB. ECON. 1065 (2004); VITO TANZI, TAXATION IN AN INTEGRATING WORLD (1995) (arguing that rates of tax on capital should approach zero). *See also* my discussion in Chapter 4.

[79] Empirical evidence does not clearly indicate that the race to the bottom is a serious problem; *see, e.g.,* Sijbren Cnossen, *Tax Policy in the European Union* (CESifo Working Paper

plausible scenarios,[80] it is now widely acknowledged that tax competition restricts the ability of states to redistribute wealth domestically.[81]

In the most extreme case, driving down tax rates on mobile residents and on the mobile factors of production will shift the tax burden to the less mobile (and often less well-off[82]) factors. This may lead to a reduction in the state's tax revenues and thereby erode its ability to sustain public goods and services and, in particular, redistribution. Moreover, as Reuven Avi-Yonah established, "if capital cannot be effectively taxed, the tax base will generally shift – regressively – toward labor. Thus, tax competition impairs the income tax's ability to redistribute wealth from the rich to the poor."[83] In any event, tax competition indisputably brings pressure to bear on states to reduce their taxes and restrict redistribution or else pay the overall welfare price.[84]

Several factors serve as counterweights to competition's downward pressure on redistribution. One central factor is the actual costs of relocation for individuals and businesses. People must take into consideration

No. 758, Category 1: Public Finance, Aug. 2002); Thomas Plümper, Vera E. Troeger & Hannes Winner, *Why Is There No Race to the Bottom in Capital Taxation? Tax Competition among Countries of Unequal Size, Different Levels of Budget Rigidities and Heterogeneous Fairness Norms*, 53 INT'L STUD. Q. 761 (2009). "No doubt, the prediction of zero capital tax rates was not in line with reality when it was first formulated and it did not come true since." James R. Hines, Jr., *Will Social Welfare Expenditures Survive Tax Competition?* 22 OXFORD REV. ECON. POL'Y 330, 331 (2006); Vivek H. Dehejia & Philipp Genschel, *Tax Competition in the European Union*, 27 POL. & SOC'Y 403, 409 (1999); Philipp Genschel & Peter Schwarz, *Tax competition: a literature review*, 9 SOCIO-ECONOMIC REVIEW, 339.

[80] *See, e.g.,* Hines, id., at 331 (arguing that it is also possible that globalization will invigorate advanced economies, thereby making them more able to support significant social welfare spending).

[81] For a detailed analysis of the phenomenon, *see* Reuven S. Avi-Yonah, *Globalization, Tax Competition, and the Fiscal Crisis of the Welfare State*, 113 HARV. L. REV. 1573, 1575–1603 (2000). It has been argued that tax competition will drive tax rates down to a suboptimal level, where states are forced to under-provide public goods. For a formal model supporting this argument, *see* George R. Zodrow & Peter Mieszkowski, *Pigou, Tiebout, Property Taxation, and the Underprovision of Local Public Goods*, 19 J. PUB. ECON. 356 (1986). Although it is unclear what exactly constitutes the "optimal" level of public goods (*see* Julie Roin, *Competition and Evasion: Another Perspective on International Tax Competition*, 89 GEO. L.J. 543(2001)), it is pretty clear that redistribution would be reduced.

[82] This is particularly acute given that there tends to be (although there not always is) a correlation between wealth and mobility. The wealthiest people (as well as their capital) are often the most mobile people. Therefore, broad-brush rules seeking to treat the mobile more leniently will tend to limit redistribution via tax laws. Since redistribution targets the wealthiest, mobility limits states' ability to redistribute. Taxing the mobile-rich might push them away; taxing the less mobile (and not as rich) will yield less efficient redistribution.

[83] Avi-Yonah, *supra* note 81, at 1578, 1624.

[84] For a more detailed analysis of the costs and benefits of tax competition, *see* Chapter 4.

the significant costs entailed by shifting their residences, families, cultural ties and jobs as well as switching their domestic loyalties. Businesses may also bear costs related to physically or legally moving their residency or economic activities and workers to a new jurisdiction. A second important factor is a jurisdiction's specific market power. If it offers an attractive residential environment, particular loyalties (e.g., a strong sentimental preferability as a specific residential location due to historical, cultural, or national ties), a unique commitment to the welfare of fellow members of the community,[85] rich natural resources, network externalities, favorable regulation (e.g., superior corporate governance[86]), or any other comparative advantages, it should be able to allow for more redistribution. [87] Political constraints are another important factor: a political tradition that is committed to fairness will be less likely to give up on redistribution altogether.[88] All of these factors could well explain how and why states continue to collect above-zero taxes and allow for a certain level of redistribution even in the current conditions of global competition.

But whatever the degree of resilience due to these factors, the fact of taxpayer mobility implies that states (should) weigh the benefits of redistribution relative to the potential costs of driving away wealthy residents and businesses with excessive redistribution. Where tax-planning opportunities are available, they act as further constraints on states' ability to redistribute wealth. For even when a state offers advantages relative to other states or taxpayers have considerable costs of relocation, it will find it difficult to convert these advantages or inelasticities into tax revenues that facilitates significant redistribution.

---

[85] Alberto F. Alesina & Paola Giuliano, *Preferences for Redistribution* (NBER Working Paper No. w14825, Mar. 2009).

[86] *See, e.g.*, Talley, *supra* note 70 (noting that the bundling of tax with place of incorporation enabled the United States to collect taxes due to MNEs' preference for Delaware corporate laws).

[87] U.S. federal laws and local tax laws have evolved so as to limit location-specific rents, especially for businesses operating in more than one jurisdiction, thereby making redistribution via local tax rules relatively inefficient. *See* Galle, *supra* note 11, at 534–37 and references cited therein.

[88] Plümper, *supra* note 79, at 783:

> Holding everything else constant, countries in which governments are least restricted by fairness considerations implement the lowest tax rates on mobile capital and become capital importers. This result remains valid for the opposite case: governments which are most restricted by fairness norms implement the highest tax rates on mobile capital and become capital exporters. Accordingly, fairness norms come at a price; the price a country with an egalitarian electorate has to pay is the highest when fairness norms are weaker in other countries.

c. Personal and Collective Identities

Competition also transforms the relationship between states and their constituents by challenging national identities, putting domestic loyalties to the test, and altering forms of political participation. When taxpayers are offered viable residency alternatives that are less costly in terms of their tax liability, they – or at least the marginal group thereof – will (almost inevitably) have to weigh their local commitments against the costs and benefits of moving (or shifting their tax base) to a different tax jurisdiction. This evaluation of their loyalties in monetary terms could have commodifying consequences. Taxpayers, faced with income tax liabilities, are pushed to compare (the liability costs of) their local affiliation with commodities they can purchase with the tax money they will save. Those taxpayers who have the capacity to relocate to another jurisdiction will need to choose between their domestic loyalties and the benefits of the alternative residency.

States face a similar dilemma: they must choose between adhering to their original criteria for the inclusion and taxation of their members and the need to recruit new, desirable residents.[89] The competitive setting brings to the forefront two attributes that would generally not be considered components of the taxpayer's identity in other contexts: taxpayers' attractiveness to the state and their degree of mobility. When competing for residents, states are more likely to pursue attractive taxpayers and to offer more generous tax deals to the mobile among them. In highlighting attractiveness and mobility, the competitive context places emphasis on people's willingness to exit their current communities as well as on their use value. By taking into account the use value of potential residents and investors, states evaluate them in terms of their prospective contribution (mostly economic[90]) to the country, assessing how beneficial they are for

---

[89] The United States' unique focus on citizenship as a main characteristic of its income-tax system could be explained as making a clear distinction between "us" and "them," with "us" referring to whoever is an American citizen (even if not residing in the U.S.). For additional explanations of the citizenship criterion and a critique of citizenship as a test for nonresidents' membership, see Mason, supra note 27, at 121–24. States that determine local taxpayer status based on residency (and the United States, which taxes residents in addition to U.S. citizens and green-card holders) use different (mostly technical) criteria. Some use a number-of-days test; others look to the location of the individual's "tax home" or her center of vital interests, using such criteria as permanent place of abode, her bank accounts, where her family members reside, where her professional ties are, etc. For a compilation of the residency rules of various countries, see http://www.oecd.org/tax/automatic-exchange/crs-implementation-and-assistance/tax-residency/.

[90] The form of encouragement – tax incentives – highlights the economic value of the "transaction." Tax benefits are monetary payments, and tax policy confers larger monetary

"us." This criterion reduces the notion of being a viable part of a community to members' costs and benefits and induces states to offer more favorable deals to more desirable prospective residents as well as to current residents regarded as most beneficial to the country and most receptive to fiscal incentives to stay.

This use-value perspective affects both personal and national identities. On the personal level, it associates one's civic identity with a narrow, commodified version of political membership. Interestingly, this takes income taxation almost full circle back to its early stages, where benefit taxation reigned as a key justification. In fact, benefit taxation was marginalized as a justification for income taxation at the end of the nineteenth century precisely because its consumeristic and commodified understanding of income taxation was incompatible with a modern, highly interdependent society.[91] Tax competition's emphasis on consumer-like choices, preferences, and transactional quid pro quo seems to bring back the commodified version of taxation and thereby undermine civic identity and political belonging.

On the national level, this old-new perspective calls into question our ideas regarding who comprise "us." Are "we" in any meaningful sense a cohesive group with a shared sense of solidarity, commitment, and belongingness? Or are "we" simply a group of people with a shared interest in increasing our collective net-worth? The emphasis in the global competitive setting on recruiting the most beneficial new residents supports the latter, more commodified version of "us." Tax competition, in other words, leads us to consider national identities in market terms.

---

payments upon people with larger incomes. Thus, it would be the wealthiest potential residents who find it beneficial to immigrate to a country that offers them tax benefits. Paying according to one's economic worth can be viewed as bluntly trading political affiliation for monetary consideration (in cases where the new recruits are best serving the political interests of decision makers), or alternatively – if political power is not what decision makers are after – tax benefits simply put higher emphasis on the economic worth (rather than other qualities) of new recruits.

[91] Ajay Mehrotra *supra* note 14, at 114 describes the shift away from benefit taxation in the United States as follows:

> If the reform-minded economists concurred that the benefits rationale was obsolete for a modern, highly interdependent society, they also disapproved of benefits doctrine because it was framed in an idiom of market relations. With their emphasis on the importance of ethical duty and social bonds, these theorists loathed how the benefits doctrine commodified the relationship between citizens and the state . . . taxation based on a transactional notion of mutual exchange or barter . . . seemed to contradict the ethical responsibility and social solidarity that tax activists and economic theorists believed was at the center of a new sense of political belonging.

Like the use-value perspective, taxpayer mobility also raises a set of new – related, but not identical – concerns about taxpayer identity as part of the political community of the state. Mobility per se focuses on taxpayers' provisional status and rewards it. The more impermanent taxpayers are, the better taxation deal they can expect from their own state and from other states that are competing for them. Rewarding mobility, however, creates the risk that national communities may become tenuous: more dependent on the quality and extent of the services the state provides and less related to a sense of belongingness based on a shared commitment among community members.

The aspiration to tax community members based on their ability to pay, on the one hand, and the desire to offer attractive deals to in-demand mobile taxpayers, on the other, clash head-on when the mobile are also the wealthier residents with greater foreign-source income and greater opportunities elsewhere. Such individuals are more likely to weigh their national membership against the domestic taxes and benefits they are offered by the state, and as a result, states may also wish to limit taxation of these individuals. This will weaken what membership implies in terms of responsibility toward co-members of the political community.

A final effect of both the mobility of existing citizens and the pursuit of attractive newcomers is their potential bearing on the state's political processes. Specifically, when the state functions as a recruiter, traditions of political participation could be altered as a result. Taxpayer mobility leads to greater emphasis being placed on exit over voice and thereby elevates the one form of democratic participation over the other.[92] Rather than trying to influence the political system using their voice and resorting to exit only as a fallback position, taxpayers with easily available exit options may be less inclined to facilitate change from within and more inclined to exit (or threaten to exit). At a certain level, the emphasis on exit might be even more destructive, for it will cease to be a means of conveying one's discontent with current policies and will instead become an independent factor in the decline of the state. The exiting of strong segments of society also means that there will be less public funds (and fewer public services) for the remaining residents.

Stronger emphasis on exit may also imply that capital owners as well as young or talented individuals might exercise more influence over the national decision-making process than other taxpayers. Decision makers may be incentivized to internalize the narrow interests of such mobile individuals into policymaking. Indeed, if the preferences of mobile

---

[92] ALBERT O. HIRSCHMAN, EXIT, VOICE AND LOYALTY (1970).

individuals or investors are not catered to and they exercise exit, there could be substantial negative externalities on local factors of production. Thus, in order to prevent damage to the interests of other segments of society (those without an exit option), the interests of mobile individuals should be advanced. Furthermore, because of the competitive pressure to recruit attractive residents and investors, non-citizens may also have significant political influence over national tax, expenditure, and wealth-distribution policies. The very presumption that such benefits are necessary to attract desirable non-residents to the state could have a significant effect on domestic policies. Hence, such foreign investors and potential residents may play an important role in local decision-making without formally having a voice in the process. In fact, it is not actually the foreign investors or potential residents themselves who influence this process but what policymakers imagine their preferences to be. In other words, at best, decision makers can only estimate the preferences of foreign residents and investors, to whom they are not even accountable.

The ability to opt out of a state's taxation system without actually exiting its territorial jurisdiction further erodes political participation. Integral to the state's power, indeed its very legitimacy, is its ability to impartially apply its coercive powers to its equally participating constituents.[93] It is this quality that legitimizes the state's imposition of its power on its residents and its acting in the name of its constituents. Subordinating the requirements of equality to the market power of individual participants in the political community undermines the legitimacy of the state as a political unit that treats its subjects with equal concern and respect.

Under competition, decision makers are forced to choose between recruiting new members and their old constituents and forced to decide whether they must use monetary incentives to lure new recruits or can afford not to do so. They have to choose between supporting an open, yet commodified and somewhat tenuous community and a community that is bound by the sense of no viable alternative. They have to eyeball the preferences of foreigners (to whom they are not accountable) and grant them benefits beyond what is offered to their current constituency, in the hope that the positive externalities from the prospective investments and residency will outweigh the costs of those benefits.

The global competition among states for residents and investments has inevitably transformed the foundation of domestic tax policies. It has altered the way in which we (should) approach the classic normative goals

---

[93] For more on this, *see* Chapter 6 on global justice.

of income tax policy. This new perspective has given rise to new dilemmas regarding efficiency, redistribution, and concepts of (personal and collective) identity. Under competition, tax is increasingly ceasing to be a coercive tool used by the state to overcome collective action problems and is increasingly becoming a means for competing for residents and capital.

The incentive to attract mobile residents and investments drives policymakers to limit tax's redistribution functions. It leads them to prefer more attractive taxpayers, as well as those more prone to and capable of unbundling states' packaging of public goods and taxes, over their original constituents and to rely less on voice-based and more on exit-based practices, with mobility gaining particular weight as a criterion for receiving economic rights and benefits. Under these conditions, tax policy does not merely set the level and distribution of tax and restrict itself to determining the types and level of services provided by the state. Rather, to an increasing extent, tax policy decides who counts and who doesn't. By inevitably providing higher incentives for some taxpayers and lower incentives for others, tax policy in fact participates in determining who belongs to "us."

Whereas this chapter focused on the internal effect of competition – its effect on domestic tax policies – the next chapters will start our discussion of the interaction of such policies with the policies of other, competing, countries. In order to analyze this complex interaction and for purely methodological reasons, I will assume in the next chapters – contrary to my discussion hitherto and despite the contestability of such an assumption – that a "national interest" does exist. Chapter 2 will discuss the interaction of unilateral strategies; Chapter 3 will discuss the bilateral interaction; and Chapters 4 and 5 will consider multilateral interactions. After this analysis of the interaction on these three different levels, I will relax the assumption of a national interest, in an effort to combine the domestic and external complexities.

2

Global Planners and Strategic Players

After considering the complexities of globalization and tax policy on the domestic level, this chapter moves on to the international level. It analyzes the structure of international taxation (leaving aside, for the time being, the complexities of the domestic level) in order to explain the unique dynamics that the interdependent decentralized international tax regime creates. The chapter exemplifies this with one of the most dominant issues on the international tax policy agenda – the prevention of double taxation. It analyzes two prominent episodes in the history of international tax policymaking. The first is the League of Nations' deliberation of double taxation during the early 1920s, which yielded a model for allocating tax rights among states on cross-border economic activities. The second is the more modern debate that has dominated much of the literature since it was launched by Peggy Richman-Musgrave in the 1960s, which advocates promoting welfare by adopting national policies that do not distort cross-border activities (so-called "neutrality"). Each of these episodes offers important lessons for the analysis of international tax policy that will be relevant to the rest of the book's chapters. Considering these two episodes at this stage in tandem is useful because it helps to understand the predominant global-normative perspective through which the field of international taxation has been analyzed and policymakers have formulated recommendations.

This chapter criticizes the League of Nations' recommendations as well as the neutrality debate, offering a third approach for designing international tax policy, one that pursues national interests and taxing strategically. To be sure, my critique of the global-normative perspective does not imply that it should be rejected. In fact, this perspective lies at the focus of the two last chapters of this book. But if we are to fully appreciate the challenges of the *ought*, we need to first properly understand the implications of the *is*. The *is* of international taxation – which is the reality at present and which will likely persist for the foreseeable future – is not structured around a centralized global government that can assess and implement such policy recommendations. Rather, the field is deeply decentralized, comprised of a host of national states, each with its own interests and agendas, each making its own decisions, which, together, shape the landscape of international taxation. In analyzing the field, therefore, the interaction between and among these players must be accounted for using, as this chapter does, strategic tools as the basic methodology. Accordingly, the chapter focuses on the national actors as the key game-makers and examines their unique position in shaping the decentralized yet interdependent regime of international taxation.

The critique offered in this chapter is essentially a positive one. Since in practice, the international taxation regime is determined by national sovereigns, the rationale underlying the analysis in this chapter is that focus must be placed, first and foremost, on their interests to fully understand international tax policy. It is the interaction between interests and the competitive nature of the international tax market that sets the parameters of the international tax playing-field. National interests determine what tax policies sovereigns pursue, while global tax competition constrains sovereigns in pursuing those interests. Thus, the preferred outcome on the state level – that is, in terms of national interests – should be the point of departure in discussing international tax policy and where this chapter begins. The next stage is determining the best strategy for promoting national interests: choosing between cooperative or non-cooperative measures. This chapter considers the available unilateral strategies. Looking at the dominant policy considerations of different states, the chapter analyzes the international recommendations for preventing double taxation and the debate at the national level over the preferable method for unilaterally alleviating it. The bilateral and multilateral cooperative options will be addressed in Chapters 3, 4, and 5.

2.1 The League of Nations Solution: Allocating Rights

Double taxation – when two or more states tax the same income[1] – has dominated taxation scholarship and policymaking for decades. It is

---

[1] States tend to tax income based on taxpayers' personal affiliations (such as the worldwide income of residents or citizens), on territorial criteria (e.g., if the income is produced within the state's territory), or a combination of the two. Thus, there are a number of contexts in which double taxation can occur. For example, two states may consider a certain taxpayer's income as produced within their respective territories, and consequently, both will tax it. This scenario usually arises when there is a conflict between the two states' definitions of sources of income and/or of the location of the relevant source. Similarly, double taxation can occur when two states both regard a particular taxpayer to be a resident of their jurisdictions and both tax her on a personal basis. The classic case of double taxation, however,

perhaps the most notorious product of the inconsistencies between states' tax policies in a decentralized regime. This phenomenon limits cross-border economic activity and distorts it. Thus, double taxation is a challenging issue for policymakers in setting international tax policies and deciding on the optimal strategy for alleviating it.[2]

The need to contend with double taxation has been at the center of the public debate on international taxation since the 1920s, when rising income tax rates intensified the problem. Seeking to address this phenomenon, the League of Nations Provisional Economic and Finance Committee appointed a panel of four academic tax experts[3] to study the issue. In their final report, submitted in 1923,[4] the panel of experts assumed the (hypothetical) role of global planner. This was most prominently manifested in their conception of a desirable international tax regime, set out in their report as follows:

> The ideal solution is that the individual's whole faculty should be taxed, but that it should be taxed only once, and that the liability should be divided among the tax districts according to his relative interests in each. The individual has certain economic interests in the place of his permanent residence or domicile, as well as in the place or places where his property is situated or from which his income is derived. If he makes money in one place he generally spends it in another.[5]

The report takes as a given that a person's entire "faculty" should be taxed by one state. In order to prevent taxation of the same income by more than one state, the experts focused on the question of which state should

and on which the literature and policymaking tend to focus, is when one state taxes an item of income based on the taxpayer's residency and another state taxes the same item for being produced within its territory.

[2] The use of the term "double taxation" to refer to this phenomenon may imply that there is something inherently wrong with it and something inherently correct about only one of the involved countries imposing its taxes. I prefer to view international taxation as a continuum of combined levels of taxation imposed by residence and host countries. At one end of this continuum is no taxation whatsoever, followed by different mechanisms for alleviating double taxation in the host and residence countries, and ending with both countries imposing their taxes without any alleviation at all. No one point along this continuum is more "right" or "normal" than any other point. Tsilly Dagan, *The Tax Treaties Myth*, 32 NYU J. INT'L L. & POL. 939, 975–92 (2000); Daniel Shaviro, *The Two Faces of the Single Tax Principle* (NYU School of Law Public Law Research Paper No. 15–47, 2015).

[3] The committee members were as follows: Professor Bruins of Rotterdam, Professor Senator Einaudi of Turin University, Professor Seligman of Columbia University, and Sir Josiah Stamp of London University. Their final report weighed several options for allocating taxing rights among residence countries, countries of citizenship, and source (or host) countries. G.W.J. Bruins et al., League of Nations Econ. & Fin. Comm., *Report on Double Taxation: Submitted to the Financial Committee*, League of Nations Doc. E.F.S.73. F.19 (1923).

[4] *Id.*   [5] *Id.* at 20.

be granted the right to tax which income and the consequent duties of individuals to pay taxes to different states. In this context, the report stressed the decline of political allegiances and the rise of new (and modular, it seems) allegiances based on economic ties. Because the latter allegiances can arise in any number of jurisdictions, the report sought to identify the jurisdiction most deserving of the right to tax. Here, again, the panel of experts took on the role of global decision maker with the power to select a "winner." The experts weighed the relative strengths of the various allegiances – political ties, temporary residency, permanent residency, location of wealth[6] – and concluded what has become widely accepted ever since: that a state is justified in taxing income where the taxpayer owes it a certain degree of economic allegiance even if he or she does not reside in the state's jurisdiction.[7] The report then analyzed the implications of economic allegiances for various categories of wealth and income, in an effort to establish what constitutes an economic tie robust enough to justify imposing a duty to pay taxes and a right to tax at source.[8]

The approach expressed in the experts' report recognizes the possibility of taxpayers' having multiple allegiances based on economic affiliations. But while it seemingly prescribes allocating tax revenues according to

---

[6] *Id.* at 18–19.

[7] *Id.* at 19:

> Practically . . . apart from the question of nationality, which still plays a minor role, the choice lies between the principle of domicile and that of location or origin. Taking the field of taxation as a whole, the reason why tax authorities waver between these two principles is that each may be considered as a part of the still broader principle of economic interest of economic allegiance, as against the original doctrine of political allegiance. A part of the total sum paid according to the ability of a person ought to reach the competing authorities according to his economic interest under each authority.

[8] What is economic allegiance? The report (*id.* at 19) states that it is

> where the true economic interests of the individual are found. It is only after an analysis of the constituent elements of this economic allegiance that we shall be able to determine where a person ought to be taxed or how the division ought to be made as between the various sovereignties that impose the tax.

See also Kim Brooks, *Tax Treaty Treatment of Royalty Payments from Low-Income Countries: A Comparison of Canada and Australia's Policies*, 5 eJOURNAL TAX RES. 168, 173 (2007) (noting that the report "concluded that for land and business property, the country in which the taxpayer had a fixed location had the strongest claim to the taxpayer's economic allegiance; in contrast, for both tangible and intangible personal property, the predominant claim of economic allegiance was held to rest with the country in which the owner resided").

the relative economic interests of the competing jurisdictions,[9] it in fact recommended that states split the revenues by reciprocally waiving their rights to tax. "[T]he reciprocal exemption of the non-resident" is, concluded the report, "the most desirable practical method of avoiding the evils of double taxation and should be adopted wherever countries feel in a position to do so."[10] Furthermore, it was suggested, where mutual exemption "is repugnant owing to a reluctance to abandon the principle of origin," classification and assignment of sources through conventions could be adopted.[11] Thus, Reuven Avi-Yonah has explained, "while pure residence-based taxation may be an ideal for the future, in practice source-based taxation would persist and therefore there should be a division between source and residence jurisdictions based on the degree of benefits accorded different types of income."[12]

An economic-allegiance rights-based allocation of taxing privileges among states is troubling for at least two reasons.[13] The first relates to

[9] *See* Bruins et al., *supra* note 3, at 22–23:

> On the assumption, therefore, that economic allegiance is the basis upon which the total tax paid by the individual should reach the competing authorities, we have to ask what is the true meaning of economic allegiance and what are the ways in which it can be subdivided. In what ways and to what extent can a man be served by two or more governments that he should owe them any duty? In the attempt to discover the true meaning of economic allegiance, it is clear that there are three fundamental considerations: that of (1) production of wealth; that of (2) possession of wealth; that of (3) disposition of wealth. We have to ask where the wealth is really produced, i.e., where does it really come into existence; where is it owned; and, finally, where is it disposed of?

[10] Bruins et al., *supra* note 3, at 51.

[11] *Id.* at 51. The report further stated as follows:

> [L]looking forward…as semi-developed countries become more industrialized…the principle of personal faculty at the place of residence will become more widely understood and appreciated and the disparity between the two principles will become less obvious, so that we may look forward to an ultimate development of national ideas on uniform lines toward method 2 [exemption], if not as a more logical and theoretically defensible economic view of the principles of income taxation, at least as the most practicable solution of the difficulties of double taxation.

Id. at 51.

[12] Reuven S. Avi-Yonah, *All of a Piece Throughout: The Four Ages of U.S. International Taxation*, 25 Va. Tax Rev. 313, 323 (2005). *But see* Wei Cui, *Minimalism about Residence and Source*, 38 Mich. J. Int'l L. (Forthcoming, 2016). Available at SSRN: https://ssrn.com/abstract=2677429 (offering a minimalist functionalist reading of the source and residence concepts adopted by the League of Nations' experts).

[13] These two lines of criticism correspond roughly to Michael Sandel's formulation of the two objections to the market in general: coercion and corruption. Michael J. Sandel, Justice: What's the Right Thing to Do? 75–101 (2009).

commensurability. The report listed factors that its authors considered intuitively relevant to establishing a state's right to tax and then identified those that they deemed the most justifiable basis for determining what an individual owes to a given state. Yet this is premised on the assumption that allegiances can be shared as well as ranked or proportioned. However, as explained in Chapter 1, it is not self-evident that political and economic allegiances and domicile and residency choices can (and, indeed, should) be measured on the same scale. Nor is it in any way obvious how states can negotiate the allegiances that will determine how the tax base will be split between them in a bilateral arrangement. Placing allegiances on the same scale frames them as commensurate. But is it actually possible to prorate individuals' political allegiances, their connections to the jurisdiction in which they reside, and their ties to the location of their business activities? Can people's political connection to their state of citizenship be compared to their ties to their state of residence, which supplies them with such public benefits as personal security, healthcare, and education? Can, moreover, these allegiances be compared to their economic ties to a host country, which provides them with a facilitating business environment? Comparing differing scales of valuation and balancing among incommensurable goods is something policymakers are often required to do. But the report seems to have avoided this complex balancing act and instead chosen to settle for a single scale – the scale of economic allegiance. Defining people's allegiances based on their economic ties and measuring the relative strength of those allegiances by the (economic) benefits they derive from a jurisdiction may be more practical, but it commodifies the allegiances. Rather than through the plurality of their scales of valuation, these allegiances are construed through the narrow prism of instrumental economic value.

Treating political allegiances, residency, and income production as comparable and measuring them by their economic value reduces personal and community affiliations to purely instrumental terms. As explained, this can transform the individual's perception of political participation as well as the state's perception of its interaction with and commitments to its constituents. In addition, this conception of loyalty in economic terms also leads states to prioritize policy options that yield economic benefits to potential constituents that will establish their affiliation to their jurisdiction. While this quid pro quo approach of providing economic benefits and collecting taxes in return could be appropriate in the context of a deal cut between governments and purely economic actors (e.g., foreign investors), it might be problematic for taxing constituents. If states have the right to tax individuals based on a compelling economic affiliation to their jurisdiction, they will be incentivized to invest in reinforcing those ties rather than in the cultural, political, and social aspects of being a member of their communities. If we take the global-planner perspective seriously, we may want that planner to make room for criteria other than the market scale of valuation and to support states in their choice to apply criteria that digress from the economic scale of valuation.

This brings us to the second reservation regarding the rights-based approach in the League of Nations report: its potential distributive outcomes among states. The report's recommendations rely heavily on the contracting states' mutual consent to the taxing rights allocation in the agreement between them. But this consent may not be as neutral as may appear at first glance. As Chapters 3, 4, and 5 will demonstrate, this reliance on the parties' consent in both bilateral and multilateral negotiations could have significant distributive ramifications. This was purportedly simply a recommendation from a body without any official authority. Yet the framing of consent as the focal point of the League of Nations report, its reinforcement by other international organizations at later stages in the development of international taxation, and probably the fact that the experts were from countries with significant international clout and thus able to impose their objectives on many other countries, significantly impacted the shape the international tax regime took, particularly its distributive outcomes.[14]

Perhaps the most significant problem for our purposes, however, is the limited range of the modes of operation the League of Nations experts considered. Although they took the perils of double taxation on cross-border economic activity very seriously, they seem to have related to the idea of a single tax as axiomatic: every individual should pay tax only once. The experts completely disregarded the possibility that no tax, low tax, or benefit taxes might better serve some states. For example, a state might derive greater benefit from a particular economic activity than from the tax revenues it can collect from that activity. Under the report's approach, if host countries willingly waive their right to tax, they do so solely for the purpose of allowing countries of residence to fully tax cross-border income in return for a reciprocal exemption. If they find the exemption of source income combined with residence base taxation repugnant – to use the report's terms – this is simply because they prefer to collect more tax revenues. In other words, the League of Nations report seems to

---

[14] This will be discussed at greater length in Chapters 3 and 5.

presume that one (single) tax should be imposed on any given taxpayer for any given income and leaves the allocation of the revenues from that tax to be negotiated between the contracting states. The desirability of setting a single tax as a global goal is at the heart of the competition-versus-cooperation debate in international taxation, a normative issue that I will return to in Chapter 4 of this book.

2.2   Solutions at the National Level: Attempted Neutrality

Like the League of Nations, national policymakers also were troubled by double taxation and contemplated unilateral measures for its alleviation. They, too, gave source countries precedence in taxing income[15] and assigned the burden of contending with double taxation to residence countries.[16] A significant range of mechanisms were considered for alleviating double taxation, including the options of a complete exemption of foreign source income, a credit for taxes paid to the source country, and a deduction for foreign taxes paid. The U.S. credit system, the first of its kind, became a particularly popular model among states.[17]

As part of the attempt to determine which policy would best promote economic efficiency, the rights-based approach that had dominated tax policy canon was replaced by a focus on what was famously formulated by Peggy Richman as different types of "neutrality."[18] Policymakers and scholars debated the efficiency of the different types of so-called neutrality as rationales for addressing double taxation on the national level: predominantly capital export neutrality (CEN), capital import neutrality

---

[15] See Michael J. Graetz & Michael M. O'Hear, *The "Original Intent" of U.S. International Taxation*, 46 Duke L.J. 1021, 1037 (1997), quoting Thomas S. Adams, the originator of the foreign tax credit: "Every state insists upon taxing the nonresident alien who derives income from source [sic] within that country, and rightly so, at least inevitably so." Thomas S. Adams, *International and Interstates Aspects of Double Taxation, in* 22 Proceedings of the Annual Conference on Taxation under the Auspices of the National Tax Association 193, 197 (1929).

[16] *See, e.g.,* Reuven S. Avi-Yonah, *The Structure of International Taxation: A Proposal for Simplification*, 74 Tex. L. Rev. 1301, 1306 (1996); David H. Rosenbloom, *The David R. Tillinghast Lecture: International Tax Arbitrage and the "International Tax System,"* 53 Tax L. Rev. 137, 140 (2000).

[17] Graetz & O'Hear, *supra* note 15, at 1022.

[18] Peggy B. Richman, The Taxation of Foreign Investment Income: An Economic Analysis (1963). Avi-Yonah, *supra* note 12, at 324 ("Gone was the old emphasis on benefits and fairness; instead the argument was henceforward based on the economic concept of efficiency, which in the international context translated into neutrality (and in particular, capital export neutrality).").

(CIN), national neutrality (NN), and, more recently, competitive neutrality or capital ownership neutrality (CON). Although focused on unilateral national policies, the neutrality debate took a global perspective (except in the context of national neutrality). Proponents of neutrality implicitly assumed that the goal of international taxation policy – despite being designed and set by individual states – is the promotion of global welfare; this policy goal, they hold, should guide national policymakers[19] and can be achieved, so the argument suggested, through their independent unilateral actions even in a decentralized international tax regime.

Advocates of neutrality seek a solution that will least distort the allocation of global resources and will thereby maximize (global) welfare. This idea can be seen as the natural extension of discussions of efficiency in domestic tax policy, according to which taxes should be optimally designed to minimize distortions of the market allocation of resources. Similarly, in the international context, the neutrality-supporters' view is that if taxes did not distort market allocation, global investments would flow to where they would be most efficiently used,[20] global welfare would increase, and the resulting efficient allocation of resources would be to the benefit of all countries.[21] A neutral system of international taxation could presumably preserve such an efficient allocation of global resources. If taxes were neutrally applied, they would have no impact on where investors and capital consumers decide to invest or from which investors and in which countries consumers choose to borrow funds. In contrast, when different countries apply different rates of taxation and varying levels of taxation are imposed on different categories of taxpayers or on different

---

[19] *See* DANIEL N. SHAVIRO, FIXING U.S. INTERNATIONAL TAXATION 121 (2014):

> [T]he mystery is not that [Musgrave] chose to identify and emphasize particular global welfare norms, which very usefully helped to orient the field. Rather, it lies in the widespread assumption, for decades thereafter, that choosing which global welfare norms to implement was the right way to go about international tax policy making.

[20] *See* PAUL R. KRUGMAN & MAURICE OBSTFELD, INTERNATIONAL ECONOMIC THEORY AND POLICY 113 (1991). But *see* Joel Slemrod, *Tax Principles in an International Economy, in* WORLD TAX REFORM: CASE STUDIES OF DEVELOPED AND DEVELOPING COUNTRIES 11, 13 (Michael J. Boskin & Charles E. McLure, Jr. eds., 1990) ("[O]penness is a mixed blessing when the taxing authority has limited ability to tax cross-border movements of factors and goods. A discussion of tax principles in an international economy must come to terms with the real world, where the implementation of certain tax systems, which may be desirable in theory, is extremely difficult.").

[21] *See*, A. Lans Bovenberg et al., *Tax Incentives and International Capital Flaws: The Case of the United States and Japan, in* TAXATION IN THE GLOBAL ECONOMY 283, 291–92 (Assaf Razin & Joel Slemrod eds., 1990).

sources of income, the optimal allocation of global resources is distorted. This leads, in turn, to a decrease in the overall size of the global welfare pie.

Yet this analysis misses the mark in advocating maximization of the global welfare pie as a domestic goal. Based on a familiar stance taken in the literature, this section criticizes the neutrality discourse.[22] It explains that much of the neutrality analysis simply presumes (without explanation) that increasing global welfare would best serve national interests. It further assumes states' cooperation and ignores the possible interaction among the national policies of different states that could undermine such cooperation. Absent cooperation among states, neutrality cannot prevail. Thus, as I explain further on in this chapter, the decentralized structure of international taxation renders global neutrality a virtual impossibility.

Were there an international regime or institution that facilitates and ensures cooperation between states in setting their international tax rules, it might also seek to promote global welfare by minimizing distortions. But such a framework for international cooperation does not exist on the global level, and the quandary for neutrality proponents is how neutrality can be achieved in the current decentralized international tax regime, where states unilaterally set their international tax policies.

In addressing this question, scholars have generally limited the debate to concepts of partial neutrality, which target specific types of choices, and determining which of these concepts is preferable. In other words, they are concerned with which partial neutrality model does a better job of enhancing global welfare. In this context, too, the dominant background assumption seems to be that states should cooperate toward (partial) global neutrality. If all states were to adopt a policy that supports some type of partial neutrality, the argument goes, global neutrality would emerge and prevail. Only here, as well, there is no reason to assume that countries would indeed adopt a neutral policy. The rest of this section reviews and criticizes the different concepts of partial neutrality that have been advocated in the literature. It shows why partial neutrality does not make sense as a policy recommendation for a single state in setting its unilateral policy on double taxation. Instead of choosing among concepts of partial neutrality as an alternative, the section concludes, individual

---

[22] *See* Tsilly Dagan, *National Interests in the International Tax Game*, 18 VA. TAX REV. 363 (1998); Michael J. Graetz, *Taxing International Income: Inadequate Principles, Outdated Concepts, and Unsatisfactory Policy*, 26 BROOK. J. INT'L L. 1357, 1367 (2000); SHAVIRO, *supra* note 19, at 108–41 (providing both a comprehensive explanation and a sharp critique of the various neutrality concepts and entitling the entire debate as "alphabet soup").

states should discard the neutrality premise altogether and promote their national interests.[23]

a. Partial Neutralities

The debate over the best method for alleviating double taxation has traditionally focused on mechanisms that residence countries can adopt, under the presumption that the host country taxes. Three unilateral mechanisms for preventing double taxation have been presented as the key candidates: exemptions, credits, and deductions. An exemption allows residents investing in foreign countries to exclude foreign-source income earned when calculating the residence country tax to be paid on their income.[24] A credit system allows taxes paid in a foreign host country to be credited against residence country tax levied on such income.[25] Under a deduction

---

[23] In contrast, analysis of neutrality at the EU level could be much more promising due to the mutual interest, promoted and enforced by the ECJ, to maximize EU welfare. Michael Knoll & Ruth Mason, What Is Tax Discrimination?, 121 YALE L.J. 1014, 1098–1099 (2012), convincingly explain that

> a competitive neutrality interpretation of nondiscrimination would improve welfare, compared to a situation in which member states face no constraints . . . [A] competitive neutrality interpretation of tax discrimination would discourage states from enacting tax laws that tilt the playing field for jobs against cross-border workers. Because workers have different skills, nonuniform tax laws interfere with the efficient matching of workers and jobs. Thus, we believe that there would be welfare gains from adopting a competitive neutrality interpretation of tax nondiscrimination. Indeed, such gains (even if only understood intuitively) may be what the founders of the EU hoped to secure by implementing the prohibition on discrimination.

Importantly, however, they stress that they do *not* argue that

> the ECJ should adopt a competitive neutrality interpretation of nondiscrimination because a competitively neutral tax system would best promote EU welfare. Other more extensive and intrusive tax measures than what we propose here – such as imposing the same tax base and rate structure on all member states – might best promote EU welfare.

Id. at 1098.

[24] To illustrate, let us consider an investor who is a resident of Country A with regular tax rates of 40 percent, who earns $100 of income in Country B. An exemption will mean that she will not pay any taxes to Country A on the income produced in Country B. Assuming that Country B collects $20 in taxes on that income, the investor will have a net income of $80.

[25] Using the example from *supra* note 24, the taxpayer will tentatively owe $40 in taxes to Country A, but will be allowed to credit the $20 she paid to Country B in taxes against her tax liability in Country A. Thus, she will pay only $20 in taxes to Country A in addition to the $20 she already paid to Country B, leaving her with a net income of $60. Most countries granting a credit limit it to the amount of taxes owed on foreign-source income.

system, residents can deduct from their taxable income in their residence country the taxes they paid to a host country.[26] Each of these mechanisms creates a different degree of incentive for a country's residents to invest abroad. All things being equal, the lower the overall tax burden (i.e., the taxes in the country of residence and in the host country combined), the more inclined residents will be to invest abroad. Therefore, generally speaking and assuming that the tax rate in the host country is lower than the rate in the country of residence, a resident will be most inclined to invest abroad under an exemption system, less inclined under a foreign tax-credit system, and least inclined under a tax-deduction system.[27] Each method is associated with one of three originally defined types of neutrality: capital export neutrality, capital import neutrality, or national neutrality.[28] Capital export neutrality supports a system of tax credits; capital import neutrality (joined more recently by CON) supports a system of tax exemptions; and national neutrality supports a tax deduction system.

Capital export neutrality ("CEN") is aimed at preventing tax considerations from distorting investors' decisions on where to invest.[29] It is achieved when the total tax imposed by the country of residence and the host country combined is equal to the tax imposed on domestic investments in the country of residence. The implicit assumption here is that global welfare would increase were all countries to apply a CEN-promoting policy, which would be to the benefit of each individual

---

[26] Using the example in *supra* note 24, the investor's taxable income in Country A will be only $80 since the $20 she paid to Country B in taxes will be deducted from her taxable income of $100. Thus, she will have to pay an additional $32 in residence country taxes (40 percent of $80), leaving her with a total tax payment of $52 and a net income of $48.

[27] The discussion in this section sidesteps the issue of the possible impact on investors' decisions regarding tax deferral through foreign entities.

[28] *See* Daniel J. Frisch, *The Economics of International Tax Policy: Some Old and New Approaches*, 47 TAX NOTES 91 (Apr. 30, 1990).

[29] *See* Hugh J. Ault & David F. Bradford, *Taxing International Income: An Analysis of the U.S. System and Its Economic Premises, in* TAXATION IN THE GLOBAL ECONOMY 27 (Assaf Razin & Joel Slemrod eds., 1990) ("If all the tax authorities in the international system adhere to export tax neutrality, a perfectly competitive international capital market will leave no gain from reallocation of (any *given* stock of) world capital unexploited."). *See also* SHAVIRO, *supra* note 19, at 123:

> The case for CEN is relatively straightforward. It is simply global production efficiency, albeit as separately determined for the residents of each country (a qualification that, as we will see shortly, ends up being extremely important). Again, if your tax rate is the same everywhere, presumably you will look for the highest available pre-tax return, which should be the "best" investment if markets are functioning properly.

country as well.[30] Given that host countries tax foreigners on income produced within their territory, CEN can be secured by allowing (perfect) foreign tax credits. Under such a regime, taxpayers would be taxed on balance according to the rate of their country of residence, whether the income were produced at home or abroad. Thus, their decision-making regarding the location of their investment would not be affected by tax considerations, for regardless of where they were to invest, their tax liability would be the same.

Capital import neutrality ("CIN") focuses on taxation in the host country. The aim of this type of neutrality is that the total tax imposed on investment returns in a given country remains constant irrespective of the investor's country of residence.[31] CIN is achieved if all investments in a certain jurisdiction are subject to the same tax rate (when all taxes paid are combined).[32] A residence country with a CIN policy will exempt the foreign income earned by its residents, thereby allowing them to enjoy the same tax rate imposed on local investors in the host country. CIN is often enlisted by MNEs as an argument for supporting their "competitiveness," which may be impaired if they are forced to pay higher taxes than competitors residing in low-tax jurisdictions.[33] However, although lower taxation would certainly boost the net gains of MNEs and perhaps

---

[30] *See* Frisch, *supra* note 28, at 584 ("In short, one of the principles on which tax policy should be based is that the U.S.' own interests are best served by rules that lead to worldwide economic efficiency."); Ault & Bradford, *supra* note 29, at 36 ("[A] policy of capital export neutrality by all countries may lead to an outcome that is better for all than would obtain if policy were made separately on the assumption of no foreign interactions.").

[31] *See* Joint Comm. on Taxation, *Staff Description (JCS-15–91) of H.R. 2889, "American Jobs and Manufacturing Act of 1991," Relating to Current U.S. Taxation of Certain Operations of Controlled Foreign Corporations, and Related Issues* (scheduled for Oct. 3, 1991, House Ways & Means Comm hearing) (Oct. 2, 1991), *reprinted in* Daily Tax Reporter (BNA), at L-37 (Oct. 3, 1991); *see also* Michael J. Graetz, *Taxing International Income: Inadequate Principles, Outdated Concepts, and Unsatisfactory Policy*, 26 BROOK. J. INT'L L. 1357, 1367 (2000); Shaviro, *supra* note 19, at 123.

[32] RICHARD E. CAVES, MULTINATIONAL ENTERPRISE AND ECONOMIC ANALYSIS 227 (1982). *Cf.* PEGGY B. MUSGRAVE, TAXATION OF FOREIGN INVESTMENT INCOME 109–14 (1969). In Musgrave's opinion, Capital Import Neutrality is grounded on the rationale that the tax on the investor is shifted to the consumer. By her definition, international tax neutrality is achieved when there is no excess tax on either local or foreign investments, which would reduce the investor's net return. If the tax burden is passed on to the consumer, the investor's return is not impaired, but her price becomes less competitive. International tax neutrality therefore requires that tax be imposed only in the host country, for otherwise investors will be prevented from making efficient investments purely because the tax will compel them to charge higher prices.

[33] *See* SHAVIRO, *supra* note 19, at 123.

even increase their incentives to reside in the country, the increased taxes imposed under CEN would not distort their investment decisions, as under CEN, MNEs would still follow pretax rates of return.[34] Hence, while the competitiveness argument may be persuasive politically, the academic rationale offered for adopting this type of neutrality is based on the savings disincentive CEN policies may create. Under the latter argument, the increased taxes imposed under CEN distort savings decisions in the country of residence due to the lower net rate of return.[35]

National neutrality is the only type of partial neutrality that sets national, and not global, prosperity as its target. Advocates of this type of neutrality assert that a national government cannot be indifferent regarding which country gets to collect taxes on a given income, since tax revenues collected by the home country increase national welfare, whereas foreign taxes do not. Thus, they contend, investors should be encouraged to invest abroad only if both the investor and the residence country's fisc benefit from the investment. Accordingly, national neutrality proponents seek to maximize national prosperity by raising the effective tax rate on residents' foreign investments to a level where it encourages them to invest abroad only when the total of their net returns and the residence country's tax returns exceeds what would be generated by an equivalent investment in the residence country.[36] Allowing investors to deduct foreign taxes from their domestic taxable income is one way of achieving this.[37]

Lastly, a new addition to the neutrality debate is the concept of competitive neutrality, or capital ownership neutrality (CON). Mihir Desai and James Hines, who coined the latter term, argue that the ownership of assets must be the focus in determining the efficiency results of taxes, as opposed to the location of investments (as in CEN) or how taxes affect savings (as in CIN). To achieve capital ownership neutrality, tax systems should not distort ownership patterns; CON arises when "it is impossible to increase output by trading capital ownership among

---

[34] The increased tax under CEN (as compared to CIN) and the lower net gains it produces for investors could constrain MNEs growth, as internal investment resources will be lower. Shaviro, *supra* note 19, at 125–26, however, makes a compelling argument that this claim is esoteric.

[35] *See, e.g.*, Thomas Horst, A *Note on the Optimal Taxation of International Investment Income,* 94 Q.J. ECON. 793 (1980); Graetz, *supra* note 31, at 1369.

[36] Some have criticized this as a "beggar-thy-neighbor policy" (*see, e.g.*, Frisch, *supra* note 28, at 583) in the sense that it is a noncooperative policy that is bound to fail since it seeks to benefit the residence country at the expense of other countries.

[37] *See* Julie A. Roin, *The Grand Illusion: A Neutral System for the Taxation of International Transactions,* 75 VA. L. REV. 919, 926–27 (1989).

investors."[38] Michael Knoll and Ruth Mason, who termed this type of neutrality "competitive neutrality," use labor rather than capital to explain that "a competitively neutral tax system does not interfere with the matching of workers to jobs, whereas a system that violates this neutrality is one in which workers sort into jobs not only on the basis of comparative advantage, but also residence."[39] Desai and Hines recommend exempting foreign-source income, since under an exemption system, "the tax treatment of foreign investment income is the same for all investors and competition between potential buyers allocates assets to their most productive owners."[40] Knoll and Mason use competitive neutrality to explain the logic behind the nondiscrimination principle. Specifically, they explain that the ECJ decisions, which impose nondiscrimination obligations at both source and residence, are consistent with competitive neutrality.[41]

b.   The Flaws of Neutrality

Conventional wisdom suggests that a truly neutral system simultaneously achieves CIN, CEN, and CON. Only such a system can achieve neutrality

---

[38] Mihir A. Desai & James R. Hines Jr., *Evaluating International Tax Reform*, 56 NAT'L TAX J. 487, 495 (2003). *See also* Michael P. Devereux, *Taxation of Outbound Direct Investment: Economic Principles and Tax Policy Considerations*, 24 OXFORD REV. ECON. POL'Y 698 (2008); David Weisbach, *The Use of Neutralities in International Tax Policy*, 68 NAT'L TAX J. 635 (2015) (explaining that "Devereux's market neutrality (MN) is a generalization of this concept.... It requires that if two firms compete with each other in the same market, they should face the same overall effective tax rates on their investments.").

[39] Knoll & Mason, *supra* note 23, at 1034.

[40] Desai & Hines, *supra* note 38, at 494. As Daniel Shaviro *supra* note 19, at 131, recently noted, this neglects broader issues of ownership, for

> in a territorial world, multinationals may have a tax advantage over purely domestic businesses, given the opportunity to use commonly owned operations in low-tax jurisdictions as a magnet for reported taxable income:
> One might therefore expect multinationals to outbid purely domestic owners for the ownership of assets that would offer special income-shifting synergies, even if this reduces global output. Adverse effects on output could result, not just from multinationals holding the wrong assets, but from excessive multinational activity in response to the availability of sourcing-based tax synergies.

For a discussion of Hines' CON policy prescriptions, *see* Mitchell A. Kane, *Ownership Neutrality, Ownership Distortions, and International Tax Welfare Benchmarks*, 26 VA. TAX REV. 53, 76–78 (2006); Mitchell A. Kane, *Considering "Reconsidering the Taxation of Foreign Income,"* 62 TAX L. REV. 299 (2009).

[41] Knoll & Mason, *supra* note 23, at 1054–55. They further explain *id.* that

> Violations of competitive neutrality occur when states assess nonuniform source taxes or nonuniform residence taxes. Source taxes are nonuniform if they do not apply on

in investors' decisions regarding where to invest, where to reside, and where to incorporate. To attain such a globally neutral system, all countries must not only uniformly implement the same method for alleviating double taxation but also apply a single worldwide rate of taxation.[42] The international allocation of resources would not be neutral if countries were to apply different tax rates even if all adopt, say, a territorial system of taxation. Similarly, even if all countries were to apply a personal system of taxation, different rates of taxation would thwart capital import neutrality. From a practical perspective, such global neutrality – whose actual desirability I dispute further on – is far from being attained. At the same time, none of these partial neutrality approaches purports to be able to achieve full efficiency.[43] The traditional debate in international tax policy has, therefore, centered on which concept of neutrality yields the least distortions. There is little consensus in the literature as to which of the versions is most desirable as a policy, although CEN seems to enjoy the widest support.[44]

Regardless, however, of which neutrality approach is advocated, it cannot prevail absent cooperation among states. Significantly, all the

the same basis to all workers in the jurisdiction, both residents and nonresidents. Residence taxes are nonuniform if they do not apply on the same basis to all residents, no matter where they earn their income.

In the absence of cross-border harmonization of tax rates and bases, competitive neutrality requires that all states must agree on one of two methods for avoiding double taxation: unlimited foreign tax credits and what Knoll & Mason call "ideal deduction," which includes territorial taxation. Moreover, they add, all taxes must be uniform – i.e., applied in the same manner to all income from the same source state without regard for the residence of the taxpayer who earns that income and in the same manner to all income earned by a resident regardless of source.

[42] See Horst, *supra* note 35.
[43] As Daniel Shaviro notes, these norms merely define "a single margin of choice at which the tax system ostensibly ought to be neutral, so taxpayers will make choices based on pre-tax profitability ... none purports to address the whole picture...." Shaviro, *supra* note 19, at 103. See also Weisbach, *supra* note 38.
[44] See Graetz, *supra* note 31, at 1366 (concluding that CEN is the dominant approach but noting that "[t]he conversation is not unanimously in favor of CEN"); Dep't of Treasury, *The Deferral of Income Earned Through U.S. Controlled Foreign Corporations* 42–54 (2000); Robert J. Peroni, *Back to the Future: A Path to Progressive Reform of the U.S. International Income Tax Rules*, 51 U. MIAMI L. REV. 975 (1997). Daniel Shaviro recently summarized the fifty years of debate as follows: "There remains no consensus, among either policymakers or experts, regarding the end towards which countries should cooperate in international tax policy. Indeed, even when there was a relatively high level of expert consensus in favor of CEN, there was no general move to adopt it comprehensively in practice." Shaviro, *supra* note 29, at 133. See also id. at 127: "In sum, the traditional analysis seemed to lead in a definite direction, suggesting that global welfare would be highest if all countries followed CEN."

efficiency arguments made by proponents of partial neutrality collapse without the cooperation of a large enough number of countries. With CEN, for example, so long as a certain number of countries exempt the foreign-source income of their residents, the worldwide investment flow will be distorted in favor of low-tax jurisdictions irrespective of whether any particular country offers a credit.[45] Consequently, even if (as is often claimed) CEN is the best partial neutrality option for improving world-wide welfare, its success hangs on broad cooperation among states to uni-laterally adopt a credit mechanism. For an individual country, however, cooperation might not necessarily be the best unilateral strategy, even if neutrality is a plausible option on the global level and even if global wel-fare would increase, were such neutrality to prevail.[46] When states pursue their national interests, strategic considerations and coordination prob-lems may prevent them from promoting global neutrality.

The bottom line is that the neutrality debate is misguided. In the current decentralized international tax regime, complete global neutral-ity is unattainable and partial neutrality highly doubtful. Thus, instead of pursuing the elusive goal of neutrality, states should pursue poli-cies that support their national interests. As Daniel Shaviro succinctly summarizes,

> the international tax policy literature took a significant wrong turn by giv-ing so much focus to global welfare considerations in general, and to the alphabet soup of CEN, CIN, and CON in particular. While global welfare considerations may be important when multilateral cooperation is suffi-ciently feasible, in the main countries must and will make international tax policy choices in a largely unilateral setting.[47]

Advocating a position supporting national interests as I do may have a protectionist, isolationist ring to it, seemingly calling for ignoring other states and their policies. But in the absence of a global decision-making process, the individual state has no viable option other than to think strate-gically and design its international tax policy in line with its own values and goals. The interests of other states should definitely be considered and their anticipated responses taken into account. Ultimately, then, states' policy preferences should be determined by their competitive positions in

---

[45] Shaviro, *supra* note 19, at 135, explains that even if as large a country as the United States were to unilaterally pursue CEN, it would be undercut by clientele effect, cross-border shareholding, and the use of non-American companies to invest in low-tax jurisdictions.

[46] *See* Graetz, *supra* note 31, at 1378 (explaining the difference between international trade, where free trade improves not only worldwide efficiency but also benefits each state employing it, and international tax, where no such harmony exists).

[47] *See* Shaviro, *supra* note 19, at 141.

the markets for investments and residents. Section 3 explores these interests and considerations.

The view that international tax rules should advance some sort of neutrality no less blurs the competitive strategic nature of the international tax game than the League of Nations' rights-based conception does. Consequently, a different line of thinking about international tax is necessary to properly reflect the decentralized yet interdependent nature of the international taxation regime. Accordingly, the next section introduces game theory's strategic analysis as a particularly useful methodology in order to analyze the complex interaction of states' unilateral policies. It explains that in this interdependent decentralized market, each state should set its international tax policy to maximize its own benefits from this market *given* its competitors' potential responses. In other words, states should tax strategically. The game theoretical analysis will be put to work again in the two-actor setting of Chapter 3, when I discuss bilateral tax treaties. The first stage of any strategic analysis, however, is presenting the actors' preferences. The rest of this chapter will therefore discuss the complexity of determining the national interest with regard to a state's level of outbound investment.

2.3   Taxing Strategically

The decentralized structure of international taxation and the relative competitive positions of states in the international tax arena dramatically impact the policies that can serve national goals. In the absence of some global organization that can allocate taxing rights and determine relative allegiance, states need to act on their own, to pursue their own goals. At the same time, contrary to the conventional neutrality debate, states should not automatically aim for any type of "neutral" position – as CIN, CEN, and CON assume, too simplistically, that states should promote global welfare. Instead, in designing their policies and pursuing their interests, states need to act strategically. More specifically, they should design their tax policies to maximize their benefits from the competition for investments, residents, and tax revenues given their competitors' expected responses.

Methodologically, I contend that the world of international taxation should be understood in game theoretical terms.[48] The game theoretical

---

[48] Dagan, *supra* note 22; Dagan, *supra* note 2 949–51 (2000). For further examples of the use of game theory in international taxation, *see* Reuven S. Avi-Yonah, *Globalization, Tax*

analysis treats states like rational players in a strategic game.[49] It outlines their *preferences* and potential *strategies* and analyzes the *interaction* of those potential strategies with those of other state-actors. The complex picture this analysis portrays captures the insight that in this game, as in real life, international tax policies are not crafted in a vacuum. Rather, one country's policies affect the outcomes of another country's policies and vice versa. Therefore, policymakers need to be aware of actions taken by other countries that may influence domestic economic behavior and devise their country's policies in a way that best serves its national interests.

I apply this approach in the context of the mechanisms for preventing double taxation (first unilaterally in this chapter and, next, in a bilateral setting in Chapter 3), asking which mechanism a given country should select. The initial step of this analysis is, as noted, presenting the (national) actors' preferences in the context of alleviating double taxation. Such preferences are shaped by the national interests involved, which include, of course, the tax revenues collected but, importantly, also a variety of interests that are affected by the level of outbound investment. In what follows, therefore, I delineate states' national interests in terms of cross-border

---

Competition, and the Fiscal Crisis of the Welfare State, 113 HARV. L. REV. 1573, 1583 (2000) (comparing LDCs' lack of cooperation to a stag hunt game); Julie Roin, *Competition and Evasion: Another Perspective on International Tax Competition*, 89 GEO. L.J. 543, 568 (2001); Adam Rosenzweig, *Thinking Outside the (Tax) Treaty*, 2012 WISC. L. REV. 717; Adam H. Rosenzweig, Harnessing the Costs of International Tax Arbitrage, 26 VA. TAX REV. 555, 583–86 (2007); Eduardo A. Baistrocchi, *The Arm's Length Standard in the 21st Century: A Proposal for Both Developed and Developing Countries*, TAX NOTES INT'L 241, 241–55 (2004); Diane M. Ring, *International Tax Relations: Theory and Implications*, 60 TAX L. REV. 83 (2007); Allison Christians, Steven Dean, Diane Ring & Adam H. Rosenzweig, *Taxation as a Global Socio-Legal Phenomenon*, 14 ILSA J. INT'L & COMP. L. 303 (2008). For a similar analysis that arrives at the opposite conclusion, see C.M. Radaelli, *Game Theory and Institutional Entrepreneurship: Transfer Pricing and the Search for Coordination International Tax Policy*, 26 POL'Y STUD. J. 603 (1998) (using transfer pricing to illustrate the claim that the international tax regime cannot be reduced to mere game theory and the prisoner's dilemma and that sometimes, the willingness to use a common standard is stronger); Robert Green, *Anti Legalistic Approaches to Resolving Disputes Between Governments: A Comparison of the International Tax and Trade Regimes*, 23 YALE J. INT'L L. 79, 104–05, 122 (1998) (discussing the relevance of the prisoner's dilemma in a tax regime and concluding that the use of retaliatory strategies in the tax arena, although not unheard of, is extremely rare).

[49] There are many players in the international tax game: countries of source, countries of residence, regional and international organizations, and interest groups within countries. All contribute to the complexity of policy analysis in this area. For the sake of clarity, I start out in this and the next chapter by focusing on two primary players: residence countries here and host countries in the next chapter.

level of investment. Next, I explore the strategies available to states for best promoting those interests given the possible reactions of other actor-states. Residence countries' policies for preventing double taxation traditionally took as a given that host countries would tax foreign investments. Although the actual policies adopted by the latter are – or at least should be – a major factor in how residence countries design their tax policies, I will assume initially (similarly to traditional discussions) that host countries do tax foreign residents on income produced within their borders. The strategic framework for analyzing international tax policies in this chapter sets the stage for the analysis of the interaction between pairs of residence and host states in Chapter 3. There, I will relax this assumption and look more closely at the interests (and, thus, preferences) of host countries, so as to more realistically demonstrate the strategic interaction between the policies of residence and host countries.

a. National Preferences

For countries of residence, an important role is played by double taxation and the mechanisms for alleviating it, since they affect outbound investments and the economic activities of domestic taxpayers abroad. Different mechanisms for contending with double taxation impose different overall levels of taxation on outbound investments and thereby create different incentives for such investments. Consequently, these mechanisms also affect the incentives of residents with significant international activity to remain in a particular country or to relocate. The higher the total level of taxation in the country of residence and abroad combined, the lower the incentive for local taxpayers to invest and produce income overseas and the lower the incentive for individuals and businesses with considerable international activity to reside in such country. Accordingly, in determining its preferred mechanism for alleviating double taxation, a country must first decide on a desired level of incentive for outbound investment.

The decision regarding the "proper" level and kind of outbound investment for a country entails many social, political, and economic considerations. Policymakers may find it relevant to distinguish between different types of outbound investments which may yield different benefits and respond to differing incentives. Thus, for example, they may wish to distinguish between portfolio investments and direct investments–that is, investments that involve control over operations overseas. The benefits these two types of investment provide, their political support, and their elasticity can differ. The same is true for different types of industries. For example, industries that involve R&D and intellectual property are considered more elastic (and more desired) than others.[50] In addition, policymakers may distinguish between individuals, whose residence decisions are sometimes inelastic, and corporations, in particular MNEs, which can be more easily relocated or can incorporate subsidiaries overseas and make greater use of tax-planning mechanisms such as transfer pricing and earning stripping. Policymakers may further weigh the possible impact of the level of outbound investment on domestic wages, unemployment, and quality of jobs.[51] Other considerations could include the expected impact on the balance of trade,[52] balance of payments,[53] availability of

---

[50] Michael J. Graetz & Rachael Doud, *Technological Innovation, International Competition, and the Challenges of International Income Taxation*, 113 COLUM. L. REV. 347 (2013).

[51] Given that labor is relatively immobile and assuming that investment abroad is at the expense of domestic investment, the traditional approach was that investment abroad lowers the productivity of labor at home and, thereby, lowers wages. *See* Musgrave, *supra* note 32, at 14–15. But *see* the more recent Mihir A. Desai, C. Fritz Foley & James R. Hines, *Domestic Effects of the Foreign Activities of U.S. Multinationals*, 1 AM. ECON. J.: ECON. POL'Y 181, 201 (2009) finding that manufacturing firms that expanded their foreign operations between 1982 and 2004 simultaneously expanded their domestic operations. Foreign investment that is triggered by foreign economic growth is associated with growing domestic-capital accumulation, employment compensation, R&D, and exports to related parties. Other economists generally believe that overall unemployment levels would not be significantly affected by investment abroad, but that the export of capital abroad can affect the type and quality of jobs (U.S. firms, for example, tend to export low-quality jobs) and can lead to lower wages. *See, e.g.*, Jane G. Gravelle, *Foreign Tax Provisions of the American Jobs Act of 1996*, 72 TAX NOTES 1165, 1166 (1996). *See also* Joint Comm. on Taxation, *supra* note 31, L-48-L-49:

> There are unfortunately few economic studies addressing this issue. One…paper examines the effect of outbound investment on domestic employment and finds some evidence that increases in overseas activities by U.S. multinational corporations reduce their domestic employment…. The authors attribute it largely to the allocation of more labor-intensive activities abroad and more skill and capital-intensive activities to the United States. Therefore, although multinational corporations may have fewer domestic employees as a result of their overseas production they also provide greater compensation per domestic employee as a result of their overseas production.

[52] Economic research has not found any negative impact of increased foreign investment on exports by U.S. multinationals. In fact, to the extent that there is any impact at all, increased foreign affiliate production tends to increase exports by U.S. parents to their foreign affiliates. These results do not, however, necessarily serve as evidence that the existence of foreign affiliates improves the overall U.S. trade balance. It is possible that increased production by foreign affiliates crowds out exports by purely domestic firms. *See* Joint Comm. on Taxation, *supra* note 31, L-48.

[53] Limiting outbound investment can improve the balance of payments in the short run but may lower future receipts of foreign currency. *See* Musgrave, *supra* note 32, at 5; William W. Park, *Fiscal Jurisdiction and Accrual Basis Taxation: Lifting the Corporate Veil to Tax Foreign*

raw materials,[54] development of advanced technology,[55] and even national security.[56] Naturally, considerations evolve and change over time, and a combination of considerations is also quite possible.

Significantly, a decision regarding the desirable level of outbound investment and preferred tax mechanism also has distributive implications. This relates to how the tax burden and the economic resources are allocated among different groups within the country and the impact on solidarity among the members of the national community.[57] For example, the policy decision can affect the distribution of the tax burden between domestic capital and labor[58] and also between those who have the capacity to invest and produce income overseas (owners of mobile capital or intellectual property, people with skills and qualifications in high demand overseas, etc.) and those who do not.[59] This could lead to a conflict of

---

Company Profits, 78 COLUM. L. REV. 1609, 1622 (1978); Martin Feldstein, *The Effects of Outbound Foreign Direct Investment on the Domestic Capital Stock, in* THE EFFECTS OF TAXATION ON MULTINATIONAL CORPORATIONS 43, 45–46, 49–55 (Martin Feldstein, James R. Hines Jr. & R. Glenn Hubbard eds., 1995).

[54] *See*, for example, FRED BERGSTEN ET AL., AMERICAN MULTINATIONALS AND AMERICAN INTERESTS 160–63 (1978), recommending a policy that would promote service contracts for American companies to countries with natural resources instead of a policy that promotes ownership of foreign natural resources (which places the investors at risk of having their assets expropriated by the foreign country).

[55] Many countries are interested in the establishment of R&D centers, which are a source of high-paying professional jobs as well as incubators of human capital, training people who may later contribute to other domestic firms. *See* GARY C. HUFBAUER & ARIEL ASSA, U.S. TAXATION OF FOREIGN INCOME 14–15 (2007); Graetz & Doud, *supra* note 50.

[56] Sometimes security considerations make it necessary to keep certain industries or know-how within a country's borders or under friendly control. At other times, it is the interrelatedness of the markets of two countries that lowers significantly the chances of war.

[57] Differences in the levels of taxation imposed on constituents could undermine their sense of social solidarity. *See, e.g.*, Marii Paskov & Caroline Dewilde, *Income Inequality and Solidarity in Europe* 13–17 (GINI Discussion Paper No. 33, Mar. 2012).

[58] Exporting capital without any increase in domestic capital or operations might reduce the productivity of local labor, thereby lowering wages. Yet at the same time, it can improve the position of local capital by reducing the amount of capital invested within the country. *See* Bergsten et al., *supra* note 54, at 177; Gravelle, *supra* note 51, at 1166; Joint Comm. on Taxation, *supra* note 31; STAFF OF JOINT COMM. ON TAXATION, 102D CONG., FACTORS AFFECTING THE INTERNATIONAL COMPETITIVENESS OF THE UNITED STATES 234, 236 (Comm. Print 1991); Feldstein, *supra* note 53, at 43–46.

[59] For example, an exemption for foreign-source income means that taxpayers investing abroad bear a lower tax burden than those investing (or otherwise producing income) at home. Significantly, not everyone enjoys the same capacity and opportunities to invest abroad. Hence, investment overseas is not merely a choice of taxpayers, which would translate into an economic distortion, but, rather, more of an attribute that translates into a distributive disparity.

interest between different sectors of the population as well as with foreign stakeholders with a domestic influence. Since the final decision on the optimal level of outbound investment is made at the political level, it is unavoidably impacted by the relative political power of the different interest groups at play.

Tax revenues are another factor a residence country's policymakers might take into account when selecting a tax mechanism. The various mechanisms for alleviating double taxation have different revenue outcomes for the residence countries that apply them as well as for host countries. Depending on the chosen mechanism, a gap could arise between what the country of residence collects and what its residents pay in taxes due to the taxes collected by the host country. Residence and host countries compete not only for investments, then, but also for their respective share of tax revenues.

b.   National Strategies

As explained above, the three predominant mechanisms for alleviating double taxation are exemptions, credits, and deductions. These roughly represent what is commonly held to be the policy options available to residence countries. However, the international tax system has produced a much more nuanced variety of mechanisms, each of which can have a different impact on both the level of outbound investments and the nature of those investments and, as a result, on the interests involved. Take a foreign tax credit limitation, for example, which allows a taxpayer a credit for foreign taxes she paid up to a limit. Absent any limitation, a credit mechanism would align residents' incentives for outbound investment with pretax rates of return. Typically, however, such a credit is limited to the level of the residence country's tax liability.[60] This limitation still aligns taxpayers' investment decisions with pretax rates of return, but only in countries with tax rates that are lower than the residence country's rate. The credit limitation thus creates a negative incentive to invest in jurisdictions with tax rates that exceed the limitation.[61] The two most popular types of foreign tax credit limitations – an overall limitation and a per-country limitation – along with the baskets system (which limits the credit for foreign taxes per type of income) produce further nuances, for they result in

---

[60] Thus, taxpayers will not be credited for the foreign taxes that exceed their residence-based tax on the same income.

[61] For a critique of this rationale, see Dagan, *supra* note 22, at 397.

tax-planning opportunities (by way of averaging) that could increase the
level of outbound investments of those who are able to tax plan their foreign operations. These limitations de facto create a price-discrimination
mechanism, enabling the state to distinguish between taxpayers for whom
the rate of tax on outbound investments is too high (and who would therefore plan to avoid them) and taxpayers who can tolerate this level of tax.[62]

Deferral, which allows taxpayers to defer paying taxes on the profits of foreign corporations until their repatriation, distinguishes between
mature and immature investments and encourages the former.[63] States'
CFC rules – that is, the rules under which a state can tax profits from foreign corporations owned by domestic taxpayers – further exemplify how
the nuances of domestic tax policies can have different effects on different
types of investments. In addition to distinguishing between foreign incorporated and unincorporated businesses, these rules also tend to distinguish (indeed, price discriminate) between business and non-business foreign income of domestically owned foreign corporations (as typically they
apply only to non-business foreign-source income), as well as between different types of ownership (the level of foreign ownership in the foreign
corporation often makes a difference in this context).

The interests of the specific countries involved set the background for
selecting among these (and other) available strategies to promote the outcomes that they most prefer. Furthermore, because in the international
tax context the different national policies impact one another, in order to
attain these desirable outcomes each country should take into account the
expected policy choices of other countries. This means that policymakers
should design their country's tax policies to best serve national interests
given the possible reactions of other countries. In other words, countries
should tax strategically.

The foreign tax credit limitation demonstrates nicely how the interde-
pendence between tax policies operates. When a residence country allows
a credit for foreign taxes paid by its residents for activities abroad, it

---

[62] For more a detailed account of these mechanisms and their potential effect on outbound
investments, see Dagan, *supra* note 22.

[63] *See* David G. Hartman, *Tax Policy and Foreign Direct Investment*, 26 J. PUB. ECON. 107,
116 (1985). Specifically, this creates a mid-level incentive for immature investments (as the
proceeds will be taxed in full but only at a later stage) while creating high incentives similar
to those produced by exemptions for mature investments. According to Hartman, *id.*, this
stems from the fact that the tax on the return of money paid to the home country will be
imposed in any event, whether it is repatriated immediately or only after x years. Assuming
a fixed rate of tax on the money repatriated, the only matter of concern for the investor is
the net rate of return in her home country compared to the net rate of return abroad.

creates an incentive for other countries to raise their taxes even if they would have preferred not to tax foreign investors were no credit offered in the residence country. Assuming an unlimited credit in the residence country, an investor will not incur any additional tax liability by investing in a foreign country, regardless of the tax rate in the latter. The host country could, consequently, generate sizeable tax revenues without deterring foreign residents from investing. As the taxes paid by the foreign investors to host countries increase, the extent of the credit offered by their country of residence will necessarily increase as well. This would, in effect, amount to a wealth transfer from the residence country to the host countries. A credit limitation, which many countries adopt, reduces the incentive of the host country to raise its taxes in excess of the existing (limited) credit.[64] A residence country might also offer a tax-sparing mechanism, whereby its residents can credit the taxes they would have paid in the host country absent a specific incentive provided by the latter to encourage investment. In such circumstances, host countries will have an incentive to limit the tax they impose on residents of the residence country that allows tax sparing, in order to attract their investments.

There are subtler ways in which host countries can take advantage of residence countries' mechanisms for alleviating double taxation. Years before the onset of the current stage of globalization, Charles Kingson[65] demonstrated the variety of ways in which host countries can de facto discriminate between domestic and foreign taxpayers in order to exploit the interests of countries of residence. A host country can refrain from collecting a genuine tax or collect a non-genuine tax so as to de facto exempt residents of a credit-providing country.[66] A popular technique among oil-producing countries, at the time, for example, was to disguise commercial payments (mostly mineral royalties) as taxes. If approved as taxes, the royalty payments could be credited against residence taxes. Such manipulative tactics dramatically influence the effectiveness of a credit mechanism. A state providing a credit mechanism cannot ignore the potential of other states taking exploitative measures. It should, therefore, try to protect its

---

[64] See, e.g., Roin, supra note 37 930 (1989); Graetz & O'Hear, supra note 15. For a critique of the limitation as a "defensive neutrality" policy, see Dagan, supra note 22, at 395.

[65] Charles I. Kingson, *The Coherence of International Taxation*, 81 COLUM. L. REV. 1151 (1981).

[66] In an effort to reduce the interest rates charged by foreign lenders, Brazil, for example, at one time imposed a 25 percent withholding tax on lenders, giving 85 percent of the amount to the borrower as a subsidy. This measure failed when the IRS ruled that only tax in excess of the subsidy is creditable. See Kingson, supra note 65, at 1263.

system against such abuses and, if this is not possible, reconsider grant-ing a credit.[67] The bottom line is that when designing its international tax policy, a state should take into account the details of the policies of other states, as well as their potential reactions to its own policies. This interaction among the unilateral tax policies of different states shapes the contours of the international taxation landscape.

c. Is Cooperation a Plausible Strategy?

Cooperation, whether formal or informal, is commonly recommended as a strategy for countries given the less-than-optimal results rendered by unilateral policies.[68] It has been asserted that whereas the uncooperative strategic interactions harm both global and national welfare (as in a pris-oner's dilemma scenario), cooperative measures could work to improve both. Although cooperation has proven to be a desirable strategy in many contexts, it is unclear whether it would be a superior solution here.[69] Moreover, and of particular relevance to our discussion, even if cooper-ation were to emerge as the better global strategy, it would not necessarily always be in the best interests of an individual state to adopt a cooperative strategy.

To begin with, the proper target for international cooperation is in no way self-evident. There is no textbook answer to the question of how to optimally tax internationally. As demonstrated in Chapter 1, even at the domestic level, the decision on taxation rates is guided by a wide combina-tion of considerations that are based on a country's unique and divergent characteristics and norms. Coordinating states' policies toward a desir-able strategy on the international level is thus far from obvious. Even from the limited perspective of the neutrality debate (which I criticize), there is little likelihood of coordinating a joint strategy for promoting neutrality or even a less distortive international tax regime. I explained above that a truly neutral system will attain CIN and CEN simultaneously through the harmonization of tax rates and mechanisms for double-taxation relief across all states. But given the diversity of states' goals and preferences, coordinating their tax rates might prove to be an impossible task. More-over, it is questionable whether this would in fact be a desirable policy,

---

[67] For more detailed examples, see Dagan, *supra* note 22, at 390.
[68] This chapter considers informal cooperation. Chapters 3–5 will consider more formal forms cooperation on the bilateral and multilateral levels.
[69] For more on the desirability of cooperation *see* Chapters 4 and 5.

for the multiplicity of national taxing and spending systems seems to better serve individual and national preferences, global justice, and political participation.[70]

Since complete global neutrality is not a viable option, opinions vary as to the desirable international tax policy from a global perspective. There is no international consensus regarding which partial neutrality will produce the least distortions. In the absence of consensus as to the global target, it is likely that different countries will select different mechanisms, thereby hindering the emergence of cooperation among states. Countries, in other words, are not expected to converge on one single solution.

Finally, even if there were broad agreement on a global policy goal, cooperation that supports a certain positive tax rate might not be possible for strategic reasons. If there are states that grant their residents who invest abroad a credit for the foreign taxes they pay, then other individual countries will have incentive to exempt their own residents and thereby attract new residents (e.g., MNEs that prefer to reside in a jurisdiction that allows them to invest in other countries tax-free).

Should the fact that the international tax game is an infinite game change the incentive to cooperate or defect? Conventional wisdom holds that states' incentives to defect in a single-round simultaneous game (i.e., a game in which all countries select their strategies simultaneously and the game ends after the completion of this single round) are quite different from the defection incentives in an infinitely repeated game (which better describes the international tax game).[71] In particular, infinitely repeated games often facilitate cooperation. Consequently, it is claimed, if countries were to opt for a long-term cooperation strategy, with the inclusion of a

---

[70] For more on the debate over harmonization and competition, *see* the discussions in Chapters 4 and 6.

[71] An infinitely repeated game incorporates different considerations. The fundamental difference is that in deciding which action to take at any given stage, players will take into account the effect each action will have on their opponents' behavior at future stages of the game. Players in an infinitely repeated game can "punish" other players if they act uncooperatively. The possibility of punishment may create an incentive for other players to cooperate provided that their losses from punishment will be greater than the potential defection gains. Game theory has devoted much effort to the analysis of collective-action scenarios similar to the situation described above. Under this analysis, cooperation may prove profitable in infinitely repeated games. One famous example of such a "punishing" strategy in an infinitely repeated prisoner's dilemma game is the "tit for tat" strategy, whereby each player begins the game cooperating but shifts to defection in response to the defection of the other. The next round will start again with cooperation. In experiments conducted by Robert Axelrod, this strategy was found to be highly effective in the long run. ROBERT M. AXELROD, THE EVOLUTION OF COOPERATION 27, 54 (1984).

punishment mechanism for players who defect from the collective "deal," global cooperation would eventually evolve.[72]

Yet broadly supporting a cooperative strategy under these circumstances ignores important complexities.[73] First and foremost, infinitely repeated games can yield cooperative results if they are contending with strategically uncooperative behavior (e.g., beggar-thy-neighbor strategies). In international taxation, however, the reason for noncooperation might – as I explained above – not be strategic but rather a lack of consensus as to the best result. As Daniel Shaviro explains, "This is not a 'cooperate versus defect' choice. It is a 'how best to cooperate' choice."[74] But even assuming that consensus could emerge and the desirable solution could evolve and that reaching this solution is purely a strategic matter, the conditions necessary to facilitate long-term cooperation do not commonly arise. Not only is perfect coordination necessary, but extremely sensitive mechanisms for detecting a player's defection are also crucial,[75] as is the willingness of all participants to submit to and enforce the defection sanction, irrespective of political coalitions or other "irrelevant" factors. Thus, the optimal strategy for any given state will be determined by the potential gains it can reap from that strategy, as well as the potential harm other states could inflict on it if it adopts the strategy. The bottom line is, therefore, that cooperation is most certainly not the only rational option available to states even in an infinitely repeated game.

None of what has been claimed here regarding the unlikeliness of the emergence of cooperation among states means that states should not

---

[72] Indeed, "[t]he main idea behind the theory of repeated games is that if the game is played repeatedly then the mutually desirable outcome ... is stable if each player believes that a defection will terminate this cooperation, resulting in a subsequent loss for him that outweighs the short-term gain." MARTIN J. OSBORNE & ARIEL RUBINSTEIN, A COURSE IN GAME THEORY 133 (1994). However, as explained below, despite the apparent appeal of the idea of cooperation, I tend to be skeptical about the possibility of achieving global cooperation.

[73] In fact, the number of possible strategies (and possible outcomes) is huge. See id. at 134 ("[T]he set of equilibrium outcomes of a repeated game is huge, so that the notion of equilibrium lacks predictive power."). Game theory cannot, therefore, help us in predicting the outcome of such a game.

[74] SHAVIRO, supra note 29, at 138.

[75] The price of monitoring such defections could be very high since it entails on-line inspection of the tax laws of all states. Tax laws are, of course, notoriously complicated and difficult to monitor, especially given that reductions in payable taxes can be applied on an individual (informal) basis. I therefore suspect that worldwide coordination of the international tax system, even if achieved, would not be long lasting due to monitoring problems.

consider the possible responses of competing states when setting their international tax policies. On the contrary: it is vital that strategic considerations be factored into the policymaking process. Contextualizing international taxation as a competitive and strategic game brings to the forefront the need for states to formulate policies that promote their own interests. But the game structure also entails that states act strategically and adopt policies that anticipate the reactions of other states. Cooperative behavior – which is required by most neutrality-based approaches – is, of course, a viable strategy for states to pursue. But as explained, its results are not necessarily superior *and* it is difficult to achieve and sustain in conditions of competition.

The next chapter will examine bilateral negotiations as an alternative to unilateral solutions for alleviating double taxation. Looking more deeply at the strategic interaction between unilateral policies, it will present the background conditions in which bilateral tax treaties are negotiated and operate. Chapter 4 will then offer a detailed account of the possibility of larger-scale interstate cooperation and the limits of such cooperation.

3

The Tax Treaties Myth[1]

For many years, the prevailing view regarding tax treaties emphasized their role as *the* indispensable mechanism for alleviating double taxation. Policymakers simply assumed that tax treaties benefit all parties involved. By reducing the burden of double taxation, the treaties presumably facilitate the free movement of capital, goods, and services and help achieve allocational efficiencies. Although under a tax treaty regime, countries are required to forego potential tax revenues and although treaty negotiations are often quite cumbersome, tax treaties were considered to be well worth the effort because of the significant benefits they allegedly create for all participants once they are implemented.

In accepting without question this "benefits all" position, scholars and policymakers have for many years[2] overlooked the question of whether tax treaties are in fact required for preventing double taxation. If not – that is, if unilateral mechanisms can prevent double taxation in an efficient and stable way – is it possible that the treaties serve primarily to redistribute tax revenues? And if tax treaties are redistributive, who are the winners and who are the losers?

This chapter shows that treaties are not the only workable solution for alleviating double taxation. I argue that the benefits countries derive from easing the double-taxation burden on their residents investing abroad are sufficient to induce them to alleviate double taxation on a unilateral basis. Using the game theory methodology introduced in Chapter 2, I analyze the interactions between the unilateral policies of different types of countries and demonstrate how these interactions reduce tax levels to as great an extent as treaties do. Without offering any significantly greater degree

---

[1] This chapter is a reviesed and updated version of Tsilly Dagan, *The Tax Treaties Myth*, 32 NYU J. Int'l L. & Pol. 939 (2000).

[2] This attitude seems to be changing recently. See text accompanying *infra* notes 16–18, as well as Chapter 5 for a more detailed description of this change.

of stability, treaties often simply replicate the mechanism that countries are already using unilaterally to contend with double taxation.

There is, however, one substantial distinction between the unilateral solution and the treaty mechanism. Whereas the former tends to enable host countries to benefit from collecting tax revenues, tax treaties generally allocate the revenues more to the benefit of residence countries.[3] The revenue disparity between the two mechanisms is likely insignificant in the context of two developed countries, but with treaties between developing and developed countries, which are usually host and residence countries respectively, the reallocation of tax revenues produces regressive redistribution – to the benefit of the developed (residence) countries and at the expense of the developing (host) countries.

This chapter challenges the myth that double taxation treaties are an essential tool for alleviating double taxation. Section 3.1 begins by telling the conventional story of why tax treaties are necessary. Section 3.2 then considers how cross-border investment would be taxed in a world without tax treaties. Addressing separately host and residence countries, it analyzes their respective interests, unilateral policies, and the equilibrium that emerges from the interaction between their policies. Lastly, Section 3.3 compares the treaty mechanism to the unilateral mechanism and considers the gains and losses produced by the former.

3.1   The Conventional Story

The conventional story of tax treaties stresses their critical role in preventing double taxation. Embedded in this account is the assumption that absent tax treaties, double taxation would inevitably occur. It thus asserts the indispensability of *mutual* cooperation for preventing the harms of double taxation.

As explained in Chapter 2, double taxation has long been considered one of the most acute problems in international taxation and is often cited as a major obstacle to unfettered economic progress. Historically, countries have taken two approaches to alleviating double taxation: a unilateral approach and a bilateral approach. Under the unilateral approach, a country can choose from a range of policies to affirmatively reduce (or completely eliminate) the double taxation burden borne by its residents,

---

[3] The host country is where the income is produced; the residence country is where the income-producer resides.

irrespective of the host country's policy or any bilateral treaty provisions. Under the bilateral approach, in contrast, tax treaties are formulated and implemented by two contracting countries, designed to alleviate double taxation on the investments of the residents of the one state in the other state.

It has long been overwhelmingly presumed that when countries are left to their own unilateral devices, double taxation results. Tax treaties, from the perspective of this conventional wisdom, have been considered vital and effective tools (indeed, the most effective tools) for preventing double taxation. This viewpoint has been widely expressed by state officials, international agencies, and regulatory bodies, as well as by scholars.[4] The American Law Institute, for instance, opened its report on U.S. income tax

---

[4] See, e.g., STAFF OF S. COMM. ON FOREIGN RELATIONS, 105TH CONG., EXPLANATION OF PROPOSED PROTOCOL TO THE INCOME TAX TREATY BETWEEN THE UNITED STATES AND CANADA 4 (Comm. Print 1997) ("The traditional objectives of U.S. tax treaties have been the avoidance of international double taxation and the prevention of tax avoidance and evasion."); OECD COMM. ON FISCAL AFFAIRS, MODEL TAX CONVENTION ON INCOME AND ON CAPITAL, at 7(2010) (declaring that eliminating the "harmful effects" of double taxation is the main purpose of the OECD Model Tax Convention) [hereinafter OECD MODEL TAX CONVENTION 2010]; UN DEP'T OF INT'L ECON. & SOC. AFFAIRS, MANUAL FOR THE NEGOTIATION OF BILATERAL TAX TREATIES BETWEEN DEVELOPED AND DEVELOPING COUNTRIES 12, UN Doc. ST/ESA/94, UN Sales No. E.79.XVI.3 (1979) (emphasizing the role of model tax conventions in eliminating double taxation and coordinating international tax policies and practices); UN MODEL DOUBLE TAXATION CONVENTION BETWEEN DEVELOPED AND DEVELOPING COUNTRIES 1 (1980) [hereinafter UN MODEL DOUBLE TAXATION CONVENTION]; Rev. Proc. 91–23, 1991–1 C.B. 534 ("avoiding the double taxation of income, property or property transfers" is a main function of tax treaties); Richard L. Doernberg, Overriding Tax Treaties: The U.S. Perspective, 9 EMORY INT'L L. REV. 71, 71 (1995) ("A central purpose of an income tax treaty is to facilitate international trade by minimizing tax barriers in the exchange of goods and services across national boundaries. . . . An income tax treaty strikes a compromise by relaxing the domestic rules of both the residence and source states in order to promote international activities."); H. David Rosenbloom, Tax Treaty Abuse: Policies and Issues, 15 LAW & POL'Y INT'L BUS. 763, 768 (1983) ("The fundamental goal of tax treaties is removal of the negative effects of double taxation on the international movement of goods, services, capital, and people . . . ."); H. David Rosenbloom, Current Developments in Regard to Tax Treaties, 40TH NYU INST. ON FED. TAX'N, pt. 2, § 31.03(1), 24 (1982) ("At minimum, a tax treaty is intended to 'avoid double taxation.'") [hereinafter Rosenbloom, Current Developments]; CHARLES H. GUSRAFSON & RICHARD CRAWFORD PUGH, TAXATION OF INTERNATIONAL TRANSACTIONS 1991–1993, at 451 (1991); H. David Rosenbloom & Stanley I. Langbein, United States Treaty Policy: An Overview, 19 COLUM. J. TRANSNAT'L L. 359, 365–66 (1981). According to Rosenbloom & Langbein, id. at 365–66,

> The first question – what tax treaties are intended to achieve – was considered in the first report of the economists: double taxation represents an unfair burden on existing investment and an arbitrary barrier to the free flow of international capital, goods and

treaties with the statement, "The principal function of income tax treaties is to facilitate international trade and investment by removing – or preventing the erection of – tax barriers to the free international exchange of goods and services and the free international movement of capital and persons."[5] In a similar vein, the OECD's model tax convention used to declare that "[t]he principal purpose of double taxation conventions is to promote, by eliminating international double taxation, exchanges of goods and services, and the movement of capital and persons."[6] Moreover, it stated that:

> International juridical double taxation['s] harmful effect on the exchange of goods and services and movements of capital, technology, and persons are so well known that it is scarcely necessary to stress the importance of removing the obstacles that double taxation presents to the development of economic relations between countries.[7]

Under the traditional approach, the contracting states consent to relinquishing taxes in order to alleviate double taxation instead of collecting taxes at their regular levels of taxation. The residence country is usually willing to grant its residents a credit for the taxes paid to the host country (although an exemption is also feasible), provided that the latter either reduces the taxes it collects on investments from the residence country[8] or

---

persons. Nations should therefore seek to eliminate – or at least alleviate – these undesirable consequences of double taxation. The second question concerned the choice of bilateral approaches to eliminating double taxation . . . The early work of the league revealed the justification for bilateral approaches. Multilateral agreement is difficult when countries are in different legal or economic circumstances; unilateral measures, on the other hand, are almost inevitably ineffectual . . . .

[5] ALI, FEDERAL INCOME TAX PROJECT: INTERNATIONAL ASPECTS OF UNITED STATES INCOME TAXATION II, PROPOSALS ON UNITED STATES INCOME TAX TREATIES 5 (1992). The report further stated that "[p]erhaps the most important policy which income tax treaties are designed to implement is to avoid the double taxation of income which can arise when two (or more) countries seek to levy a tax on the same income base." *Id.*

[6] OECD MODEL TAX CONVENTION 2010, *supra* note 4, at 59. But note the change in the recent introduction to the 2014 OECD model tax treaty, described in the text accompanying *infra* note 19. OECD, MODEL TAX CONVENTION ON INCOME AND ON CAPITAL: CONDENSED VERSION 2–14 (2014), http://dx.doi.org/10.1787/mtc_cond-2014-en [hereinafter OECD MODEL TAX CONVENTION 2014].

[7] *Id.* at 7.

[8] This is usually the case with passive income. See, e.g., OECD MODEL TAX CONVENTION 2014, *supra* note 7, art. 10 (Taxation of Dividends); *id.* art. 11 (Taxation of Interest); *id.* art. 12 (Taxation of Royalties).

else grants a reciprocal credit.[9] The tax revenue losses to the residence and host countries are, as depicted by the traditional view, the price of enjoying the benefits of higher levels of cross-border investment, accompanied by the benefits of greater exports, higher wages, and increased standard of living.[10]

At first blush, this story makes a lot of sense. Since both contracting countries can gain more from free trade than from the tax revenues they could collect by limiting free trade, it seems reasonable to give up tax revenues in favor of the benefits of cross-border investment. The problem, however, is that this rests on the false premise that double taxation would inevitably occur in the absence of tax treaties. In fact, however, countries have incentives to reduce double taxation unilaterally, without the cooperation of other countries secured through tax treaties. Thus, if every country were to act unilaterally, the interaction between the policies of the residence and host countries would (as I show below) result in a stable equilibrium under which double taxation is alleviated. That is to say, there is no reason why cross-border investment should be expected to be lower in a world without tax treaties than in a world with treaties. If this is in fact the case, there must be another explanation for the existence of tax treaties.

Not all commentators subscribe to the conventional story. Some are skeptical as to the actual contribution treaties make to relieving double taxation. Already in 1963, Elisabeth Owens argued that "U.S. income tax treaties play a very marginal role in relieving double taxation ... [since] the U.S. has unilaterally provided for the avoidance of double taxation for its own citizens, corporations, and residents through the foreign tax credit provisions of the Internal Revenue Code."[11] In addition, she claimed, "for most taxpayers the amount of relief is minimal compared with that

---

[9] This would usually be the case with business income or personal services. *See, e.g., id.* arts. 7, 15; UN MODEL DOUBLE TAXATION CONVENTION, *supra* note 4, arts. 7, 15; US DEP'T OF TREASURY, TREASURY DEPARTMENT'S PROPOSED NEW MODEL INCOME TAX TREATY OF JUNE 16, 1981, arts. 7, 15, 1 Tax Treaties (CCH) §§ 211.07, 211.15 [hereinafter US MODEL INCOME TAX TREATY].

[10] *See, e.g.,* ALI, *supra* note 5, at 2:

The loss (or potential loss) of revenue which this entails is accepted as the price of obtaining the perceived benefit to the participating countries of assuring taxpayers of neutral tax treatment with respect to their international activities, thus promoting international commerce and contributing to the optimal allocation of world resources.

[11] Elizabeth A. Owens, *United States Income Tax Treaties: Their Role in Relieving Double Taxation,* 17 RUTGERS L. REV. 428, 430 (1963).

provided under United States internal law."[12] Owens' stance did not gain much prominence in the literature, perhaps because it concentrated solely on the United States. However, unilateral prevention of double taxation is certainly not a uniquely American practice. Quite the contrary, the majority of countries apply such mechanisms alongside tax treaties. Thus, double taxation would appear to be not as great a problem as conventional wisdom would have us believe.

Other commentators have also noted the relatively marginal role of tax treaties in preventing double taxation,[13] but like Owens, they have not offered a theoretical explanation for their claim.[14] Interestingly, policymakers have not seemed to be significantly affected by commentators'

---

[12] *Id.* at 446.

[13] *See* JOSEPH ISENBERGH, INTERNATIONAL TAXATION: U.S. TAXATION OF FOREIGN PERSONS AND FOREIGN INCOME 55:2 (2d ed. 1996) ("[I])ncome tax treaties can easily be taken at first inspection as measures designed to confer tax relief on certain individuals or enterprises. In fact, that is rarely their function. Tax treaties are principally concerned with the apportionment of tax revenues between the treasuries of the treaty countries. . . ."); PAUL R. MCDANIEL & HUGH J. AULT, INTRODUCTION TO UNITED STATES INTERNATIONAL TAXATION 178 (1998) (noting that many countries alleviate double taxation with unilateral measures and use treaties to "refine and adapt" these measures "to the specifics of the tax relationships between the two countries involved"); Julie A. Roin, *Rethinking Tax Treaties in a Strategic World with Disparate Tax Systems*, 81 VA. L. REV. 1753, 1767 (1995) (arguing that the use of unilateral measures to avoid double taxation has "blunted U.S. taxpayers' incentives to use treaty provisions"). Roin asserts that

> these bilateral agreements typically provide for reciprocal reductions in each treaty partner's source taxation of income earned by residents of the other treaty partner. Though some of these source tax reductions are intended to benefit investors through the elimination of "excessive taxation," many are intended to effect a roughly neutral exchange of tax revenues between the source and residence countries.

Id. at 1763 (footnotes omitted). *See also Pierre Gravelle, Tax Treaties: Concepts, Objectives and Types*, 42 BULL. FOR INT'L FISCAL DOCUMENTATION 522, 523 (1988) ("While the elimination of double taxation is an objective which is usually stated in its title, in reality a treaty is more correctly described as an instrument which refines and improves existing provisions in the domestic legislation which are designed to accomplish that end. . . ."); Alex A. Easson, *Do We Still Need Tax Treaties?*, 54 BULL. FOR INT'L FISCAL DOCUMENTATION 619 (2000).

[14] One commentator who did raise these issues is Koichi Hamada, *Strategic Aspects of Taxation on Foreign Investment Income*, 80 Q.J. ECON. 361 (1966). Hamada presented a model constructed around two large countries that can both affect the world prices of capital and assumed that the only feasible mechanism for double-taxation alleviation is a deduction. He showed that the uncoordinated unilateral actions of the two countries create a prisoner's dilemma, whereas a binding agreement would produce the optimal outcome. I discuss a different situation, however. I am assuming that countries cannot impact world prices of capital (which is a much more realistic assumption regarding the majority of countries) and that in terms of countries' interests, it is profitable for them to alleviate double taxation

occasional expressions of implicit support for Owens' position. The ALI report, for example, asserted a state of general unanimity regarding the necessity of tax treaties: "There is remarkably broad and well-established consensus among governments of various political and economic persuasions that it is in their interest to enter into income tax treaties."[15] As this chapter explains, however, treaties are not necessarily in the best interests of all countries. In particular, developing countries should carefully assess the costs and benefits of a tax treaty before signing, given their typical position as net capital importers and, accordingly, primarily host countries in tax treaties.

Since the publication of the article on which this chapter is based, skepticism regarding the role of tax treaties has become more prevalent. Voices questioning their value for developing countries are increasingly being heard, even in international organizations. Accordingly, in 2014, the IMF published a policy paper urging developing countries to think twice before entering tax treaties;[16] the World Bank recently echoed this.[17] Even the introduction to the 2014 OECD model tax convention was changed[18] and now reads as follows:

unilaterally not only by offering deductions but also credits and exemptions. These conditions influence their preferences and yield an equilibrium that differs from that described by Hamada.

[15] ALI, *supra* note 5, at 12. It is noteworthy that the ALI assesses the extent to which treaties are necessary for achieving the goal of preventing double taxation and that it notes that "many of the goals . . . could be achieved in whole or major part through the legislative process, without the need to conclude treaties." *Id.* The Institute interestingly concludes, however, that "income tax treaties will remain an important part of United States law." *Id.* at 14. The most important reason for this, according to the reporters, "is the fact that a country may be prepared to modify its domestic law rules only when satisfied that it is (and its taxpayers are) deriving appropriate reciprocal concessions from the foreign country concerned." *Id.* at 13. I show in this chapter that treaties do not offer any benefit that could not be attained through the interaction between unilateral policies, excluding, of course, more favorable allocation of tax revenues from the perspective of developed countries.

[16] IMF, Spillovers in International Corporate Taxation 28–29 (2014), https://www.imf.org/external/np/pp/eng/2014/050914.pdf. ("Some would simply advise developing countries not to sign BTTs.").

[17] *See* Mindy Herzfeld, *The Backlash Against Tax Treaties and Free Trade*, 84 Tax Notes Int'l 438 (Oct. 31, 2016) ("The IMF's position that developing countries should think twice before entering into tax treaties is not new. In 2014 it released a paper with a key message that treaty shopping 'is a major issue for many developing countries, which would be well-advised to sign treaties only with considerable caution'. . . . But the recent World Bank meeting demonstrated that skepticism about the benefits of tax treaties for developing countries is growing. While many suggest that developing countries should be skeptical of tax treaties, it is difficult to find anyone making the opposite case.").

[18] Even the name of the OECD model was changed: "In recognition of the fact that the Model Convention does not deal exclusively with the elimination of double taxation but also addresses other issues, such as the prevention of tax evasion and non-discrimination, it was

[I]t has long been recognized among the member countries of the Organization for Economic Co-operation and Development that it is desirable to clarify, standardize, and confirm the fiscal situation of taxpayers who are engaged in commercial, industrial, financial, or any other activities in other countries through the application by all countries of common solutions to identical cases of double taxation.... *[T]this is the main purpose of the OECD model tax convention... which provides a means of settling on a uniform basis the most common problems that arise in the field of international juridical double taxation.* As recommended by the council of the OECD, member countries, when concluding or revising bilateral conventions, should conform to this Model Convention as interpreted by the Commentaries thereon and having regard to the reservations contained therein.[19]

The final action 6 BEPS report even recommended that the Introduction of the OECD Model Tax Convention will be revised to include "[t]ax policy considerations that are relevant to the decision of whether to enter into a tax treaty or amend an existing treaty" and to specifically indicate that

> Two States that consider entering into a tax treaty should evaluate the extent to which the risk of double taxation actually exists in cross-border situations involving their residents. A large number of cases of residence-source juridical double taxation can be eliminated through domestic provisions for the relief of double taxation (ordinarily in the form of either the exemption or credit method) which operate without the need for tax treaties.[20]

This text implies a shift away from the goal of alleviating double taxation to the need to develop a mechanism that coordinates specific international tax "building blocks."[21] And yet, the network of treaties ostensibly continues to prosper. Even among developing countries, which are the apparent net losers of such treaties, the practice of signing cooperative treaties seems to be thriving.[22] Despite assertions – that are explored

---

subsequently decided to use a shorter title which did not include this reference." OECD MODEL TAX CONVENTION 2014, *supra* note 7, at 10.

[19] OECD MODEL TAX CONVENTION 2014, *supra* note 7, at 7 (emphasis added). *See also* OECD, PREVENTING THE GRANTING OF TREATY BENEFITS IN INAPPROPRIATE CIRCUMSTANCES (2014), http://dx.doi.org/10.1787/9789264219120-en (indicating that unilateral measures could prevent most forms of double taxation).

[20] OECD, *Preventing the Granting of Treaty Benefits in Inappropriate Circumstances, Action 6 – 2015 Final Report*, OECD/G20 BASE EROSION AND PROFIT SHIFTING PROJECT 94–95 (2015), http://dx.doi.org/10.1787/9789264241695-en at 94–95.

[21] *See* Chapter 5 for more a detailed account of this shift in the rationale of tax treaties and analysis of treaties' network effect. For a more detailed explanation and support of the building blocks conception, *see* Chapter 7.

[22] IMF, *supra* note 16, at 26–27.

in some detail below – of the asymmetrical costs tax treaties entail for developing countries,[23] these countries continue to negotiate and sign them.

3.2   The Interaction between National Policies

This section hypothesizes about a world without tax treaties to fully understand their function. In such a world, states operate strategically, and the policies they choose unilaterally interact with one another. Game theory analysis can help us think about a world in which countries, acting on political, economic, and social self-interest, resort solely to unilateral mechanisms to contend with double taxation problems. We can imagine a game in which each country chooses international tax policies that maximize these interests. Since a country's national interests are affected not only by its own policies but also by those of other countries, we should try to arrive at the optimal policy for each country given the possible responses of other countries to such policy. In this world, the policies chosen unilaterally by the different countries interact to create an international taxation landscape devoid of any treaties. The contours of this landscape will, therefore, depend not only on the impact of existing unilateral policies, but also on the potential interplay between the policies of different countries with their varying national interests.

The analysis in this section will focus on the interaction between two types of actors: residence and host countries. In line with the game theoretical analysis presented in Chapter 2, it will explore their preferences and study the unilateral strategies that would best promote their interests, followed by a game-theoretical analysis of the interaction of these unilateral strategies. Contrary to the conventional wisdom predicting double taxation in the absence of treaties, the analysis here will show that such strategic interaction yields a stable equilibrium that in fact prevents double taxation.

The countries whose policies interact in unilaterally preventing double taxation vary in what they seek to promote. As we can expect, residence countries may differ in the extent to which they seek to promote outbound investment. Residence countries and host countries can also diverge in the extent to which they encourage cross-border investment,[24] as well as in the

---

[23] See text accompanying *infra* notes 68–70.
[24] Whereas the host country likely prefers the highest level of cross-border investment created by an exemption, the residence country might prefer a lower level of outbound investment.

tax revenues they seek to reap from this activity.[25] In what follows, I will present and consider different premises that have been raised regarding countries' preferences. Each of these premises yields a different possible game. The discussion tends to be fairly technical. For those inclined to press forward to the discussion of the realities of tax treaties in Section 3, the takeaway lessons from the games developed in the discussion below can be summarized as demonstrating that under all of the premises, the interaction between states' unilateral strategies produces a stable equilibrium under which double taxation is prevented. In other words, unilateral alleviation of double taxation emerges not only as a common practice among states but also as a stable condition or, in game theory terms, a stable equilibrium. Thus, a unilateral policy can be an effective and stable means for preventing double taxation.

One technical detail regarding the premises in the forthcoming analysis must be noted. As a matter of course, the contracting countries in bilateral treaties function both as a country of residence (of investors investing abroad) and a host country (where the investment or economic activity takes place), and they are assigned reciprocal rights and duties in line with these capacities. However, to simplify the analysis of the interests of residence and host countries in the context of international tax policy interactions, my discussion will assume a treaty to be an agreement signed between a residence country, as the one party, and a host country, as the other, where the former provides some alleviation of double taxation in return for the latter's reduction of its tax rates for investors who are residents of the residence country. I relax this assumption in the last section of this chapter and take treaties to be the conglomeration of reciprocal rights and duties between the contracting states.

In addition, I will assume that each country functions like a "black box" and promotes its economic and social welfare through mechanisms aimed at achieving a desired level of cross-border investment. Conceiving of the state as a body with one uniform national interest is obviously an oversimplification. To fully understand what the "interests of the state" might be, we need to decipher the interests and power relations between the different actors and groups within each country. As Eyal Benvenisti has convincingly explained, many of the pervasive conflicts of interest between nation-states are in fact more internal than external and stem from the

---

[25] Host countries might be willing to give up more tax revenues for increased cross-border investments.

heterogeneity within states.[26] I will take a somewhat closer look at these internal effects of international tax policies in Part III of the book.

a. The National Interests of Host Countries

Host countries have a genuine interest in reducing the tax wedge, which is the efficiency loss that results from the imposition of taxes. This will attract foreign investors as it will minimize the taxes they will have to pay. Therefore, the optimal policy for a small host country is to eliminate, even unilaterally, all taxes imposed on foreign investors, other than the costs of the goods and services they consume. Only in cases where eliminating taxes altogether is not possible should such a country pursue the second-best option of collecting the largest possible portion of the tax revenue pie.

Indeed, to maximize the benefits from foreign investment and avoid the welfare-reducing effects of taxes, a small, open economy should not tax foreign investments.[27] As Joel Slemrod explains,

> Capital imports should occur as long as their contribution to the domestic economy, the marginal product of capital, exceeds the cost to the economy. A small country must compete with investment opportunities elsewhere,

[26] Eyal Benvenisti, *Exit and Voice in the Age of Globalization*, 98 MICH. L. REV. 167 (1999). Moreover, Benvenisti argues, domestic interest groups often cooperate with foreign interest groups across national boundaries in order to impose their externalities on their respective rival domestic groups. Hence, many global collective action failures must be attributed to conflicts among rival domestic groups rather than to inter national competition.

[27] *See* Joel Slemrod, *Tax Principles in an International Economy*, in WORLD TAX REFORM: CASE STUDIES OF DEVELOPED AND DEVELOPING COUNTRIES 11, 13 (Michael J. Boskin & Charles E. McLure, Jr. eds., 1990). For a h discussion of the "tax wedge" and the welfare effects of a capital income tax in a small, open economy, *see* A. Lans Bovenberg et al., *Tax Incentives and International Capital Flaws: The Case of the United States and Japan*, in TAXATION IN THE GLOBAL ECONOMY 283, 291–92 (Assaf Razin & Joel Slemrod eds., 1990). In economic terms, the income tax "crowds out" foreign investment, resulting in a loss in national welfare, which may be measured by a tax wedge. This crowding-out effect *arises* because the tax makes some investments not profitable. The host country tax discourages foreign investment that would otherwise flow into the country in the absence of such a tax. The amount of investment that is crowded out is measured by the difference between the new, before-tax required return and the rate of return on world capital markets (*i.e.*, the old, before-tax required rate of return) on the amount of investment that is lost as a result of the tax. *See id.* at 290–92. This amount is referred to as a "tax wedge" so that it can be graphically depicted as a triangle on familiar supply-demand graphs. But *see* Yariv Brauner, *The Future of Tax Incentives for Developing Countries*, in TAX AND DEVELOPMENT 25, 38 (Yariv Brauner & Miranda Stewart eds., 2013) and authorities there for possible differences among host states.

so it must offer the foreign investor the going after-tax rate of return. This level of capital imports will be achieved if such imports are completely exempt from taxation by the importing nation, because in this case foreign investors will, in their own interest, invest until the domestic marginal product equals their opportunity cost, the after tax world rate of return. Any attempt to tax capital imports will cause the country to forgo domestic investment whose contribution to national income exceeds the cost to the nation.[28]

It is important to note that the tax wedge is a product of all the taxes imposed by the host county and residence country combined.[29] Reducing it therefore means reducing the combined taxes of the two countries. Accordingly, the host country should take the residence country's tax policies into consideration in determining its optimal policy for reducing the tax wedge. For example, if the residence country exempts its residents' outbound investments, the host country's best policy is to not tax these investors, since any tax will create a tax wedge.[30] If, instead, the residence country taxes its residents on their foreign-investment activities, the host country will be unable to completely eliminate the tax wedge unilaterally. However, it can capture tax revenues from foreign investments without increasing the tax wedge if the residence country allows a credit for foreign taxes paid by its own residents. In effect, the residence country will be reimbursing its residents for the taxes they pay to the host country. The host country will benefit most from this if it imposes the highest possible tax on foreign investments that the residence country is willing to credit.[31] When a residence country offers a limited credit mechanism – that is, a foreign tax credit that is limited to the residence country's tax rates – the host country should tax foreign investors at a rate that matches the rate in the residence country. Lastly, if a residence country allows a deduction for foreign taxes, the host country will be better off not taxing foreign

---

[28] Slemrod, *supra* note 27, at 13.   [29] See Bovenberg et al., supra note 27, at 288–94.

[30] A subsidy would also be undesirable, as it would create a tax wedge of its own. *See* Mark Gersovitz, *The Effect of Domestic Taxes on Foreign Private Investment, in* THE THEORY OF TAXATION FOR DEVELOPING COUNTRIES 615, 619–22 (David Newbery & Nicholas Stem eds., 1987).

[31] Imposing tax that is creditable against a foreign investor's domestic tax liability will raise tax revenues for the host country and not drive away foreign investments. In fact, in these circumstances, the best policy for the host country would be to tax foreign investments while at the same time offer foreign investors a subsidy to reimburse them for the taxes they pay. Thus, the residence country's laws permitting, the host country would effectively be able to eliminate the tax wedge even when the residence country taxes its residents on foreign-source income. *See* Gersovitz, *supra* note 30, at 619–23.

investors from that residence country. Since deductions do not fully offset the amount of foreign taxes paid by investors,[32] any tax imposed by the host country will increase the tax wedge and undermine its goals.[33]

In sum, if a host country's primary policy objective is to eliminate the tax wedge, it must sacrifice tax revenues to increase foreign investment. However, if completely eliminating the tax wedge is impossible because the residence country does not exempt its residents' foreign-source income, the host country should try to collect as large a portion of the tax revenues as possible.

Based on this analysis, we can conclude that the host country will rank its policy preferences in the following order:

1. It would most prefer that neither country imposes any taxes (i.e., an exemption in the residence country/no tax in the host country), which would completely prevent a tax wedge from forming and maximize cross-border investment.
2. It would prefer to a lesser extent a moderate level of cross-border investment and that it collect tax revenues from this investment. This would be possible if the residence country provides a credit. The host country would then tax the foreign investments at a rate equal to that imposed in the residence country.
3. It would even less prefer a moderate level of cross-border investment, but without collecting any tax revenues. This would occur when the residence country grants either a credit or deduction and when the host country refrains from taxing foreign investments.
4. It would least prefer a low level of cross-border investment, which would arise if the residence country opts for a deduction mechanism and the host country taxes foreign investments.

b. The National Interests of Residence Countries

It is more complex to determine the optimal policy for a residence country than for a host country. Although there is widespread concurrence that countries of residence should alleviate the double taxation of their

---

[32] While a credit reduces the taxes that the residence country should collect in the amount of the taxes paid to the host country, deductions only reduce the taxable income by that amount.
[33] Unlike in the case of an exemption, an increase in the host country's taxes would affect the tax wedge only partially since the host country's tax is deductible. However, the tax wedge would still grow to some extent, and therefore, the host country would be better off without increasing its tax.

residents, there is, as we saw in Chapter 2, much less consensus regarding which of the three typical unilateral mechanisms for alleviating double taxation – exemptions, credits, or deductions – best serves the interests of a residence country.[34]

Recall that these mechanisms differ in the level of outbound investment they promote, assuming that the host country taxes foreign investments. Generally speaking, assuming an equal or lower tax rate in the host country, an exemption creates the highest incentive for outbound investment; a credit supports an intermediate level of outbound investment; and a deduction provides the weakest incentive. In addition, each mechanism yields a different division of the tax revenues between the host country and residence country.[35]

In the discussion that follows, I will examine the interests of three prototype residence countries: residence countries that prefer a high level of outbound investment, even if at the cost of lost tax revenues (I will call them "exemption countries"); residence countries that prefer a moderate level of outbound investment – that is, they are willing to forego tax revenues for more investment but unwilling to create an incentive for their residents to invest abroad instead of at home (I will call them "credit countries"); and residence countries that prefer a low level of outbound

---

[34] *See* Chapter 2 for the details of the debate and the various considerations in support of each of these mechanisms.

[35] The table in this note presents some of the possible interactions between host and residence countries.

Residence Country	Host Country	Level of Incentive for Cross-Border Investment	Who Collects?
exemption	no tax	high	neither
credit	no tax	moderate	residence
deduction	no tax	moderate	residence
exemption	tax	moderate	host
credit	tax	moderate	host
deduction	tax	low	both (reduced)
no alleviation	tax	lowest	both

The first row, for example, shows that in order to create a high level of incentive for cross-border investments, it is not sufficient for the host country to exempt its foreign investors, but rather, the investors' country of residence must exempt them as well. If, however, the investors' country of residence does not offer them an exemption and instead grants a credit (as in the second row) or a deduction (as in the third row), only a moderate incentive for cross-border investment will be created, despite the exemption offered by the host.

investment, namely, are interested in the combined benefits of outbound investment and tax revenues (I will call them "deduction countries"). For simplicity's sake, I use the terms "exemption country," "deduction country," and "credit country" as codes for the types of countries. This is not meant to indicate that these are the mechanisms they each necessarily end up selecting.

1.   Deductions

If we assume that the preferred policy for a residence country is to create a low incentive for outbound investments and collect more tax revenues per investment, we have, at first glance, a forceful rationale for tax treaties. It seems reasonable to presume that the host country and residence country would both benefit from cooperating to achieve a somewhat higher level of cross border investment by reducing, through mutual agreement, the combined level of taxation. While the cost in tax revenues could be too high a price to pay if shouldered by one of them alone, it should be a reasonable burden if shared by both. Yet upon closer consideration, it emerges that the interaction of unilateral policies could create an equilibrium free from double taxation, making treaties unnecessary.

i.   **Why Might a Deduction Policy Be Preferred?**   If a residence country takes into account only tax revenues and investors' income when determining its optimal tax policy, a small, open economy would foster outbound investments so long as the return on those investments (excluding the tax paid to foreign governments) exceeds the return on domestic investments (including any tax paid to the residence country's government).[36] The residence country could encourage investment under these conditions by adopting a personal taxation system (i.e., taxing residents/citizens on their worldwide income) and allowing taxpayers to deduct foreign taxes from their taxable income. The deduction would operate as a unilateral mechanism that encourages outbound investment as long as the revenues of the residence country and its resident investors combined exceed domestic investment revenues for both.

Chapter 2 presented the criticism expressed in the literature regarding this type of policy, often labeled "national neutrality," for being shortsighted on the interaction between the policies of different countries. Implicit in this criticism is the premise that cooperative behavior – that is, mutual efforts by the host and residence countries to lower the level of

---

[36] *See* Slemrod, *supra* note 27, at 13.

taxation on cross-border investments – would be to the benefit of both. A typical example of such cooperation is the signing of a bilateral tax treaty. If, indeed, under a deduction mechanisms, there is a high combined level of taxation in the host and residence countries in the absence of a treaty between them (meaning that there is a relatively low level of cross-border investment between them), a treaty can arguably serve to reduce the total level of taxation and split the tax revenues between the host and residence countries.

There is something inherently wrong with this scenario, however – namely, that it takes as a given that the host country taxes foreign investments. Conventional wisdom tends to think of a deduction mechanism as limiting cross-border investment and, therefore, noncooperative because it presumes that the host country taxes foreign investments. If the host country does, in fact, do this and the residence country allows only a deduction for the tax, then a relatively high level of taxation (and low incentive for cross-border investment) will undoubtedly ensue. But if the host country does *not* tax foreign investments, investors will face a moderate total level of taxation in the two countries combined (and the incentive for cross-border investment will be likewise moderate), regardless of whether the residence country offers a deduction or a credit. In either event, the combined level of taxation will be equal to the tax in the residence country.

Why would this, in all likelihood, be the case? Why is it plausible to assume – contrary to conventional wisdom – that when the residence country grants a deduction, the host country does *not* tax foreign investors?

ii.   The Residence-Host Interaction under the Deduction Assumption

A closer look at the interests of the residence and host countries reveals that the outcome of their unilateral policies is not double taxation but, rather, a single level of taxation. To analyze the interaction between the policies of the two countries, we must first identify each country's order of preferences.

A residence country that chooses a deduction over a credit indicates that it prefers to collect tax revenues even if this will lead to a decrease in the level of outbound investments. The rationale underlying this preference is that tax revenues comprise part of the national welfare pie. However, this residence country would undoubtedly prefer not to forego outbound investments if it can maintain its tax revenue levels. This would be theoretically possible if, for example, the host country were to not tax income earned by foreign residents. In this case, only the residence country would collect tax from the investments of its residents in the host country. Thus, cross-border investments between the two countries would be subject to a single level of taxation (that of the residence country) and would increase in level. Moreover, the residence country's tax revenues would not drop, for a higher level of outbound investments means more income for its investors, which, in turn, means more tax revenues.

The choice of a deduction rather than an exemption, in contrast, is indication that the residence country does not want to exempt its residents from taxation in any circumstances, regardless of whether or not the host country taxes them on their investments there. Otherwise, it would simply offer them an exemption.[37]

We can infer, then, the following order of preferences for a deduction residence country:

1. It would most prefer a moderate level of outbound investments, but only provided that it (and not the host country) collects the tax imposed on its residents investing abroad. This policy would be implemented either through a deduction or a credit, but only if the host country does not tax the foreign investment.[38] Note that a deduction and a credit mechanism yield identical outcomes when the host country imposes no taxes.

2. Its second-best preference would be a low level of outbound investment, provided that its national welfare (i.e., the profits earned by its residents investing in the host country as well as its tax revenues) is maximized. This would be the outcome if a deduction mechanism is implemented in the residence country and the host country taxes foreign investments.

3. It would least prefer a moderate level of outbound investment if the host country reaps all the tax revenues. This will be the outcome if the residence country implements a credit system.

---

[37] Such an assumption could be reasonable, for example, with regard to a country that seeks to distribute equally the burden of income tax between capital owners and the immobile factors of production, such as labor and land. This assumption may also be plausible, moreover, where the bureaucracy has an independent interest in preserving a high level of tax revenues or where a specific interest group has enough political clout to promote its interests despite the accompanying national welfare loss.

[38] When a residence country adopts either a deduction system or a credit system and the host country does not tax foreign investment, the investor pays only residence country taxes. Under a credit mechanism, investors pay their residence country taxes and are not entitled to any credit since they paid no foreign taxes. Under a deduction system, when no host country taxes were paid, they pay tax to their residence country on the full amount of their foreign income.

Note that this order of preferences diverges significantly from the host country's order of preferences presented above.

iii. The Game Table 1 summarizes the interaction between the preferences of the residence country and the preferences of the host country.[39]

Table 1

action	host country taxes	host country does not tax
deduction in residence country	2;4	1;3*
credit in residence country	3;2	1;3

In this stylized game, the host country can choose between not taxing foreign investors and taxing them at a rate equal to the tax rate in the residence country. The residence country, in turn, taxes its residents on their worldwide income and can choose between allowing them a deduction or a credit for the foreign taxes they pay.

If the host country does not tax foreign investors (as in the right-hand column), the inevitable outcome will be that the investors are taxed in full

---

[39] The numbers in this table indicate the ranking of options in their order of preference, with 1 representing the most preferred option for each country and 4 the least preferred. In each pair of numbers, the left-hand number represents the preferences of the residence country and the right-hand number the preferences of the host country. The numbers with an asterisk represent the equilibrium point at which neither country has incentive to defect.

This game should actually include another scenario: when the residence country allows an exemption. However, since this would lead to the worst possible outcome for the residence country (either no taxation whatsoever, which would create a high incentive for outbound investment, or else taxation only by the host country, which is the third best option for the latter) and since the choice to allow an exemption is totally up to the residence country, I assume that a residence country whose most preferred policy is a deduction would not consider granting an exemption.

action	host country taxes	host country does not tax
residence country grants deduction	2;4	1;3
residence country grants credit	3;2	1;3
residence country grants exemption	3;2	4;1

If the residence country prefers no taxation at all out of all of these options, it will prefer an exemption policy (see my analysis in *infra* Section 3.c.iii). However, implicit in the assumption of a deduction as the residence country's preferred policy is its need to collect some taxes from its residents investing abroad.

by (and only by) their residence country, regardless of whether it grants a credit or deduction. This will result in a moderate level of taxation and, therefore, a moderate incentive for cross-border investment. In this scenario, the residence country alone will collect the taxes. This is the most preferable option for the residence country and the third-best option for the host country. The residence country will reap all the tax revenues from the cross-border investment and the host country none, while foreign investment in the latter will be moderate.

If the host country does tax foreign investments, however, the outcome of the game becomes contingent on the residence country's policy. Allowing its residents a deduction for their foreign taxes will produce a low incentive for cross-border investment, since both countries will collect taxes. In Table 1, we see that this is the second-best option for the residence country and the least-preferred option for the host country. But if the residence country allows a credit, the host country will benefit from all the tax revenues and enjoy a moderate level of cross-border investment. This is the least-preferred option for the residence country. It is the second-best scenario for the host, since it will collect all the tax revenues but the foreign investment from the residence country will be moderate.

iv.   **An Equilibrium**   It emerges from Table 1 that, given these assumptions, the residence country's dominant strategy is to allow a deduction. Regardless of what policy the host country adopts, a deduction will always be the better (or at least not the worst) policy option for the residence country. If the host country taxes foreign investments, for example, the residence country should choose a deduction over a credit, since it would prefer a lower level of outbound investment and collecting some of the tax revenues to a moderate level of outbound investment and collecting no tax revenues at all. If, instead, the host country opts not to tax foreign investments, the residence country should be indifferent to the choice between a deduction and a credit. Therefore, the preferred mechanism overall (taking into account both scenarios) is a deduction.

The best possible outcome for the host country, as Table 1 shows, will emerge if it taxes foreign investments and the residence country allows its residents a credit for foreign taxes. But given that the residence country allows only a deduction, the host country will be better off not taxing investors from that residence country. Since the host country will be responsive to the residence country's policy preferences, it will realize that the latter's dominant strategy is to offer a deduction for foreign taxes. Therefore, in effect, the host country is left with only one choice, assuming that the residence country prefers a deduction, which is not to tax foreign investors, for it would derive greater benefit from increased investment from abroad even at the cost of less tax revenues.

This outcome – namely, that the residence country allows a deduction and the host country does not tax foreign investments – would create a stable equilibrium, since neither country has incentive to defect from it as long as the other does not defect.

Two points are noteworthy at this juncture. The first is that double taxation would be prevented by the interaction of these unilateral tax policies, thus obviating the need for tax treaties for that purpose. Second, this equilibrium-forming outcome does not correspond with the reality of the mechanisms residence countries tend to prefer in practice, which are credits, exemptions, or a combination of the two (as in deferral[40]) rather than deductions.[41] This discrepancy between the policy reality and the theoretical analysis suggests that residence countries tend to think that deductions do not serve their national interests. I now proceed to scenarios in which residence countries might regard a credit to be the best mechanism for promoting their interests.

b.   Credit

Under a credit mechanism, as explained, investors can credit the foreign taxes they pay in the host country against their residence country taxes.[42] Since the credit is usually limited to the residence country's tax

---

[40] Deferral occurs when the residence country exempts foreign entities owned by their residents. This exemption allows the resident-owners to defer the realization of their income. Only when the foreign entity distributes its profits or the resident-owners dispose of their investments will their income be taxed.

[41] The recent trend among countries is toward territoriality (i.e., exemption of dividend income from foreign affiliates). In 1992, Greece, Iceland, Italy, Japan, New Zealand, Spain, Turkey, the United Kingdom, and the United States all granted credits for foreign business income. By 2010, Austria, Belgium, Canada, China, France, Finland, Germany, India, Italy, Japan, Luxembourg, the Netherlands, Russia, Spain, Switzerland, and the United Kingdom were all exempting foreign business income unilaterally by offering an exemption of at least 95 percent of the dividends received from foreign affiliates. A COMPARISON OF KEY ASPECTS OF THE INTERNATIONAL TAX SYSTEMS OF MAJOR OECD AND DEVELOPING COUNTRIES (May 10, 2010), http://businessroundtable.org/sites/default/files/BRT_14_country_international_tax_comparison_20100510.pdf. Even as early as 1992, of the states surveyed by the Committee of Independent Experts, only Ireland, Portugal, and Switzerland were allowing only a deduction for non-business income. On the strong trend toward territoriality, see REPORT OF THE COMMITTEE OF INDEPENDENT EXPERTS ON COMPANY TAXATION 267 (1992) [hereinafter REPORT ON COMPANY TAXATION].

[42] For an illustration of the operation of the credit mechanism, see Chapter 2 note 25.

rate, investors pay tax at the higher of the two rates. If the host country taxes foreign investments and the residence country provides a credit, the host country collects all the tax revenues and (assuming equal tax rates in both countries) the residence country collects none. The credit mechanism thus creates a moderate incentive for outbound investment.

i. Why the Credit Mechanism May Be the Optimal Mechanism for (Some) Residence Countries

As explained in Chapter 2, a wide variety of arguments have been offered in support of the credit mechanism for residence countries. Some see virtue in the fact that a credit mechanism promotes an efficient allocation of worldwide investments, an argument I rejected.[43] Others assert that it promotes horizontal equity, and still others contend that the credit has a positive impact on national, social, political, and economic factors such as savings, jobs, trade, and innovation.[44] Thus, a credit policy does make perfect sense for a country seeking a moderate level of outbound investment, even if at the expense of tax revenues presumably because the benefit generated from the investments outweighs the loss in tax revenues.

ii. The Residence-Host Interaction under the Credit Assumption

Let us consider again the interaction between the unilateral policies of the host and residence countries in game format, beginning with the latter's order of preferences assuming it prefers a credit over a deduction:[45]

1. The residence country would most prefer a moderate level of incentive for cross-border investment (which a credit system will yield) and that it (rather than the host country) collects all the tax revenues from this activity. In adopting a credit mechanism, however, the residence country will be willing to give up its tax revenues unilaterally in order to achieve a moderate level of outbound investment. Thus, it can be reasonably assumed that it would prefer to achieve that same moderate level of outbound investment without losing revenues.
2. The residence country's second-most preferred option would be a moderate incentive for outbound investments but that the host country

---

[43] See the text accompanying note 34 in Chapter 2.

[44] See the text accompanying notes 54–60 in Chapter 2.

[45] The preferences are described in a highly generalized manner. Certainly, different mixtures of these preferences might exist. For example, there is the possibility (which falls between Options 1 and 2 above) that the total amount of taxes paid would be the same as what the residence country would collect on the income, but that both countries would share in the revenues.

collects all taxes on these investments. This option is obviously less desirable than option 1 but preferable to a low level of outbound investment (option 3). In fact, if the residence country prefers a lower level of outbound investment, it will choose a deduction over a credit.

3. The residence country would least prefer one of the following two options: that it collects no taxes from its residents on their outbound investments (i.e., there is a high incentive for cross-border investment) or that it creates a low incentive for outbound investment (i.e., it imposes a high level of taxation).[46] A high level of outbound investment would necessarily result from no taxation and could be higher than what the residence country would consider optimal. On the other hand, a high level of taxation, as explained above, would reduce the incentive to invest abroad and be less preferable than option 2 because it would mean that the residence country is unwilling to sacrifice tax revenues to create the optimal incentive for outbound investment.[47]

A residence country can prevent the third (and worst, from its perspective) outcome by unilaterally avoiding both double taxation and no taxation on foreign investments. In order to ensure that its residents are taxed at all times, it can simply tax them on their worldwide income while taking unilateral measures to alleviate double taxation.

The question that remains, then, is whether the residence country should adopt a credit or a deduction to prevent double taxation.[48] Raising such a question may seem puzzling given my initial assumption that a credit produces the optimal level of outbound investment. But in this context, a country's preference for a credit is merely code for its preference of a moderate level of outbound investment, even if at the cost of less tax revenues. So despite this preference, this country might still make the strategic move of implementing a deduction mechanism. This could be the case, for example, if it believes that the interaction of a unilateral deduction policy with the unilateral policy of a host country will yield better results.

Table 2 depicts the interaction between the policies as the following simultaneously played game between the two countries:

---

[46] Recall that I am assuming that the residence country would rather forego its own tax revenues than subject its residents to double taxation since its national gain from facilitating more outbound investment is greater than the possible revenues from taxing it.

[47] If this is not the case, then we are dealing with a country that prefers a deduction, as discussed in Section 2.b.1.

[48] An exemption would not serve the residence country's interests under these assumptions since the optimal response from the host country would be to exempt foreign investments, thereby resulting in no taxation whatsoever on cross-border investments.

Table 2

action	host country taxes	host country does not tax
residence country grants a deduction	3;4	1;3*
residence country grants a credit	2;2*	1;3

If the residence country allows a deduction and the host country taxes foreign investments, a disincentive for outbound investment will arise, which, under the current assumption, is the worst-case scenario for both countries. In all of the other options in Table 2, a moderate level of outbound investment is encouraged, since the tax paid is equal to what would be collected in the residence country. The only point of divergence is with regard to who collects the tax revenues: the host country or residence country. If the host country does not tax foreign investments, the residence country will collect all tax revenues on that activity, regardless of whether it allows a credit or deduction. If, instead, the host country does tax foreign investments and the residence country grants a credit, all tax revenues will go to the former.[49]

iii. An Equilibrium Granting a credit emerges as the dominant strategy for a residence country in Table 2. No matter what policy the host country adopts, the residence country will be better off (or at least not worse off) allowing its residents a credit for their foreign taxes rather than

---

[49] If the host country taxes and the residence country grants a credit (assuming that the two countries have identical tax rates), the investor will pay tax to the host country and not to the residence country. To illustrate, if both countries impose a 40 percent tax, an income of $100 will be subject to $40 in tax in the host country. The tax due in the residence country will also be $40, but a credit for the $40 paid in taxes to the host country will be allowed. Thus, no taxes will be paid to the residence country, and the investor's net income will amount to $60. If the host country does not tax the foreign investment, the investor will pay tax only to the residence country under either a deduction or exemption mechanism. In this example, the investor will pay $0 in taxes to the host country. Under a deduction mechanism, this investor's taxable income would still be $100 ($100-$0), and he or she would pay $40 in residence country taxes with a resulting net income of $60. Under a credit mechanism, the analysis would be different but the results the same: an income of $100 produced in the host country would be tentatively taxed in the residence country (tentative liability of $40). A credit would be allowed for taxes paid to the host country, but since no such tax would be paid, the investor would pay only the residence country's tax of $40. Again, the investor's net income would be $60.

a deduction. If the host country does not tax foreign investments, a credit and deduction will produce the same result: a moderate level of tax revenues, collected in their entirety by the residence country. If the host country does tax foreign investments, the residence country will be better off allowing a credit rather than a deduction. In this latter scenario, the residence country will enjoy a high level of outbound investment but lose in tax revenues.[50]

Since host countries are aware of the fact that the credit mechanism is the dominant strategy for such residence countries, they will choose to tax foreign investors. This is because their best option is to reap the benefits of the credit in the residence country and collect the tax revenues on the investments from the latter's residents. Thus, the credit/tax solution creates a stable equilibrium, since neither country has incentive to adopt a different policy given the other country's policy.

iv.   **Another Equilibrium**   Interestingly, this game yields another equilibrium, when the host country does not tax foreign investments and the residence country allows a deduction for foreign income. This equilibrium is stable as well, since neither country has incentive to deviate from its chosen strategy. If the residence country allows a deduction, then the host country is better off not taxing foreign investments; if the host country does not tax foreign investments, the residence country has incentive only to allow a deduction.

However, since in this game analysis, the credit mechanism has emerged as the dominant strategy for a residence country and given that under current practice, the credit mechanism is the prevailing strategy, there is no reason to assume that a residence country would adopt a deduction policy.[51] Residence and host countries compete with peer countries for residents and investments. The competition among residence countries makes it difficult for any of them to take a leadership position and unilaterally adopt a deduction policy. If a lone residence country were to change its policy and grant only a deduction, it could incur serious

---

[50] Note that we are now focusing on a country that prefers this option to the option of higher tax revenues with lower outbound investment that would result from a deduction system.

[51] Instead of a simultaneous game, if this were a sequential one in which the residence country gets to be the first to make a move, the residence country would prefer a deduction mechanism. This would force the host country into not taxing the income produced by foreign investors. Given this, I suspect that were it not for the competition among residence countries or, alternatively, if one residence country were strong enough to take the lead on this matter, there might be a shift toward the deduction/no-tax equilibrium.

costs in competing with other residence countries. Instead of exempting investments from this residence country, host countries could simply
favor investments from credit-granting residence countries.

Thus, similarly to what we found under the deduction assumption,
with the credit assumption as well, unilateral measures produce a stable
equilibrium. Under this equilibrium, residence countries provide a credit,
thereby allowing host countries to tax foreign investments. The alternative
equilibrium (i.e., the deduction/no-tax equilibrium) is unlikely to emerge
due to the competition between residence countries. Accordingly, under
the credit assumption, unilateral measures can also effectively prevent
double taxation.

c. Exemption

The third unilateral mechanism that a residence country can adopt to alleviate double taxation is an exemption for foreign-source income. Under
this mechanism, an investor in a foreign country is subject only to the host
country's taxation and pays no taxes on her foreign-source income in the
residence country.

When a residence country adopts an exemption policy, it is indicating
that it believes it will benefit more from a higher level of outbound investment than from the tax revenues on outbound investment or from the
stronger incentive to invest domestically that would be created by a credit
or deduction. As discussed in Chapter 2, this is a policy often lobbied
for by residents who invest abroad and would most benefit from it, and
some countries view this to be sufficient reason to exempt foreign-source
income.[52]

If a residence country prefers the high level of outbound investment
incentivized by the exemption mechanism at the expense of tax revenues
and domestic investment, there is no real conflict between its interests and
those of host countries. If a host country does not tax foreign investments,

---

[52] While it is true that the residence country might lose some domestic investment that would
be made abroad because of the lower taxes, there is considerable debate over whether, on
the whole, its economy (including jobs) would benefit or be harmed by such an outbound
flow of investments. However, there is no need to take a stance in this debate for the purposes of the discussion in this chapter, as we are assuming that the interests of the residence
country would be served by eliminating the tax wedge. If this is not the case and the residence country would be better served by a lower incentive for outbound investments, then
we return to the analysis in Section 2.c.ii, with its premise that a credit best promotes the
residence country's interests.

Table 3

action	host country taxes	host country does not tax
residence country grants exemption	3;2	1;1*
residence country grants credit	3;2	2;3
residence country grants deduction	4;4	2;3

the residence country's national welfare from outbound investments will likely be maximized if it does not tax them. No taxation on all foreign-source income would eliminate any tax wedge, thereby enabling capital consumers in the host country and capital suppliers in the residence country to maximize their benefits from cross-border investments.

The order of preferences for both the residence country and host country, assuming the former prefers the high level of outbound incentive provided by an exemption, will thus be as follows:

1. Both countries would most prefer that neither taxes cross-border investments, which would maximize their benefits from this activity.
2. Both countries would next prefer that only one of them imposes a moderate level of taxation on cross-border investments, but both would want to collect the taxes.
3. Both would prefer that a less-than-moderate level of taxation is imposed on cross-border investments and collected only by the other country.
4. Both countries would least prefer a low level of outbound investment and that each collects some portion of the tax revenues.

Table 3 presents these outcomes. It shows that an equilibrium emerges when neither country taxes cross-border investments, which serves the mutual interests of both. If the host country taxes foreign investments, the residence country cannot prevent the creation of a moderate to low incentive for outbound investment, nor, obviously, will it collect the entire amount of tax revenues. Its only option is to either facilitate a moderate level of outbound investment and collect no tax revenues or else allow a low level of outbound investment and collect some portion of the revenues. If, however, the host country does not tax foreign investments, the residence country can choose to either tax (and limit) outbound investments or not tax (and maximize) outbound investments. Since I have assumed in this section that the residence country prefers the latter option, its dominant strategy will be an exemption policy. In this way, it will maximize the level of outbound investments.

The host country, aware of the residence country's dominant strategy (i.e., preference for an exemption), will prefer not to tax foreign investments, thereby attaining its best outcome and preventing its least-preferred outcome. Recall that it is in the host country's best interests to eliminate the tax wedge, since the benefit from unhindered foreign investment is greater than the potential benefit from tax revenues.

Ultimately, both the residence country and host country will opt not to tax the income earned in the host country, and both will achieve their optimal outcomes. As with the deduction and credit scenarios, here, too, a stable equilibrium emerges, as no other strategy will be more favorable for the host country. In sum, then, presuming the residence country's preference for an exemption, we find, again, that the individual interests of the residence country and host country yield an equilibrium under which double taxation is prevented.

3.3   The Reality of Tax Treaties

Existing international tax practices support my theoretical prediction that under any of the policy preference assumptions outlined above, the interaction between the unilateral policies of host and residence countries will yield a stable equilibrium under which double taxation is prevented and host countries reap all the tax revenues if any are collected. We saw that this is the outcome regardless of which policy is assumed to be the optimal one for a residence country.

The actual international tax rules of countries of residence indicate that this is not mere theoretical hypothesizing. Indeed, contrary to conventional wisdom, it emerges that tax treaties are not necessary for alleviating double taxation on cross-border investments. The majority of countries in fact apply unilateral mechanisms to prevent double taxation in conjunction with tax treaties. Most of the major developed countries (which tend to be the residence countries of investors) ameliorate double taxation by granting a credit for foreign taxes paid by their residents[53] and

---

[53] The following countries provide credits to individual taxpayers who produce income overseas: Italy, Japan, Spain, Finland, Luxemburg, Portugal, Sweden, Brazil, India, South Africa, China, New Zealand, Belgium, Israel, Ireland, Canada, Austria, the United Kingdom,

are increasingly offering a complete exemption on all (mostly business) income produced abroad.[54] Only a handful of residence countries allow their residents only a deduction for foreign taxes.[55] The majority of countries, moreover, incorporate into their tax treaties the same (or roughly the same) mechanism as what they were already applying unilaterally.[56] Even without tax treaties, then, double taxation is not the dreaded beast it is often made out to be. The prevailing international tax regime therefore supports what could not be shown definitively in the theoretical analysis: that most developed countries prefer a credit or exemption to a deduction.

Yet this notwithstanding, the format of the tax treaty solution seems to be truly tailor-made for preventing double taxation. Treaties allocate taxing jurisdiction for different sources of income between the contracting

the United States, Switzerland, Greece, and Iceland. Some of these countries also allow taxpayers to choose between a credit and a deduction, while the United States, the United Kingdom, Austria, and Switzerland allow certain exemptions. See http://taxsummaries .pwc.com/uk/taxsummaries/wwts.nsf/ID/tax-summaries-home; http://www.ey.com/gl/en/services/tax/worldwide-personal-tax-and-immigration-guide–country-list.

In recent years, many countries have shifted from a worldwide system to an exemption system for dividends local shareholders receive from their foreign affiliates. In 2009, Japan and the United Kingdom, which were two of the three G-7 countries still levying a repatriation tax on corporate foreign dividends, switched to a policy of dividend exemption (territoriality). See Thornton Matheson, Victoria Perry & Chandara Veung, *Territorial vs. Worldwide Corporate Taxation: Implications for Developing Countries* (IMF Working Paper 13/205, 2013). The United States is one of the few remaining countries that continue to levy a tax on the worldwide income of its resident multinational corporations. See Rosanne ALSHULER, STEPHEN SHAY & ERIC TODER, LESSONS THE UNITED STATES CAN LEARN FROM OTHER COUNTRIES' TERRITORIAL SYSTEMS FOR TAXING INCOME OF MULTINATIONAL CORPORATIONS (2015). But see PRICE WATERHOUSE COOPERS, A COMPARISON OF KEY ASPECTS OF THE INTERNATIONAL TAX SYSTEMS OF MAJOR OECD AND DEVELOPING COUNTRIES (May 10, 2010), http://businessroundtable.org/sites/default/files/BRT_14_country_international_tax_comparison_20100510.pdf.

[54] The following countries exempt foreign business income unilaterally: Australia, Austria, Belgium, Canada, Czech Republic, Denmark, Estonia, Finland, France, Germany, Hungary, Iceland, Italy, Japan, Luxembourg, the Netherlands, New Zealand, Norway, Portugal, Slovak Republic, Slovenia, Spain, Sweden, Switzerland, Turkey, and the United Kingdom. See Matheson et al., *supra* note 53.

[55] Today, only Turkey and Switzerland allow a deduction to their residents investing abroad.

[56] Of the countries examined, only Turkey and Switzerland allow a deduction for foreign taxes paid to a country with which they have not signed a treaty and a credit where a treaty has been signed. See Fabian Barthel et al., *The Relationship Between Double Taxation Treaties and Foreign Direct Investments*, in TAX TREATIES: VIEWS FROM THE BRIDGE – BUILDING BRIDGES BETWEEN LAW AND ECONOMICS 3, 6 (Michael Lang et al. eds., 2010) ("with a few notable exceptions, tax treaties today generally do no more than reaffirm the operation of the credit or exemption systems that most countries have unilaterally adopted to prevent double taxation").

countries. Provisions that accord both countries the power to tax meticulously set forth how the revenues will be divided between the two. In addition, on the face of it, treaties seem to not only serve a necessary function but to do so impartially. The allocation of taxing jurisdiction and revenues between the contracting countries is ostensibly symmetrical. The same rules tend to apply to both parties, and both are simultaneously host countries (for the foreign investors from the other country) and residence countries (for their residents investing in the other country). Thus, presumably the two countries give up and gain comparable parts of their taxing jurisdictions and revenues. Thus, despite the prevalence of unilateral mechanisms for the prevention of double taxation, the structure of tax treaties appears to coincide with the traditional story, namely, that countries agree to reciprocally limit their tax collection for increased investments.

In what follows, I will show that tax treaties are in fact biased against countries that are predominantly host countries *and*, furthermore, that they do not, in fact, encourage cross-border investment. The reason for this, in a nutshell, is that treaties systematically provide residence countries with higher tax revenues than what the interaction between unilateral policies described above yields, while at the same time preserving the same overall level of taxation (and the same incentive for cross-border investment). Treaties no doubt offer other advantages, which I elaborate on below and could explain their existence. But these advantages, I claim, have very little to do with the (in itself worthy) cause of preventing double taxation. Hence, I question the desirability of tax treaties, in particular, for developing countries, which are predominantly host countries.

a. Preventing Double Taxation through Tax Treaties

In a typical tax treaty, the two contracting countries agree on how to allocate the taxing jurisdiction for different types of income. The host country can tax foreign income without limitation, tax it up to a maximum, or not tax it at all.[57] Thus, for example, income from business activity can be taxed by the host country without restriction provided that the income is attributable to the activities of a "permanent establishment."[58] If, however, no such permanent establishment exists, the host will usually

---

[57] *See* PHILIP BAKER, DOUBLE TAXATION CONVENTIONS AND INTERNATIONAL TAX LAW 18 (1994).

[58] *See, e.g.*, OECD MODEL TAX CONVENTION 2014, *supra* note 7, art. 7; UN MODEL DOUBLE TAXATION CONVENTION, *supra* note 4, art. 7; US Model Income Tax Treaty, *supra* note 9, art. 7.

cede taxing jurisdiction to the residence country.[59] Similarly, foreign residents' income from personal services rendered is also typically taxed by the host country without limitation,[60] except in cases specifically excluded in the tax treaty, such as income earned by students, trainees,[61] or diplomatic staff.[62] Passive income, which usually consists of income from interest or dividend payments, is ordinarily taxed by the country in which the payment originates, that is, the "source" country, but the rate of taxation is generally limited in the treaty.[63]

A tax treaty that grants both countries the right to tax a given type of income (with or without a limitation on the rate of taxation at source) often includes a mechanism for alleviating double taxation. The UN and OECD model tax treaties, for example, recommend offering either a credit for taxes paid in the source country (the mechanism more commonly opted for by contracting countries) or an exemption for income taxed by the source country.[64] When an exemption is chosen as the double-taxation alleviation mechanism in a treaty, this has usually been based on the premise that the source country will tax the exempt income.[65]

[59] *See, e.g.*, OECD MODEL TAX CONVENTION 2014, *supra* note 7, art. 5 (defining "permanent establishment"). For a comparison of the definitions of permanent establishment under different treaties, *see* Michael Lang & Jeffrey Owens, *The Role of Tax Treaties in Facilitating Development and Protecting the Tax Base* 4 (WU Int'l Taxation Research Paper Series No. 2014–03, 2014), http://ssrn.com/abstract=2398438.

[60] *See* OECD MODEL TAX CONVENTION 2014, *supra* note 7, art. 15.

[61] *See, e.g.*, OECD MODEL TAX CONVENTION 2014, *supra* note 7, art. 20; UN MODEL DOUBLE TAXATION CONVENTION, *supra* note 4, art. 20; US Model Income Tax Treaty, *supra* note 9, art. 20.

[62] *See, e.g.*, OECD MODEL TAX CONVENTION 2014, *supra* note 7, art. 19; UN MODEL DOUBLE TAXATION CONVENTION, *supra* note 4, art. 19; US Model Income Tax Treaty, *supra* note 9, art. 19.

[63] The typical withholding rates run between 0 and 15 percent. U.S. TAX TREATIES 95 (Richard L. Dorenberg & Kees Van Raad eds., 1991).

[64] *See, e.g.*, OECD MODEL TAX CONVENTION 2014, *supra* note 7, arts. 23A, 23B; UN MODEL DOUBLE TAXATION CONVENTION, *supra* note 4, arts. 23A, 23B.

[65] Treaties are presumed to operate based on the ideal of a single tax. Hence, they seek to prevent cross-border income going untaxed in both jurisdictions. This was one of the central goals stressed in the recent BEPS report:

> Most of the provisions of tax treaties seek to alleviate double taxation by allocating taxing rights between the two States and it is assumed that where a State accepts treaty provisions that restrict its right to tax elements of income, it generally does so on the understanding that these elements of income are taxable in the other State. Where a State levies no or low income taxes, other States should consider whether there are risks of double taxation that would justify, by themselves, a tax treaty.

OECD, PREVENTING THE GRANTING OF TREATY BENEFITS IN INAPPROPRIATE CIRCUMSTANCES, ACTION 6 – 2015 FINAL REPORT, OECD/G20 BASE EROSION AND PROFIT SHIFTING PROJECT 95 (2015), http://dx.doi.org/10.1787/9789264241695-en.

Some treaties set a tax-sparing mechanism for certain host countries (typically developing countries).[66] Under this mechanism, the host country's incentive programs (designed to attract foreign investors) are ignored by the residence country, and it allows its residents a credit for taxes they would have paid to the host if not for the specially targeted concessions. This serves to reduce the total level of taxation on foreign investments that fall within the scope of the treaty. It thereby increases the level of cross-border investment and the benefits the host country derives from this activity. It is important to note that with this type of mechanism, the residence country not only gives up the tax revenues it would have collected absent the credit but also allows a higher level of outbound investment into the host country than it would ordinarily prefer. On this background, OECD countries are increasingly more reluctant to include tax sparing in their treaties.[67]

b.   The Distributive Consequences of Tax Treaties

There are important similarities – and no less significant differences – between the equilibrium achieved by tax treaties and the alternative equilibria produced by the interaction between unilateral policies described above. Unilateral mechanisms can prevent double taxation just as well as a treaty mechanism and achieve the same combined level of taxation. Yet the equilibrium reached under treaties diverges from the credit/tax and exemption/no-tax equilibria of unilateral policies primarily in how the tax revenues are distributed.

Treaties traditionally protect residence-based taxation, particularly those that are constructed on the OECD model tax convention.[68] They are

---

[66] For a review see Lang & Owens, supra note 59, at 28:

> Among the BRICS, China and India have negotiated such provisions in around half their treaties, though in some cases the provisions have expired. The middle and high income developing countries reviewed (apart from Colombia) have also been active in including tax sparing in their treaties. Among the resource rich countries Nigeria and Zambia have included such provisions in most of their treaties. Among the sample of LDCs Bangladesh, Kenya and Mozambique have negotiated tax sparing provisions in many of their treaties.

[67] See id. at 29–30.

[68] Lee Sheppard has commented, for example, that

> the international system has been set up to preserve residence-based taxation by rich capital-exporting countries at the expense of everyone else. Under the OECD model treaty, which rich countries impose on others, whenever there is a conflict or a possibility of double taxation, the source country is required to cede its primary right to tax.

formulated assuming a single tax and provide residence countries with a larger slice of the revenue pie than do the unilateral mechanisms. Given the limitation on the host country's tax rates and that taxing jurisdiction over certain categories of income is given solely to the residence country, the host country collects a smaller portion of the tax revenues. As explained, treaties tend to limit the tax rate a host country can impose on passive income. With the exception of cases in which the relevant treaty allows tax-sparing, under a credit mechanism, a reduction in host country taxation does not translate into a larger volume of foreign investment and in fact amounts to no more than a revenue shift from the host to the residence country. Therefore, a credit mechanism results in the residence country collecting taxes that the host country has relinquished.[69]

Lee Sheppard, *Revenge of the Source Countries, Part IV: Who Gets the Bill?*, 40 TAX NOTES INT'L 411, 416 (2005). Victor Thuronyi, *Tax Treaties and Developing Countries, in* TAX TREATIES: BUILDING BRIDGES BETWEEN LAW AND ECONOMICS 441, 445 (Michael Lang et al. eds., 2010), stresses the costs of treaty negotiations and concludes that most developing countries likely decide against the negotiation of tax treaties: "I am not suggesting that treaties are entirely superfluous, but given what can be accomplished by unilateral measures, the extra value from the legal protection afforded by a treaty will in many cases not be worth the costs of negotiating a treaty." *See also* Reuven Avi-Yonah, *Bridging the North/South Divide: International Redistribution and Tax Competition*, 26 MICH. J. INT'L L. 371 (2004); Kim Brooks, *Tax Treaty Treatment of Royalty Payments from Low-Income Countries: A Comparison of Canada and Australia's Policies*, 5 EJOURNAL TAX RES. 169 (2007); Robert Hellawell, *United States Income Taxation and Less Developed Countries: A Critical Appraisal*, 66 COLUM. L. REV. 1393, 1419 (1966); Karen B. Brown, *Missing Africa: Should U.S. International Tax Rules Accommodate Investment in Developing Countries?*, 23 U. PENN. J. INT'L ECON. & L. 45 (2002); H.L. Goldberg, *Conventions for the Elimination of International Double Taxation: Toward a Developing Country Model*, 15 LAW & POL'Y INT'L BUS. 833, 855 (1983) ("[D]eveloped countries in the OECD Model opted for the residence jurisdiction bias, an option which would be expected to be unacceptable to the chronic source country in the unequal income flow situation. Thus it is not surprising that the OECD Model proved unsatisfactory to the developing countries in their negotiations with developed countries."); Stanley S. Surrey, *United Nations Group of Experts and the Guidelines for Tax Treaties Between Developed and Developing Countries*, 19 HARV. INT'L L.J. 1 (1978); Eduardo Baistrocchi, *The Use and Interpretation of Tax Treaties in the Emerging World: Theory and Implications*, 4 BRIT. TAX REV. 352, 353 (2008); Mindy Herzfeld, *The Purpose of Treaties: Not Always About Double Taxation*, 81 TAX NOTES INT'L 627, 630 (Feb. 22, 2016), http://pdfs.taxnotes.com/tnipdf/2016/81ti0627.pdf. But see Hearson, *supra* note 70, at 20, who argues, "While the trend for treaties with non-OECD countries is for more source-friendly provisions, where treaties are concluded with OECD countries they are becoming more residence-based over time."

[69] *See* Roin, *supra* note 13, at 1766 (footnotes omitted): "Reductions below a 'reasonable' level of tax, by contrast, have generally been perceived as benefiting a foreign taxpayer's country of residence rather than the taxpayer when that residence country, like the U.S., uses a tax-credit system to ameliorate duplicative taxation." Of course, there may be a reciprocal revenue shift when the host country is operating in its capacity as a residence country. See the discussion in Section 3.c.i.

Another distributive divergence between the treaty outcome and uni-lateral outcomes occurs when a treaty limits the authority of the host country to tax certain kinds of income, such as business income in the pre-permanent establishment phase and certain types of income from per-sonal services. In such cases, the treaty prevents the host country from imposing any taxes whatsoever on these types of income. The outcome is that the residence country collects all of the tax revenues.

Consequently, although treaties and unilateral mechanisms achieve approximately the same reduction in double taxation, they allocate tax revenues between the host and residence countries differently. In con-straining the host's power to tax, tax treaties essentially give residence countries a larger piece of the tax-revenue pie. To be sure, as recent schol-arship has shown, host countries and their treaty negotiations with resi-dence countries are not all cut of the same cloth, and the specifics of the treaties they sign vary.[70] But when compared to the non-treaty equilibria, these treaties all constitute an inferior arrangement for source countries in terms of tax revenues and none offer the advantages of increased foreign investment.

[70] Thus, for example, Lang & Owens, *supra* note 59, at 38, have importantly demonstrated that developing countries, which tend to be host countries, are not identical in policy pref-erences. This heterogeneity suggests the possibility of divergences in bargaining power and skills:

> The evidence shows that there is a wide variety of treaty policies among the develop-ing countries. . . . The relative economic strength of the contracting states and level of economic development of the [developing and emerging economies] partner and the experience of the negotiators are all factors in determining the final provisions of the treaty.

Martin Hearson, *Measuring Tax Treaty Negotiation Outcomes: The ActionAid Tax Treaties Dataset 36* (ICTD Working Paper No. 47, Feb. 2016), http://www.ictd.ac/ publication/2-working-papers/99-measuring-tax-treaty-negotiation-outcomes-the-actionaid-tax-treaties-dataset recently conducted a nuanced study of the elements of more than 500 treaties and concluded as follows:

> Previously, it was thought that tax treaties were becoming more restrictive of develop-ing countries' taxing rights, because WHT rates in the treaties they signed were falling. This study has shown that such a conclusion is not supported once a more compre-hensive assessment is made, and once the data is disaggregated by different groups of countries. Broadly speaking, WHT rates are falling, but other parts of treaties, in par-ticular some components of the definition of PE, are becoming more source-oriented. Furthermore, while treaties between developing countries and OECD countries are curbing source taxing rights more than in the past, the trend is reversed for the growing number of treaties signed by developing countries with countries outside the OECD, which are leaving more source taxing rights intact. This points to a growing division between approaches to tax treaty negotiation in the OECD and the rest of the world.

c. Other Consequences of Tax Treaties

In addition to their distributive ramifications, tax treaties can provide the contracting countries with a number of benefits. These include greater access to tax information on residents regarding their overseas activities upon request (i.e., a contracting state can usually request information from the tax authorities of the other country regarding specific taxpayers[71]); assistance in tax enforcement; and positive signaling to investors. Moreover, tax treaties can further increase the coordination between the tax rules of the two countries.[72] By addressing specific conflicts between the tax laws of the contracting countries, treaties can improve the functioning of existing unilateral mechanisms for alleviating double taxation.[73] The 2014 BEPS report on tax treaties noted this advantage:

> A large number of cases of residence-source juridical double taxation can be eliminated through domestic provisions for the relief of double taxation (ordinarily in the form of either the exemption or credit method) which operate without the need for tax treaties. Whilst these domestic provisions will likely address most forms of residence-source juridical double taxation, they will not cover all cases of double taxation, especially if there are significant differences in the source rules of the two States or if the domestic law of these States does not allow for unilateral relief of economic double taxation (e.g., in the case of a transfer pricing adjustment made in another State).[74]

To illustrate, a treaty might lay out a set of uniform source rules for the two countries[75] or set tests of residency for tax purposes. It might also set

[71] See Chapter 5 for more on exchange of information under treaties as well as under different mechanisms.

[72] See, e.g., ALI, supra note 5, at 6 (identifying three types of coordination problems between the tax rules of the two countries: residency-residency conflicts, residency-source conflicts, and source-source conflicts).

[73] See Owens, supra note 11, at 436. But see Rebecca Kyser, Interpreting Tax Treaties, 101 Iowa L. Rev. 1387, 1418–21 (2016) (indicating that tax treaties are still incomplete instruments that require extensive interpretation by domestic courts and recommending harmonization devices for such interpretation to ameliorate the concerns of implementation and double taxation).

[74] OECD, supra note 19, at 103.

[75] See Rosenbloom, Current Developments, supra note 4, at 28–30 (suggesting that the discrepancies in source rules are among the most important problems treaties are supposed to solve); Pamela B. Gann, The Concept of an Independent Treaty Foreign Tax Credit, 38 Tax L. Rev. 1, 20–22 (1982) (describing how treaties signed by the United States often include specific source rules); Stanley Surrey, International Tax Conventions: How They Operate and What They Accomplish, 23 J. Taxation 364, 364 (1965) ("Tax treaties deal with these

rules for determining the legal status of entities and codify agreements that determine which taxes are to be considered creditable. These are issues that are extremely difficult to contend with unilaterally.

In addition, treaties can improve states' ability to collect taxes. This is particularly significant in the context of tax collection from foreign residents, whose only connection to the source country is the fact that they earned income within its territorial borders. Tax treaties enable host countries to trade the tax revenues they may have difficulty collecting (i.e., taxes owed by foreign investors) for tax revenues that are easier to collect (i.e., taxes owed by their own residents on their foreign activities).[76] Such a trade-off also makes it easier for the residence country to implement a truly progressive tax system based on its residents' worldwide income.[77]

Treaties also often serve as a framework for establishing harmonious international relations.[78] Treaties can be proof of good faith and signal a certain respectability for the signing country in the eyes of other countries. The United States, for example, will sometimes sign a tax treaty with another country as a first step toward establishing broader diplomatic relations.[79]

Lastly, tax treaties can enhance the ease and certainty with which an individual investor can assess her tax liability in a foreign country.[80] They provide a familiar language and structure for taxpayers seeking to

problems by reaching mutually acceptable rules regarding the source of income and allocations of income."). However, Owens, *supra* note 11, at 438–41, demonstrates that in most cases, the source rules in the treaties are very similar to unilateral source rules.

[76] *See* Paul D. Reese, *United States Tax Treaty Policy Toward Developing Countries: The China Example*, 35 UCLA L. REV. 369, 373 (1987):

> While the source state generally is granted the primary taxation rights, most industrialized nations, including the U.S., stress relatively greater residence-state jurisdiction, and strive to limit the taxation of income in the source state. This scheme theoretically is justified by concerns of administrative feasibility: the taxpayer's residence state, it is argued, is better able to tax accurately on a progressive basis by virtue of its easier (and less burdensome) access to the taxpayer's worldwide expense and income data.

[77] *See* Roin, *supra* note 13, at 1761 ("Residence-country taxation is thought to be preferable because it enables greater inter-taxpayer equity.").

[78] *See generally* Rosenbloom, Current Developments, *supra* note 4, at 31–52 and examples therein. *See also* Yariv Brauner, *Treaties in the Aftermath of BEPS*, 41 BROOK. J. INT'L L. 973, 988 (2016) ("Tax treaties also institutionalize lines of communications between tax authorities on both bilateral and multilateral levels, and in some cases legitimize such discourse in fiscal rather than diplomatic channels.").

[79] *See, e.g.*, Reese, *supra* note 76, at 380, considering such benefits China gained from signing a tax treaty with the United States, but attributing them to China's geopolitical importance. *Id.* at 391.

[80] *See* Lang & Owens, *supra* note 59, at 30:

determine their tax liability[81] and serve as a signal for the legitimacy of the country involved;[82] they also can clarify existing tax rules and lower (although not eliminate) the risk of future changes to existing tax laws.[83] They might also provide administrative support to taxpayers who seek assistance from their domestic tax authorities in navigating the foreign system. The dispute-resolution mechanism[84] provided for in most treaties tends to reassure investors that they can appeal to their official representatives to negotiate a reasonable solution with the tax authorities of the other contracting country.[85]

Surely all of these significant advantages of the tax treaty mechanism create a strong incentive for countries to sign treaties. None of these benefits, however, advances as commendable a goal as the prevention of double taxation.

d. Reality Check: Do Treaties Actually Increase Foreign Direct Investment?

Recall that my theoretical conclusion in the previous sections was that tax treaties do not reduce the tax burden on cross-border investments any more than the equilibrium that emerges under unilateral strategies.

> Tax treaties may help to create a stable investment climate within which FDI may take place. A tax treaty may contain a number of provisions that contribute to this climate and increase the confidence of a foreign investor, creating more certainty in relation to the tax treatment. For example, in addition to the elimination of double taxation a treaty may contain provisions in respect of non-discrimination, exchange of information and a mutual agreement procedure in the event of tax disputes.

[81] John F. Avery Jones, *The David R. Tillinghast Lecture: Are Tax Treaties Necessary?*, 53 Tax L. Rev. 1, 2 (1999) ("[o]ne can pick up any modern tax treaty and immediately find one's way around, often even down to the article number.").

[82] IMF, *supra* note 16, at 28–29 (asserting that signaling may be the only benefit of tax treaties for developing countries). *See also* Barthel et al., *supra* note 56, at 5 ("From the perspective of a source country, the most important function of a tax treaty may be its role as a signaling device, indicating to potential investors that the capital-importing nation is playing by the conventional international investment rules and is part of the global economy 'club'."); Allison Christians, *Tax Treaties for Investment and Aid to Sub-Saharan Africa: A Case Study*, 71 Brook. L. Rev. 639, 706–11 (2005); Miranda Stewart, *Global Trajectories of Tax Reform: The Discourse of Tax Reform in Developing and Transition Countries*, 44 Harv. Int'l L.J. 139, 148 (2003) (indicating specifically that the "signing of a tax treaty is often presented as an important symbol of international capitalist engagement").

[83] *See* Lang & Owens, *supra* note 59, at 33 ("tax treaties provide foreign investors with a stable and predictable tax environment since tax treaties tend on average to remain in force for 10–15 years and generally override domestic tax laws, which change much more frequently.")

[84] *See* Rosenbloom, *Current Developments*, *supra* note 4, at 31–43.

[85] *See* Surrey, *supra* note 75, at 366; Barthel et al., *supra* note 56, at 6.

Rather, they simply serve to allocate tax revenues between the contracting states. Some interesting empirical evidence that has been amassed since the publication of *The Tax Treaties Myth*,[86] which originally raised this theoretical argument, provides an opportunity for a reality check on its conclusions.

If tax treaties actually did prevent double taxation, one would expect foreign direct investments (FDI) to increase between countries once they sign them. But if all they do is allocate tax revenues between the contracting countries, there is no reason to predict such an increase. There is also one other advantage of tax treaties that can be measured empirically: even if treaties do not reduce double taxation but do bolster international economic recognition for their signatories, their benefits (and, therefore, the investment they encourage) should compound as a country's treaty network expands.[87]

The empirical evidence is inconclusive, however, as to any correlation between tax treaties and increased FDI. Over the past several years, a considerable amount of research has been conducted on the relationship between the two, with two distinct waves of studies yielding seemingly reverse findings. The first group of studies[88] examined changes in bilateral treaty status and shifts in FDI volume on a jurisdiction-by-jurisdiction basis and arrived at the general conclusion that treaties have no positive effect on FDI.[89] The next generation of studies explored whether a

---

[86] Dagan, *supra* note 1.   [87] Barthel et al., *supra* note 56, at 7.

[88] Ronald B. Davies, *Tax Treaties and Foreign Direct Investment: Potential versus Performance*, 11 INT'L TAX & PUB. FIN. 775 (2004) (not finding that U.S.-signed treaties have had any effect on FDI flows); Bruce A. Blonigen & Ronald B. Davies, *The Effects of Bilateral Tax Treaties on U.S. FDI Activity*, 11 INT'L TAX & PUB. FIN. 601 (2004) (not finding any positive effect of tax treaties on U.S. FDI flows); Bruce A. Blonigen & Ronald B. Davies, *Do Bilateral Tax Treaties Promote Foreign Direct Investment?*, in 2 HANDBOOK OF INTERNATIONAL TRADE 526 (E. Kwan Choi & James C. Hartigan eds., 2005) (finding a positive effect of old treaties on FDI flows but an insignificant negative effect for new treaties); Paul L. Baker, *An Analysis of Double Taxation Treaties and their Effect on Foreign Direct Investment*, 21 INT'L J. ECON. BUS. 341 (2014) ("despite their intentions and the significant costs of entering into DTTs, the treaties have no effect on the flows of FDI. An analysis of the treaties in conjunction with the related domestic tax legislation shows why this is the case. Developed countries unilaterally provide for the relief of double taxation and the prevention of fiscal evasion regardless of the treaty status of a host country. This eliminates the key economic benefit and the risk that these treaties would otherwise create for the FDI location decisions of multinational enterprises."). But *see* Peter Egger et al., *The Impact of Endogenous Tax Treaties on Foreign Direct Investment: Theory and Evidence*, 39 Can. J. Econ. 901 (2006) (finding a negative effect of tax treaties on FDI flows).

[89] The external validity of these studies has been questioned, as their samples were small and non-representative. Barthel et al., *supra* note 56, at 7–10. For an extensive review of the

higher treaty count is associated with higher FDI in the source country and found a positive correlation between the number of treaties signed and FDI levels.[90] A more recent study, which is something of a hybrid of the previous studies, similarly found a positive correlation between tax treaties and increased FDI. However, its authors emphasized, this is not necessarily a cause-and-effect relationship as "[t]here are a wide range of potential endogenous factors that may explain both the rise in the number of treaties and the volume of FDI, as well as the fact that increases in treaty numbers appear to precede slight increases in FDI."[91] Interestingly, another recent study confirmed both conclusions, indicating a positive correlation between the total number of tax treaties a host country has signed with the United States and American FDI outflows *as well as* a negative correlation between new and existing U.S. bilateral tax treaties and FDI outflows to the host country.[92]

empirical literature and the conclusion that there is presently no consensus, *see* Lang & Owens, *supra* note 59, at 7 ("There have been a number of empirical studies which attempt to determine the impact of tax treaties on FDI flows into DEEs. Nevertheless, at present, there appears to be no consensus.... All the studies acknowledge the difficulty in isolating the influence of treaties from other variables such as the economic and political environment. Surveys of business suggest the MNEs look at whether there is a treaty and what are its provisions when deciding where to locate. Other things being equal, MNEs will tend to favor a country with a good treaty network.").

[90] Julian di Giovanni, *What Drives Capital Flows? The Case of Cross-Border M&A Activity and Financial Deepening*, 65 J. INT'L ECON. 127 (2005) (finding a positive correlation between tax treaties and cross-border acquisitions); Eric Neumayer, *Do Double Taxation Treaties Increase Foreign Direct Investment to Developing Countries?*, 43 J. DEV. STUD. 1501 (2007) (finding a positive correlation between tax treaties and FDI at least in middle-income developing countries).

[91] For a useful review of the literature, *see* Barthel et al., *supra* note 56, at 16.

[92] Joseph P. Daniels, Patrick O'Brien & Marc V. von der Ruhr, *Bilateral Tax Treaties and US Foreign Direct Investment Financing Modes*, 22 INT'L TAX & PUB. FIN. 999 (2015). The researchers offer the following explanation:

Results, in general, indicate that both new and existing US bilateral tax treaties are associated with lower FDI outflows to the host country, while the total number of treaties a host country has in place is associated with greater US FDI outflows to the host country.... We offer as an explanation that, on the one hand, the positive multilateral effect measured by the total number of treaties is consistent with a treaty-shopping effect in which a host country with a large number of bilateral treaties facilitates income shifting by multinational firms for tax minimization purposes. On the other hand, new and existing renegotiated US bilateral tax treaties enhance tax cooperation, information sharing, and rules to reduce tax avoidance and outweigh positive aspects of the treaties thereby reducing both equity-financed FDI and reinvested earnings.... Hence, our results are consistent with Davies' observation that there exists a "mismatch" between the framing of tax treaties and how they are used in practice.

A recent IMF report summarized the situation as follows:

> The empirical evidence on the investment effects of treaties is mixed.... Identifying causality is inherently problematic, since treaties may precede investment not because they spur the latter but because they may be concluded only when there is an expectation of such investment. (This can be a deliberate feature of treaty policy, as it traditionally has been in the U.S.). Studies using macro-level data indeed find a wide range of effects, though perhaps with some signs that a positive effect on FDI is most likely for middle-income countries. Work using firm-level data finds a significant impact on firms' entry into a particular country, though not on the level of their investment once they are present.[93]

3.4   Winners and Losers

Since tax treaties tend to allocate tax revenues more generously to residence countries than their unilateral alternatives, it is clear why these countries would favor such agreements. Limiting the level of taxation a host country can impose allows the residence country to collect more tax revenues without changing the overall level of taxation on outbound investments. This, alongside the collateral benefits of treaties in terms of certainty, administrative convenience, and enforcement, quite possibly motivates residence countries to enter into tax treaties.

But why should host countries have an interest in signing tax treaties? Treaties reduce their tax revenues while doing nothing to lower the tax barriers for foreign investment from residence countries, since the total level of taxation remains the same. Can this arrangement be in any way beneficial to a host country? The answer could depend on the particular type of treaty in question. While a symmetrical treaty might be a deal worth making for any country, an asymmetrical agreement might not be advantageous to countries that are predominantly hosts, which is the case with developing countries. This latter type of country tends to lose revenues with a tax treaty, without providing increased tax incentives for cross-border investment.

---

[93] IMF, *supra* note 16, at 26. For a review of the literature, *see* Hearson, *supra* note 68, at 12. Hearson interestingly advocates a more nuanced reading of the terms of tax treaties, noting that

> [withholding tax] rates, while most easily obtainable as a dataset and undoubtedly a salient factor for investors, may not be an accurate guide to the role a particular treaty plays in investment decisions. Examples of other important provisions include tax sparing, capital gains tax, and the risk that a particular operation – whether of the investing firm or its contractors – will cross the PE threshold.

a. Symmetrical Tax Treaties

Reciprocity is one feature that can make the tradeoff between host and residence taxation in a tax treaty worthwhile for both countries. In a symmetrical tax treaty, when the levels of investment by Country A residents in Country B and by Country B residents in Country A are roughly equal, each signatory country is simultaneously and to an equal extent a host country for foreign investment and a residence country for its own residents. Thus, neither A nor B should be concerned with the taxes they collect from each individual transaction. The revenues they lose from lowering their taxes on foreign investments (in their capacity as host country) will be offset by the taxes they collect from their own residents on foreign-source income (in their capacity as residence country).[94] If the cross-border investment in the two countries is, in fact, symmetrical, the outcome of the reduction in taxes for each is no more than a switch in the identity of the tax-collecting agent,[95] which could be beneficial for both administrative and enforcement reasons. It may be easier for a residence country to collect taxes from its residents investing abroad since it can more easily enforce its taxation regime on taxpayers whose center of life is within its borders.

b. Asymmetrical Treaties

Reciprocity in the framework of a tax treaty exists only where there is mutual investment (or the potential for such investment). However, such a symmetrical flow of investments cannot always be assumed, most particularly when one of the contracting countries is a developing country and the other a developed country.[96]

---

[94] This is the case since the lower taxes in the host country enable the residence country to collect higher taxes by using a credit system.

[95] See Roin, *supra* note 13, at 1767 ("[T]hough treaties reducing source taxation below reasonable levels change the identity of each countries' taxpayers, in theory they need not, and are not supposed to, change either the total amount of tax paid by each taxpayer nor the amount of tax collected by each country.").

[96] See Roin, *supra* note 13 at 1767. See also Rosenbloom & Langbein, *supra* note 4, at 392–93, who argue,

> The OECD and U.S. models are, as indicated, designed primarily for treaties between countries where the flows of income are roughly reciprocal. The limitations of source state taxation in those models produce a revenue cost for that state. However, when investment flows are more or less reciprocal, the revenue sacrifices more or less offset each other. In a treaty between a developed and a developing country the flows are

When a developing country enters into a treaty with a developed country, the symmetry of the treaty breaks down as each of the countries takes on its typical role. Developing countries are, more often than not, capital importers. Their outbound investments are typically insignificant relative to the amount of inbound investments they receive. Therefore, in practice, when a developing country enters into a tax treaty with a developed country, it will typically serve as host country, while the developed country will tend to function as the residence country. When a treaty reduces the taxes that the host country can collect, it necessarily unevenly reduces the tax revenues of the developing country.[97] Despite what might be expected,[98] the treaty arrangement does not necessarily offer increased foreign investment,[99] nor does it offer compensation through the level of tax revenues from the foreign income of a developing country's own residents – since the number of its residents investing abroad is probably insignificant. Thus, the almost certain outcome for a developing country that shifts from a unilateral approach to a treaty regime is that it loses tax revenues that it would have collected but – as the inconclusive empirical evidence indicates – it does not necessarily attract more investments (unless the contracting country is willing to offer tax sparing).[100]

---

largely in one direction: income flows from the developing country to the developed country. Thus, a model which is in form reciprocal in fact can impose a substantial revenue burden on a developing country.

[97] This can also be the case for a developed country which becomes a capital importer. Thus, for example, when the United States became a major capital importer, there were calls to change its treaty policy. *See, e.g.*, H. David Rosenbloom, *Toward a New Tax Treaty Policy for a New Decade*, 9 Am. J. Tax Pol. 77, 83 (1991) ("We can no longer afford the luxury of assessing tax treaty policy from an unbalanced position-with the certainty that US investors abroad are so much more numerous than foreign investors in the United States that any reciprocal reduction of tax at source will surely redound to the benefit of the Treasury, U.S. taxpayers, or both.").

[98] *See, e.g.*, Reese, supra note 76, at 379 ("[A] developing country might be expected to ignore revenue goals and accept substantial limitations on source-based taxation, at least insofar as such limitations could be expected to encourage investment.").

[99] Allison Christians, *supra* note 82, at 644, demonstrates, using a case study of a hypothetical tax treaty between the United States and Ghana, that "in today's global tax climate, a typical tax treaty would not provide significant tax benefits to current or potential investors. Consequently, there is little incentive for these investors to pressure the U.S. government to conclude tax treaties with many LDCs."

[100] For the effect of tax sparing *see* C. Azémar, R. Desbrodes & Jean-Louis Mucchielli, *Do Tax Sparing Agreements Contribute to the Attraction of FDI in Developing Countries?*, 14 Int'l Tax & Pub. Fin. 543, 557–58 (2007), who offer empirical evidence of the effectiveness of tax sparing: "[W]e confirm the existence of a link between the provision [of tax-sparing] and FDI. ... Our results suggest that Japanese FDI flows in tax sparing countries were

Even benefits seemingly unrelated to whether a country is a net capital importer or exporter are not equally enjoyed by both countries when the volume of cross-border investment is asymmetrical. For example, improved enforcement or collection of information is far more significant for a residence country seeking to tax its residents investing abroad than for a host country. Since the latter seeks to reduce the tax burden on foreign investors, it has an incentive to assist them in avoiding their residence country taxes.

This does not mean that tax treaties offer no advantages to developing countries. There is a range of benefits to the treaty regime that can in fact be of far greater significance to developing countries than developed countries, including administrative convenience, certainty, and international economic recognition. A chief gain developing countries derive from a tax treaty is the friendlier and more familiar tax arrangement it offers for foreign investors, who can rely on the treaty's compatible, standardized mechanisms and familiar language rather than having to navigate an unfamiliar foreign tax system. Moreover, belonging to the "tax treaties club"[101] serves as stamp of approval[102] that bolsters its members' legitimacy in the international arena. However, unlike treaties between developed countries, whose losses are symmetrically offset by the benefits they gain, asymmetrical treaties between developing and developed countries entail that the former sacrifice tax revenues to enjoy their benefits.

c.   What Should Developing Countries Do?

Tax treaties have generally been formulated by and for developed countries with mutual interests and a shared ideology. The OECD's model tax convention, for example, was primarily designed with the interests of developed countries in mind.[103] The OECD has always regarded itself as

almost three times bigger as in non-tax sparing countries." More recently, Céline Azémar & Dhammika Dharmapala, *Tax Sparing, FDI, and Foreign Aid: Evidence from Territorial Tax Reforms 1* (Univ. of Chicago Coase-Sandor Institute for Law & Economics Research Paper No. 758, 2016), https://ssrn.com/abstract=2767184, found that "tax sparing agreements are associated with 30 percent to 123 percent higher FDI. The estimated effect is concentrated in the year that tax sparing comes into force and the subsequent years, with no effects in prior years, and is thus consistent with a causal interpretation."

[101] In Chapter 5, I elaborate on the network effect of the standardized tax treaty regime.

[102] *See* Brauner, *supra* note 78, at 988 ("The mere existence of a tax treaty seems to send a signal of normalcy and relative safety for investment.").

[103] Tsilly Dagan, *BRICS – Theoretical Framework: The Potential of Cooperation, in* THE BRICS AND THE EMERGENCE OF INTERNATIONAL TAX COORDINATION 15 (Yariv Brauner &

the representative of the interests of its member states[104] and, therefore, "unauthorized to consider interests of other countries, at least to the extent they conflict with its members' interests."[105] Hence, it is not surprising that the OECD model ignores the interests of non-members. In a certain sense, developing countries stepped into a preexisting game, where treaties are assumed to be universally beneficial and the allocation of tax revenues to the benefit of residence countries a built-in feature.

To address the troublesome distributive effects of tax treaties between developed and developing countries, the UN appointed an ad hoc group of experts to examine the issues and formulate guidelines for unbiased tax treaties between developed and developing countries as well as a model tax treaty.[106] The UN guidelines and model treaty do not, however, differ much from the OECD model[107] and therefore did not resolve the distributive issues. Developing countries found it unsatisfactory in addressing their interests, while "some industrialized countries consider the model imprecise and too generous."[108] Developed countries, for their part, claim to contend with developing countries' resistance to tax treaties by offering a more expanded, source-based taxation arrangement. This, they assert, recognizes developing countries' "need . . . to conserve revenues."[109] Yet

---

Pasquale Pistone eds., 2015); Pasquale Pistone, *Tax Treaties with Developing Countries,* in TAX TREATIES: BUILDING BRIDGES BETWEEN LAW AND ECONOMICS 422 (Michael Lang et al. eds., 2010) (arguing that the fact that tax treaties are modeled after the OECD model harms the interests of developing countries); Stewart, *supra* note 82, at 162 ("As a result of its history, the OECD model is based on a developed country tax system, and it thus has been perceived as biased toward developed countries.").

[104]   Yariv Brauner, *What the BEPS?,* 16 FLA. TAX REV. 55, 63 (2014).

[105]   *Id.* at 62.   [106]   *Supra* note 58.

[107]   *See* SOL PICCIOTTO, INTERNATIONAL BUSINESS TAXATION: A STUDY IN THE INTERNATIONALIZATION OF BUSINESS REGULATION 56 (1992) 56:

> [T]he UN Guidelines did not make any new departure in the approach to tax treaties. They took as their starting point the 1963 OECD draft, and merely noted the differing views expressed by experts . . . . Neither the Guidelines, the Manual nor the Model Treaty could be said to challenge the basic principles of the OECD model. Although the report of the UN experts stressed the primacy of taxation at source, this was not expressed in any general principle . . . .

> *See also* A.H. Figueroa, *Comprehensive Tax Treaties,* in 15 DOUBLE TAXATION TREATIES BETWEEN INDUSTRIALIZED AND DEVELOPING COUNTRIES: OECD AND UN MODELS, A COMPARISON 9, 12 (1992) ("After twelve years, in 1979, the ad hoc group of experts approved a model that is known as the United Nations model (the yellow book). Notwithstanding the different color of its cover, this model shows definite and clear similarities with the OECD model.").

[108]   Figueroa, *supra* note 107, at 12.

[109]   Rosenbloom & Langbein, *supra* note 4, at 393.

recent data show that developing countries, in particular African states, are often unable to negotiate source-friendly terms.[110]

In any event, as we saw, the lower level of tax revenues is not what essentially concerns developing countries but, rather, the need for a higher level of inbound investment. Collecting more tax revenues is only a second-best solution absent the possibility of reduced overall tax rates on foreign income. And since a unilateral credit regime already enables developing countries to collect more tax revenues, a treaty that offers them less arguably makes no sense for them.

Developing countries try to encourage foreign investment by pressuring developed residence countries to either grant exemptions to the latter's residents who invest in the developing (host) country or else allow them tax-sparing credits for the host country taxes they would have paid on the foreign income. Some developed countries have agreed to include a tax-sparing arrangement in their treaties with developing countries.[111] Others – most notably the United States – have persistently rejected tax sparing. They often describe countries seeking to include tax sparing or exemptions in treaties as aggressive or as expecting that the residence

---

[110] Lang & Owens, *supra* note 70; Hearson, *supra* note 70. Hearson, *id.* at 19–20, also notes that

> treaties signed by Asian countries have consistently more source-friendly taxing provisions than African countries, and that the gap appears to be widening over time: since the mid-1990s, no African country has concluded a treaty with a source index greater than 0.7, in contrast to numerous Asian countries.... While the trend for treaties with non-OECD countries is for more source-friendly provisions, where treaties are concluded with OECD countries they are becoming more residence-based over time.

[111] *See, e.g.,* PICCIOTTO, *supra* note 107, at 57 ("At the same time, some developed countries became willing to make concessions.... Thus, the tax sparing credit has been accepted by many OECD countries, other than the US."); Reese, *supra* note 76, at 379. For a detailed description of the use of tax sparing, *see* Kim Brooks, *Tax Sparing: A Needed Incentive for Foreign Investment in Low Income Countries or an Unnecessary Revenue Sacrifice?*, 34 QUEEN'S L.J. 505, 539–40 (2009). Brooks argues that tax-sparing provisions may be based in good intentions but can ultimately have bad results, among the most serious of which is the erosion of the tax revenues that low-income country governments badly need.

The effectiveness of tax sparing has certainly been debated. *See, e.g.,* William B. Barker, *An International Tax System for Emerging Economies, Tax Sparing, and Development: It Is All about Source*, 29 J. INT'L L. 349, 362–63 (2007) ("Indeed, the complexity of tax sparing has created uncertainty among MNEs as to tax sparing's value. The most important consideration, however, is the growing evidence of tax sparing's underlying premise that emerging economies are being helped by tax sparing is incorrect. Instead, emerging economies are being harmed because tax incentives work poorly. The evidence strongly indicates that it encourages repatriation of earnings, tax competition and a substantial loss of revenue without appreciably increasing investment.").

country subsidize investments within their borders[112] and favor them over other countries.[113] Developed countries sometimes will request specific concessions in return for agreeing to tax sparing, which makes the arrangement less attractive to the developing countries.[114] However, if we consider the tax-sparing solution in relation to the unilateral alternative, developing countries' demand for more inbound investment can be regarded as merely quid pro quo for their willingness to lower their taxes, and tax-sparing mechanisms seem like a workable solution to encourage the FDI they seek.[115]

Some developing countries realized that tax treaties with developed countries are inherently biased against them[116] and became reluctant to

---

[112] *See* Surrey, *supra* note 75, at 366:

> In our view [the exemption and tax sparing] approaches are undesirable. Thus, tax exemption of income ... would be viewed as a highly inequitable provision. ... It would be basically inconsistent with the principle of the foreign tax credit .... A tax sparing credit would operate capriciously, providing the largest tax benefits to investors in countries having the highest nominal tax rates and without any necessary relationship to the fundamental economic needs of a country.

[113] *See* Rosenbloom & Langbein, *supra* note 4, at 380:

> When the first U.S. treaty with such a provision – the treaty with Pakistan – was submitted to the Senate for ratification, the "tax sparing" idea was greeted with hostility by the Foreign Relations Committee .... Three other treaties with tax sparing provisions ... were never reported out by the Committee.

> *See also id.* at 392 ("We think it inappropriate to use tax treaties to favor foreign investment over domestic investment. Moreover, given the history of this issue, we believe that a treaty reflecting a different view would be unlikely to achieve ratification.").

[114] Lang & Owens, *supra* note 59, at 38, predict the demise of tax-sparing mechanisms:

> Many developing countries originally favored tax sparing and often sought to negotiate a tax sparing clause in treaties with developed countries; but the benefits of tax sparing may now be seen as less valuable when weighed against the other concessions that may have to be made in treaties in return for tax sparing.

[115] *See* Azémar et al., *supra* note 100; Azémar & Dharmapala, *supra* note 100.

[116] *See, e.g.*, Figueroa, *supra* note 107, at 9:

> [D]espite the many agreements that were signed, mainly at the initiative of the industrialized countries, developing countries soon realized that the stipulations imposed on them in negotiations, equivalent to those being used in the industrial countries' agreements among themselves, did not sufficiently take regard to the legitimate fiscal interests of the developing countries.

> *See also* references in *supra* note 68. It is not entirely clear whether the tax-treaty bias was merely the product of the history of tax treaties or whether developed countries were trying to maximize their self-interests in a bargaining process. *See* Rosenbloom & Langbein, *supra* note 4, at 364.

sign them;[117] some even canceled and renegotiated their treaties.[118] Yet as the IMF recently indicated, "There has been a proliferation of BTTs over the last twenty years – driven by an increasing number that involve developing countries. . . . Initially, almost all BTTs were between advanced economies. The tripling of the number of treaties since the early 1990s, however, almost entirely reflects an increase in the number to which at least one party is a non-OECD country – many of which, of course, will have few capital exports."[119]

I contend that developing countries' averseness to entering into tax treaties with developed countries is justified. Developing countries are not guided by some noncooperative whim and hostility to a purportedly "benefit-to-all" solution. Rather, they reject an arrangement that could harm them in terms of the tax revenues they can collect, without improving the flow of foreign investment into their economies. They can certainly be expected to give up some of their tax revenues in order to enjoy more foreign investment. But this cannot be justified without increasing the incentive for foreign investment in these countries, which is what occurs when residence countries collect the tax revenues that the hosts forego.

---

[117] *See, e.g.*, Surrey, *supra* note 75, at 366 ("Under these circumstances, less developed countries are reluctant to enter into the standard type of tax treaty, even though the rules are eminently reasonable and equitable, because those rules involve a revenue loss to them without an adequate offset."); PICCIOTTO, *supra* note 107 at 55 (1992) ("Although some attempt was made by the developed countries (DCs) to extend the tax treaty network to these underdeveloped or less-developed countries (LDCs) . . . these efforts met with relatively little success . . . . The general inappropriateness of the tax treaty system for LDCs . . . was reflected in the paucity of treaties negotiated with them."); Roin, *supra* note 13, at 1767 (footnotes omitted) ("The United States has found it difficult, if not impossible, to enter into treaty agreements with countries where such apparent reciprocity is unavailable due to differences in investment and revenue flows. For example, lesser-developed countries . . . balk at relinquishing source tax jurisdiction because they are unlikely to be able to enjoy anything close to offsetting residence tax increases.").

[118] *See* Hearson, *supra* note 70, at 7 (references omitted):

> A number of developing countries have recently begun to reconsider their approach to tax treaties. South Africa, Rwanda, Argentina, Mongolia and Zambia have all cancelled or renegotiated agreements since 2012, and others, such as Uganda, are undertaking reviews. The Netherlands and Ireland have also reviewed the impact of their treaty networks on developing countries, and offering renegotiations to some of their treaty partners as a result.

[119] IMF, *supra* note 16, at 25. *See also* Yariv Brauner, *An International Tax Regime in Crystallization – Realities, Experiences and Opportunities*, 56 TAX L. REV. 259 (2003) (arguing that developing countries are happily joining the tax treaties regime); PICCIOTTO, *supra* note 107, at 57 (indicating that in the early 1990s, some developing countries did sign tax treaties, most prominently with their colonial mother countries).

Over the last fifteen years, skepticism regarding the benefits of tax treaties has increased.[120] Even the IMF recently argued that a

> [c]ritical decision for any primarily capital-importing country is whether it can achieve more by signing a treaty than it can simply through its own domestic law. . . . The reciprocal benefits that a treaty could provide to such a country may actually be of relatively little value. . . . Some would simply advise developing countries not to sign BTTs. . . . What is clear is that countries should not enter treaties lightly – all too often this has been done largely as a political gesture – but with close and well-advised attention to the risks that may be created.[121]

Thus, arguably, there are good reasons why developing countries should be hesitant to sign tax treaties or, at the very minimum, be extremely wary of them. And yet, they do sign these treaties. As Chapter 5 will explain, strategic reasons may drive them to agree to tax treaties and join the "tax treaty club" despite the fact that they could be better off in the absence of this entire regime and despite the lack of any direct coercion to sign.

3.5 Conclusion

Tax treaties are an important mechanism for an array of good reasons. They coordinate the tax rules of the contracting parties. They provide investors with a significant measure of certainty and signal that the contracting countries are committed to supporting cross-border investment.

---

[120] *See, e.g.*, Christians, *supra* note 82, at 712 ("Tax treaties represent a significant opportunity cost for LDCs, diverting attention and resources away from the exploration of more direct ways to increase cross-border investment. Thus, every potential tax treaty relationship with LDCs should be approached critically."); Barthel et al., *supra* note 56, at 4 ("The main role of modern tax treaties is to allocate taxing rights, primarily by shifting rights from capital-importing nations to capital-exporting nations."); Brooks, *supra* note 68, at 171; Pistone, *supra* note 103, at 424 (suggesting that treaties should be used to support developing countries); Thuronyi, *supra* note 68; Sheppard, *supra* note 68. *See also* Mindy Hertfeld, *supra* note 17, citing Stephen E. Shay of Harvard Law School as follows:

> Shay . . . , the keynote speaker at the World Bank event, argued that while treaties were originally intended to mitigate double taxation, they are now primarily used by multinationals engaged in tax avoidance and rent seeking. He urged developing countries to be skeptical until it can be shown that the costs of entering into tax treaties – including both forgone revenues and administrative costs – outweigh the benefits. And he said that if countries find they have entered into a bad treaty, they might be well advised to terminate it or override it through domestic legislation. While those approaches might be considered to violate international law, Shay argued that an occasional breach of international law could be harmless.

[121] IMF, *supra* note, at 27–28.

They ease bureaucratic hassle, (somewhat) facilitate information-gathering and sharing, and advance diplomatic relations between the signatory countries. But what does emerge is that tax treaties are most certainly not crucial for preventing double taxation and unilateral mechanisms do so just as effectively. Residence countries and host countries alike apparently have strong incentive to alleviate double taxation unilaterally. The interaction between their unilateral policies, we saw, creates a stable equilibrium under which double taxation is prevented. Yet while this strategy reduces double taxation to the same extent and as effectively as a tax-treaty regime, the two solutions differ in how they allocate tax revenues between the interacting or contracting countries.

This leads to the conclusion that the contribution tax treaties make to preventing double taxation is highly overrated. While countries do gain administrative, economic, political, and social benefits from signing treaties, the costs of these benefits differ for developed countries and developing countries. Developed countries do not have to bear any costs for the benefits of the treaty beyond what they would pay if they were to act unilaterally to reduce double taxation. Developing countries, in contrast, sacrifice more to become members of the treaty club. The empirical analysis described in this chapter has hinted at a possible positive network effect, when countries sign increasing number of treaties. The discussion in the ensuing chapters will explore in detail the emergence, development, operation, and outcomes of this network and evaluate its consequences. These chapters will further explain why developing countries might sign treaties that they would have been better off were those treaties not to exist at all.

4

Costs of Multilateral Cooperation

After considering the unilateral policies set by individual states and how they interact bilaterally with other states, this chapter moves to the multilateral level. On this level too, tax competition is one of the key issues that policymakers must grapple with. As described, this competition has been generated by the decentralization of international taxation and drives states to design rules that attract both prospective residents and foreign investment. The preceding chapters emphasized the impact tax competition has on national-level policymaking and on the strategic interaction between host and residence states. This chapter will now take a closer look at tax competition among peer states: competition among host states for capital and among residence states for residents.

Tax competition – or, to be more precise, fiscal competition – for investments and for residents is, as previously noted, often accused of sending countries on a race to the bottom. Host countries struggle to attract investments by lowering their tax rates on foreign residents; residence countries try to lure foreign residents (individuals as well as multinational enterprises) with appealing taxing and spending deals. The result is that residence and host countries steadily reduce their tax rates and thereby weaken their ability to redistribute wealth. Despite inconclusive empirical evidence,[1] this premise of tax competition is widely supported; it is evoked, moreover, to support policy recommendations endorsing harmonization as a means for assisting states in regaining their ability to redistribute and for improving the efficiency of taxation in a globalized world.

Policymakers and scholars who are troubled by this idea of a tax race to the bottom tend to advocate a cooperative multilateral solution that will enforce universal standards of taxation. This chapter takes a critical look at such notions of cooperation, arguing that it can be problematic on both efficiency and distributive grounds. Despite the lack of decisive empirical evidence for the existence of such a race to the bottom, I assume

---

[1] *See* the discussion in Chapter 1, note 77.

in this chapter that it does, in fact, exist so as to make the strongest critical argument against tax competition. I will claim that (even) such a well-supported case against tax competition and its potential harms does not necessarily mandate tax coordination.

To demonstrate this, the chapter analyzes a highly stylized (and admittedly hypothetical) scenario of cooperation:[2] worldwide coordination of tax rates, some basic definitions that construct the income tax base and set standards for its measurement, and uniform mechanisms for alleviating double taxation. The analysis compares this hypothetical regime to a case of perfect competition. Although both the cooperation and competition sides of this debate are indisputably hypothetical since neither perfect competition nor complete coordination is currently even remotely plausible, their theoretical consideration allows us to examine their desirability on an abstract level. A possibly more realistic (and, I will argue, more desirable) version of coordination will be discussed in Part III of the book.

Section 4.1 of this chapter begins with a review of the arguments against tax competition, clarifying the claim that coordination would enable countries to collect enough taxes to sustain (or restore) the welfare state and simultaneously promote both equity and efficiency. Section 4.2 criticizes coordination on two grounds. One is the infeasibility of a comprehensive cooperative regime, the argument being that significant collective action problems would likely hinder both the attaining and sustaining of such a regime. The second argument against coordination is its questionable normative appeal: even if feasible, multilateral cooperation is not necessarily desirable because of its inefficiencies and its potentially regressive effects both among and within states. Thus, although coordination is indeed likely to improve countries' ability to collect taxes for public goods, tax competition (its antithesis) may be normatively preferable.

4.1   The Costs of Tax Competition

The decentralized structure of international taxation affects states' ability to redistribute wealth. As explained in Chapter 1, because tax is increasingly a factor weighed by corporations and individuals when making their investment and residence decisions,[3] it has become a competitive tool in

---

[2] In Chapter 5, I will discuss the actual efforts being made toward cooperation and coordination by the international tax community.

[3] *See* Chapter 1, text accompanying notes 35–44.

the game states play in the global arena.[4] The pressure to lower taxes is created by peer countries that reduce their taxes in response to the lower taxes in other countries that incentivize investors and residents to invest, reside, or shift their income to their jurisdictions.[5] This competitive setting is accused of constraining states in pursuing distributive justice. As Reuven Avi-Yonah argues, it "threatens to undermine the individual and corporate income taxes . . . and . . . lead to fiscal crises for countries that wish to continue to provide social insurance."[6]

In conditions of tax competition, countries strive to draw (and keep) investors and residents by providing, among other things, attractive taxing and spending packages.[7] This means, on the one hand, offering competitive tax rates to the most mobile elements and, on the other hand, offering the public goods and services that will be most attractive to them. Investors, for example, will presumably seek goods and services that the state can supply more efficiently than the free market (such as infrastructure, personal security, and the rule of law, all classic public goods). They will likely be less interested, however, in state services aimed at assisting the weaker segments of society (such as welfare, public health, and, perhaps, education). Hence, tax competition pushes states to lower taxes on capital while, at the same time, curb services that target non-investors.[8]

Residents, too, are mobile to a certain extent.[9] They may therefore also be influenced by state tax and welfare policies. Assuming that there is some elasticity in residents' decisions, countries can compete for mobile residents by offering attractive tax and benefits packages. Under the Tiebout

---

[4] For comprehensive surveys of the research on tax competition, *see* John D. Wilson, *Theories of Tax Competition*, 52 NAT'L TAX J. 269, 270 (1999); John D. Wilson & David E. Wildasin, *Capital Tax Competition: Bane or Boon?*, 88 J. PUBLIC ECON. 1065 (2004); Michael Keen & Kai A. Konrad, *The Theory of International Tax Competition and Coordination* (Max Planck Inst. for Tax Law & Pub. Fin. Working Paper 2012, July 6, 2012).

[5] But *see* Keen & Konrad, *supra* note 4, who note that it is unclear whether the strategic game between countries will necessarily drive them to reduce their tax rates.

[6] Reuven S. Avi-Yonah, *Globalization, Tax Competition, and the Fiscal Crisis of the Welfare State*, 113 HARV. L. REV. 1573, 1575–1603 (2000).

[7] This is an insight famously captured in the local government context in the classic Charles M. Tiebout, *A Pure Theory of Local Expenditures*, 64 J. POL. ECON. 5 (1956).

[8] Other factors may have the opposite effect, which is why, some assert, tax rates do not actually race to the bottom. *See* Thomas Plümper, Vera E. Troeger & Hannes Winner, *Why Is There No Race to the Bottom in Capital Taxation?*, 53 INT'L STUD. Q. 761 (2009) (arguing that while tax competition does drive tax rates downward, other factors, such as budget rigidity and fairness norms, have a countereffect).

[9] See my discussion in Chapter 1 around notes 39–44. On the (more limited) mobility of individuals, see notes 36–38 in Chapter 1.

model (which assumes admittedly unrealistic conditions of perfect mobility, among other things),[10] states try to attract residents with packages of public services and prices (the taxes they have to pay for those services), while residents "vote with their feet" by moving to the state that offers the most favorable package for the best "price." Unlike investors, residents might prefer better education and health services, stronger environmental protection, and greater public spending on the arts and culture. But similarly to the competition for investments, this competition for residents may have problematic distributive effects if, as seems plausible, residents who benefit from the welfare state have a stronger preference for it than those who have no need for it or are at a lower risk of requiring its benefits. Rich taxpayers who are on the contributing side of redistribution will, for example, likely prefer less distribution to more distribution. In fact, even the more altruistic among this group of taxpayers might prefer to fund charities of their own choosing rather than support governmental redistribution. Taxpayers on the receiving end of redistribution will presumably have a preference for greater redistribution. But greater redistribution may attract too many welfare-seeking residents[11] and entail higher taxation to finance the welfare state, possibly driving wealthy residents away.

Consequently, although there may be variances between features that are attractive to prospective residents (e.g., environmental protection and public parks) and features that appeal to future investors (e.g., lower environmental standards), a certain degree of aversion toward redistribution is probably common to both types of sought-after taxpayers. If this assumption is valid, and competition is fierce, competing states are forced to balance between two options, as explained in Chapter 1: between keeping taxes (and redistribution) high and risking losing the wealthy, on the one hand, and reducing taxes (and redistribution) and holding on to the

---

[10] Tiebout, *supra* note 7. For a critique of the applicability of the Tiebout model to international income taxation *see* Ian Roxan, *Limits to Globalisation: Some Implications for Taxation, Tax Policy, and the Developing World* (LSE Working Paper, 2012), http://eprints.lse .ac.uk/46768/1/Limits%20to%20globalisation%20%28lsero%29.pdf, convincingly arguing that the assumptions required do not apply when only income moves.

[11] The U.S. federal system faced some interesting issues with regard to welfare at the state level. The unrestricted mobility of residents between states created a risk of turning states with extensive welfare systems into "welfare magnets," which would significantly impair their ability to sustain their welfare systems. For a discussion of whether this trend actually exists, *see* William D. Berry, Richard C. Fording & Russell L. Hanson, *Reassessing the "Race to the Bottom" in State Welfare Policy*, 65 J. POL. 327 (2003). *See* also Roderick M. Hills Jr., *Poverty, Residency, and Federalism: States' Duty of Impartiality toward Newcomers*, 1999 SUP. CT. REV. 277.

wealthy, on the other. Either way, assuming wealthy taxpayers are mobile and that they prefer lower to higher taxes, redistribution will be curtailed. If, indeed, the wealthy leave, it will mean, in practical terms, shifting taxes to mid-level taxpayers. Although the outcome would be a smaller wealth gap within the country (as the wealthy taxpayers have left), it would also mean a decrease in the collective welfare pie. Accordingly, competition and its resulting race to the bottom are often accused of harming justice.[12] At its extreme, it is claimed, this competition will drive down the tax rates for mobile residents and the mobile factors of production, shift the tax burden to the less mobile factors (most importantly, to low-skilled labor), lead to a reduction in tax revenues, and undermine the welfare state and, in particular, redistribution.[13] But even in its less extreme form, tax competition indisputably creates pressure for countries to lower their tax rates and limit redistribution or otherwise pay a (political and overall welfare) price.[14]

Significantly, the race to the bottom is driven not only by the actual shift of activities and residencies but also by taxpayers' ability to paper-shift their tax bases through tax planning.[15] Taxpayers tax plan through such tactics as incorporating and reincorporating their foreign activities,

---

[12] *See* Avi-Yonah, *supra* note 6.

[13] Avi-Yonah, *supra* note 6, at 1624, focuses on capital mobility, asserting that "a shift in the tax burden from capital to labor tends to render the tax system more regressive. Such a tax system is also less capable of redistributing resources from the rich to the poor."

[14] Plümper, *supra* note 8, at 771, explains this as follows:

> [H]olding everything else constant, countries in which governments are least restricted by fairness considerations implement the lowest tax rates on mobile capital and become capital importers. This result remains valid for the opposite case: governments which are most restricted by fairness norms implement the highest tax rates on mobile capital and become capital exporters. Accordingly, fairness norms come at a price; the price a country with an egalitarian electorate has to pay is highest when fairness norms are weaker in other countries.

[15] A recent study conducted by the IMF developed "an empirical approach for assessing base spillovers, relating (proxies of) the corporate tax base in 103 countries, over the period 1980–2013, to both their own statutory CIT rate and the rates of others." The study concluded that

> [s]pillover base effects through real activities are significant and large ... [A] one point reduction in the statutory CIT rate in all other countries reduces the typical country's corporate tax base by 3.7 percent. With corporate tax rates having fallen, on average, by 5 points or so over the last 10 years, this implies a sizable effect.... Spillover base effects through profit shifting are also large – and no less significant.

IMF, *Spillovers in International Corporate Taxation*, Policy Paper 19 (2014), http://www .imf.org/external/pp/longres.aspx?id=4873.

shifting income through transfer pricing, treaty shopping, and stripping mechanisms, sheltering financial assets through foreign trusts, and sometime even outright tax evasion.[16] As discussed in Chapter 1, tax planning enables residents and investors to enjoy lower tax rates in foreign jurisdictions even without changing the location of their actual activities and residence. Although paper-shifting does not significantly benefit the state that attracts the "paper" income (other than, perhaps, a "toll charge" in tax revenues and increased demand for white-collar jobs), it does impinge on the ability of states in general to collect taxes and, hence, exerts an additional pressure on them to engage in the tax competition. Thus, it is not only the mobility of investments, capital, and taxpayers that sends the race to the bottom, but also taxpayers' ability to lower their effective tax rates through tax planning. The latter pushes states to provide tax benefits for the extra mobile factors of production and planning-prone attributes (e.g., patent boxes and financial instruments) so as to collect greater volumes of the tax planners' taxes even if at lower rates.[17]

Not only redistribution is affected by tax competition. Tax competition has also been accused of undermining efficiency. To begin with, some claim that tax competition will drive tax rates down to a suboptimal level, where states will be forced to under-provide public goods.[18] This argument envisions a situation in which a state's choice of its tax rates (and, accordingly, the level of public goods it provides) is affected by the competition for mobile capital. Raising tax rates drives capital away (and harms immobile factors of production) but could enhance the state's ability to provide public goods. Lowering tax rates, in contrast, attracts foreign capital (and leads to an increase in the demand for local factors of production) but could impair the state's ability to provide public

---

[16] For a more detailed review of tax planning tools, *see* Chapter 1.

[17] *See* Omri Marian, *The State Administration of International Tax Avoidance*, 7 HARV. BUS. L. REV. (forthcoming 2016) Available at SSRN: https://ssrn.com/abstract=2685642 (describing the rogue behavior of tax haven countries in facilitating tax planning opportunities and exemplifying it with the Luxemburg leaked ATAs). See also Peter Dietsch, Catching Capital (2016) distinguishing between states' "luring" investments and the illegitimate "poaching" of foreign jurisdictions.

[18] WALLACE E. OATES, FISCAL FEDERALISM 143 (1972), *cited in* John D. Wilson, *Theories of Tax Competition*, 52 NAT'L TAX J. 269, 270 (1999):

> The result of tax competition may well be a tendency toward less than efficient levels of output of local services. In an attempt to keep taxes low to attract business investment, local officials may hold spending below those levels for which marginal benefits equal marginal costs, particularly for those programs that do not offer direct benefits to local business.

services.[19] While the optimal level of public services would ordinarily be the point at which the marginal benefit from such services equals their marginal cost, the effect of capital mobility modifies this efficiency rule and makes investment in public goods less attractive.[20] Thus, even when the interaction between unilateral strategies under competition yields an equilibrium that is production efficient (that is, resources are allocated efficiently), states might benefit from collectively increasing their tax rates.[21] As Michael Keen and Kai Konrad have phrased it,

> Relative to the social optimum, there is thus under-provision of the public good, and too low a tax rate, in the Nash equilibrium. The symmetric Nash equilibrium does have production efficiency: all countries charge the same tax rate, so the allocation of capital is first best. But the decentralized tax-setting means that countries fail to properly exploit what is, from the collective perspective, a perfectly inelastic tax base, access to which makes the first best feasible.[22]

Inefficiencies may further arise in the provision of public goods and services when one country's tax choice has an external effect on the welfare of another country. Thus, for example, when the benefits from a public good provided by one country (e.g., support for R&D) spill over to another jurisdiction, the former country may be less inclined to provide that public good.[23]

Two additional arguments for why tax competition may be inefficient have been raised, both of which relate to state decision makers' failure

---

[19] Under the classic Zodrow & Mieszkowski model, a country considering whether to impose tax rates that are higher than those of its competitors must weigh the loss to domestic immobile factors of production caused by the outflow of capital against the benefits from potentially higher revenues. Intuitively, the optimal reaction to other countries' lower rates would seem to be to reduce tax rates. But this is not necessarily the case, since the benefit in tax revenues from increasing tax rates could be greater than the loss from capital flight. See George R. Zodrow & Peter Mieszkowski, *Pigou, Tiebout, Property Taxation, and the Underprovision of Local Public Goods*, 19 J. URBAN ECON. 356 (1986).

[20] Under competition, increasing tax in order to supply additional public services entails extra costs for immobile factors of production (beyond the costs of producing the public goods) due to the increased outflow of mobile capital that the higher tax encourages. This outflow of mobile capital imposes a cost on local factors of production (*e.g.*, labor), which may make their benefits from an extra unit of public good less than the costs of producing it.

[21] The simplicity and sharpness of these results made this symmetrical analysis – where competing states are presumed to be identical – the prevalent assumption in the literature. However, its premises – regarding both the identical nature of the countries involved and the optimal use of public funds – are highly unrealistic. These premises will be discussed further below.

[22] Keen & Konrad, *supra* note 4, at 12.   [23] *Id.* at 1.

to properly evaluate the marginal costs of the public goods the state provides.[24] The first argument refers to the winner's curse, whereby the highest bidders tend to pay an excessive price (or, in our context, collect too low a tax), which, post factum, they regret. The reason for this outcome is that bidding involves a certain degree of guesswork, and since winners are outliers they are often wrong.[25] From this perspective, competition might drive tax rates – and public services – down to a suboptimal level. The second argument is that tax competition could generate agency costs: decision makers might prefer their own interests (be it public reelection or personal gain) when they set tax rates and favor the unrepresented few over the public good.[26]

Another reason why tax competition may yield inefficiencies is the externality created by tax avoidance through tax planning and the consequent ability of certain individuals and corporations to free ride on the public goods of a jurisdiction without paying its taxes. Absent competition, the state is presumably able to overcome collective-action problems in the provision of public goods by imposing its collective financing through taxation.[27] When, however, taxpayers are able to avoid this taxation but the government is incapable of excluding them from enjoying the domextic public goods, the collective action problem reemerges. Although a small number of defectors might not undermine the provision of public goods, a large enough group of defecting taxpayers could lead to the collapse of the state's capacity to provide (efficient) public goods. This brings us back to square one, namely, where the market underprovides

---

[24] Julie Roin, *Competition and Evasion: Another Perspective on International Tax Competition,* 89 GEO. L.J. 543, 564 (2001).

[25] *Id.* at 564:

> In an auction format, the winners are those that bid most aggressively. In the tax context, this is the jurisdiction that imposes the lowest effective tax rate. Because jurisdictions should be willing to lower their bids to the rate that will allow them to recoup the marginal costs of hosting the investment, the nominal winner should be the jurisdiction with the lowest marginal cost. However, because determining the amount of some key determinants of marginal cost involves guesswork, the winner is really the jurisdiction that guesses it will have the lowest marginal cost. As the lowest cost projection, this guess is an outlier – and like all outliers, likely to be wrong. And indeed, both field studies and experimental data show that auction winners often find out that they have overpaid.

[26] *See id.* at 565–67.

[27] The market, in contrast, is unable to sufficiently provide such goods due to collective action problems – each individual actor has an incentive to free ride on others' provision of non-excludable services.

public goods and the state is unable to supply them. Thus, the state's inability to exclude free riders impairs both its incentive and ability to provide public services.

Lastly, the decentralized structure of the international tax regime is responsible for significant conflicts between jurisdictions. These conflicts, in turn, have led to the creation of loopholes. Loopholes are prominently abused by tax planners seeking to reduce their effective tax rates through what has been colloquially termed "tax arbitrage."[28] The loopholes not only create free-riding opportunities but also entail major planning costs (for taxpayers) and enforcement costs (for the government). In social welfare terms, these are pure transaction costs that reduce the collective welfare. Any effort to streamline the various taxing jurisdictions will necessarily reduce these transaction costs and thereby increase efficiency.

The obstacles tax competition has created for the redistribution of wealth and the promotion of efficiency have led many to advocate for a coordinated – perhaps even harmonized – multilateral international taxation regime as the best means of promoting efficiency and distributive justice. Harmonization certainly seems like a textbook response to the need to curtail tax competition in order to fight competition-based inefficiencies as well as to bolster the ability of states to promote distributive justice. If the race-to-the-bottom prediction is accurate, it is the decentralized structure of international taxation, where competition thrives, that is to blame for hampering efficiency and obstructing states in their pursuit of distributive justice. If states were to cooperate to avoid the downward pressure of tax competition, it is asserted, they would be able to pursue redistributive goals and – presumably – supply efficient levels of public goods and services. This has led many to support multilateral cooperation to curtail tax competition, claiming that countries must cooperate to set and enforce a high enough level of tax to sustain their tax base and support their welfare states.[29]

---

[28] See, e.g., Diane M. Ring, One Nation Among Many: Policy Implications of Cross-Border Tax Arbitrage, 44 BOSTON COLLEGE L. REV. 79 (2005); Adam Rosenzweig, Harnessing the Costs of International Tax Arbitrage, 26 Va. Tax Rev. 555 (2007).

[29] See, e.g., Avi-Yonah, supra note 6; Yariv Brauner, An International Tax Regime in Crystallization – Realities, Experiences and Opportunities, 56 TAX L. REV. 259 (2003); Yariv Brauner & Pasquale Pistone, Introduction, in BRICS AND THE EMERGENCE OF INTERNATIONAL TAX COORDINATION 3 (Yariv Brauner & Pasquale Pistone eds., 2015). This was also the reason for supporting the current BEPS initiative. See, OECD, Explanatory Statement, OECD/G20 Base Erosion and Profit Shifting Project 4 (2015), https://www.oecd.org/ctp/beps-explanatory-statement-2015.pdf:

For multilateral coordination to be truly effective in preventing tax competition, states would have to agree on the common basic building blocks of their tax systems (specifically defining who should be taxed, on what income, and when).[30] This would enable them to close the loopholes that arise from the inconsistencies between different jurisdictions and facilitate tax avoidance. Moreover, to curb the race to the bottom, states must coordinate not only their tax rules but also their tax rates (at least with regard to taxes collected beyond the value of the state-provided public services), so as to prevent price-based competition for residents and investments. Accordingly, the type of coordination I will consider in the rest of this chapter is a hypothetical regime in which countries have agreed to impose a harmonized tax rate, beyond benefits taxes (i.e., beyond the costs of the public goods and services provided to taxpayers), along with a standardized tax base and effective mechanisms for preventing double taxation.

Supporters of such coordination might claim it promotes both efficiency and distributive justice. A harmonized international tax regime is considered more efficient than a tax competition regime because, according to some, it would prevent states from driving their taxes down to a suboptimal level[31] and falling victim to the winner's curse, as well as limit agency costs. Moreover, by inhibiting tax arbitrage, coordination would

In a globalised economy, governments need to cooperate and refrain from harmful tax practices, to address tax avoidance effectively, and provide a more certain international environment to attract and sustain investment. Failure to achieve such cooperation would reduce the effectiveness of CIT [corporate income tax] as a tool for resource mobilisation, which would have a disproportionately harmful impact on developing countries.

See also, *e.g.*, Testimony of Robert B. Stack, Deputy Assistant Secretary (International Tax Affairs) U.S. Department of the Treasury before the Ways and Means Subcommittee on Tax Policy (Dec. 1, 2015), https://waysandmeans.house.gov/wp-content/uploads/2015/12/2015–12–01-TPS-Testimony-Bob-Stack.pdf:

failure in the BEPS project could well result in countries taking unilateral, inconsistent actions, thereby increasing double taxation, the cost to the U.S. Treasury of granting foreign tax credits, and the number and scale of tax disputes. Indeed, notwithstanding the BEPS project, some countries have taken unilateral action, and it is our hope that they will reconsider those actions in the post-BEPS environment.

Yariv Brauner, *Treaties in the Aftermath of BEPS*, 41 BROOK. J. INT'L L. 974, 981 (2016), also notes that "[t]he BEPS project . . . reflects a realization that more coordination and even some harmonization may be beneficial to both developed and developing (productive) countries."

[30] This will be discussed in Chapter 7.
[31] Recall, however, that the assumption of a suboptimal race to the bottom is based on the premise of identical competing jurisdictions.

reduce the costs produced by tax planning and the distortions created by income shifting for tax purposes.

Important as the efficiency considerations may seem, however, the strongest justification for coordination of tax policies seems to be distributive justice concerns. Coordination could help states shift the tax burden from less mobile labor back to more mobile capital,[32] as well as enable them to finance their welfare states. This would make redistribution something that countries could afford.[33] Avi-Yonah elaborates on this:[34]

> In a world in which capital can move freely across national borders and MNEs are free to choose from among many investment locations, the ability of any one country (or any two countries in cooperation) to tax (or otherwise regulate) such capital is severely limited. . . . A multilateral solution . . . is therefore essential if the fundamental goals of taxation are to be preserved. Only organizations with an equally global reach can regulate or tax private market activities.

4.2   The Problems with Coordination

Undoubtedly, a successfully operating coordination regime would enable states to collect more tax revenues, which could prevent suboptimal provision of public goods and facilitate redistribution. This regime would also arguably improve efficiency by reducing externalities and other costs. This does not, however, necessarily make coordination superior to tax competition. This section focuses on two drawbacks of a coordinated regime. First, coordination is extremely hard to achieve and sustain, for its costs could be prohibitive. Second, and perhaps of greater significance, even if actually attained, coordination would not necessarily yield normatively superior outcomes.

a.   Coordination Is Hard to Achieve and Sustain

Coordination is obviously extremely difficult, if not completely impossible, to achieve. Chapter 2[35] discussed the obstacles to attaining cooperation among states in the relatively narrow context of the adoption of a uniform mechanism to alleviate double taxation. Similar – indeed even worse – hurdles would arise in any attempt to harmonize entire tax policies.

---

[32] *See* Avi-Yonah, *supra* note 6, at 1616–25.   [33] *Id.* at 1631–48.
[34] *Id.* at 1675.   [35] *See* the text accompanying notes 45–49 and 69–75 in Chapter 2.

To begin with, it would be extremely challenging for states to reach an agreement on the details of the coordination regime, that is, on a uniform mechanism that includes a single rate of taxation beyond the costs of public goods. Countries differ in their economic and political characteristics as well as in their expectations of their tax systems. Their decisions regarding tax rates – in particular in relation to redistribution – are strongly anchored in the divergent characteristics and beliefs (and, sometimes, simply the means) of their citizenry and leadership. The variety of interest groups within each country complicates the picture even further.[36] Countries can therefore be expected to diverge and even conflict in terms of their positions and interests vis-à-vis a multilateral accord,[37] and the prospects of arriving at a collective agreement on a single solution seems problematic at best.[38]

Furthermore, even if such coordination were to be achieved, sustaining it would be difficult given the possible incentives of individual countries to defect. As with cooperative efforts in general, any given country

[36] For an analysis of the influence of interest groups on inter-nation conflicts, see Eyal Benvenisti, *Exit and Voice in the Age of Globalization*, 98 MICH. L. REV. 167 (1999).

[37] In the IMF Policy Paper, *supra* note 15, at 43, the following argument was made:

Countries' interests diverge widely, most obviously between low and high tax countries, but in other respects too. Countries that are primarily capital exporting, for instance, are likely to be more sensitive to the interests of the residence country, while resource-rich countries may attach more importance to source rights. This diversity of interest need not preclude identifying mutually advantageous forms of coordination. Minimum effective tax rates, for instance, can prove beneficial even for low tax countries initially below the minimum, since an enforced increase in their own tax rates may lead to an induced increase in tax rates elsewhere from which they can benefit. But diversity clearly does make securing agreement on coordination measures harder.

[38] *See* Tsilly Dagan, *Just Harmonization*, 42 U.B.C. L. REV. 331, 379 (2010); Roin, *supra* note 24, at 557–61. *See also* STEVEN A. DEAN, *More Cooperation, Less Uniformity: Tax Deharmonization and the Future of the International Tax Regime*, 84 TUL. L. REV. 125, 152 (2009–2010) describing the difficulties in promoting homogeneity in a heterogeneous world; Katharina Holzinger, *Tax Competition and Tax Co-Operation in the EU: The Case of Savings Taxation*, 17 RATION. & SOC. 475, 497–98 (2005). Holzinger describes the strategic results of the heterogeneity of countries as a possible explanation for why the EU could not agree on a harmonized system for taxing savings. She models the interaction as an asymmetric dilemma:

The strategic constellation is an asymmetric dilemma. This does not only tell us that we need co-operative institutions and binding contracts, but also that we face a negotiation problem in trying to find a co-operative agreement. . . . In the asymmetric dilemma it is more difficult to find an agreement in the first place. Some governments have a strong incentive to negotiate a fully co-ordinated solution based on a harmonized system, for example, that all apply a withholding tax, all use the same tax rate,

could derive greater economic benefits from defecting even if the over-all world welfare increases due to the cooperation.[39] Defection can take the form of imposing taxes that are lower than what was cooperatively agreed upon, in order to attract residents and investors (as is the case of a tax haven); alternatively, a defecting country could offer better public goods without raising its tax rates or specific economic benefits not pro-vided by coordinating states.[40] To prevent defection, sensitive monitoring mechanisms must be set in the cooperation agreement, and all participat-ing countries must be willing to submit to and uphold the sanction against defection. The price of monitoring defection may be excessive since ongo-ing online scrutiny of the tax laws and public expenditure programs of all participant states is required, as well as monitoring for concessions made either on an individual basis or simply by nonenforcement of existing norms.[41]

It is therefore reasonable to assume that attaining and maintaining cooperation among states regarding redistribution would be an extremely formidable task. Moreover, the accompanying curtailment of competition would entail significant drawbacks. Surprisingly, given its positive conno-tations, cooperation could conceivably give rise to distributive concerns as well as undermine efficiency.

b. The Distributive Biases of Coordination

The distributive challenges of coordination are disturbing. To begin with, one of the principle purposes of a coordinated tax regime is to facilitate the implementation of higher tax rates across the board so as to allow coun-tries to collect enough taxes to fund their welfare states. For some states,

---

> or all use an information exchange system. Other governments have an incentive to resist full co-ordination. Even if they prefer full coordination over tax competition, their most preferred solution is non-coordination.

Id. at 497.

[39] Holzinger, id., describes this as a "weakest link" game, where no critical mass exists to make all other countries prefer cooperation to defection. This, in turn, makes spontaneous coop-eration unlikely. See also Wolfgang Eggert et al., Tax Competition and International Tax Agreements: Lessons from Economic Theory, in TAX TREATIES: BUILDING BRIDGES BETWEEN LAW AND ECONOMICS 161 (Michael Lang et al. eds., 2010) (suggesting that a single country will find it profitable to free ride on the harmonization efforts of other countries).

[40] Charles I. Kingson, The Coherence of International Taxation, 81 COLUM. L. REV. 1151, 1158–67 (1981).

[41] See the recent IMF policy paper, supra note 15, at 43.

this could mean gaining greater tax revenues but foregoing the domestic benefits of attracting foreign investments through lower tax rates. Yet some of these states might have more pressing needs than maintaining a social welfare net. Alternatively, some might simply value more the benefits of an unobstructed inflow of capital, as opposed to greater tax revenues. For these countries, lowering tax rates – especially if it will attract more investments into their borders – could be more beneficial than collecting more taxes. A coordinated mechanism, in other words, is bound to suit some states more than others, thereby creating a bias against the latter.[42]

Second, restraining the decentralized, marketized competition among states to enable them to collect more taxes requires that they consent to a multilateral regime. In the absence of a central global government, the terms of such multilateral coordination would most likely entail multilateral negotiations.[43] This shift from competition to negotiation is not insignificant. In multilateral negotiations, countries are no longer relatively small players guided by the invisible hand of the market; rather, their relative bargaining power is impacted by such factors as cultural, diplomatic, and military strength. As will be explained in greater detail in Chapter 5, shifting from competition to negotiated coordination produces costs that derive from asymmetries in the relative bargaining power of the negotiating states and their ability to forge coalitions with other states. Some states – notably developed countries – enjoy a relatively superior position in the international community. Moreover, the resource they compete for (i.e., residents) is far less mobile than the capital sought by developing countries. The combination of these two attributes makes developed-residence countries far less vulnerable to defection than

---

[42] Holzinger, *supra* note 38, for example, distinguishes between revenue-oriented governments that prefer tax revenue to market benefits (*e.g.*, governments faced with serious budget deficits or countries with a small and relatively unimportant financial sector) and financial market-oriented governments that see greater value in political benefits from the financial sector (*e.g.*, if the financial sector accounts for a large share of the national product or is extremely active in lobbying), as well as between large and small countries. Modeling this as an asymmetric game, she concludes that "[g]overnments of large countries and/or those which value tax revenue more highly than financial sector benefits prefer tax cooperation; governments of small countries and/or those which value financial sector benefits more highly prefer tax competition." *Id.* at 497; Philipp Genschel & Peter Schwarz, *Tax competition: a literature review*, 9 SOCIO-ECONOMIC REVIEW, 339, 354: "small, poor, low-tax countries tend to suffer less from tax competition and may actually gain from it."

[43] Chapter 5 discusses the option of a standard developing through the facilitation of network externalities.

developing-residence countries. Hence, developed countries as a group can be expected to wield relatively more power in negotiations and, as a result, have greater influence over the design of the regime. This influence can be expected to translate into the setting of favorable conditions in the coordination agreement that serve their interests. Specifically, these more powerful countries can use their advantageous negotiating position to secure for themselves a larger share of the tax revenues collectively imposed.

Lastly, even if developed-residence countries do not have superior cooperating abilities or greater bargaining power and even if collecting more tax revenues serves the best interests of all involved countries, a multilateral tax agreement could still have disturbing distributional ramifications. This is due to another divergence between host and residence countries, namely, the divergences in how local groups gain and lose from cross-border investments and the taxation of that activity. While some factors of production in certain countries might gain from tax coordination, others might lose if coordination curbs cross-border investment.[44]

In some countries (I'll call them "rich" countries), mainly capital-exporting countries, the government will be better able to collect taxes from capital owners (and therefore better able to redistribute wealth) under the coordinated regime. In contrast, in "poor" countries, which are by and large capital-importing countries and, more typically, developing countries, immobile local factors of production (most importantly, labor) benefit most from foreign investments. The increased tax that would be imposed by a multilateral coordinated regime on cross-border investments (as well as the tax wedge it would create) reduces the level of investment in such countries along with the demand for local labor. It thus inflicts costs on local labor.

Certainly, under such a tax regime, poor countries would be able to gain some tax revenues from the incoming investments and collect more taxes from their own capital owners. These revenues, however, would not necessarily alleviate the costs borne by local factors of production in these countries (most importantly, labor) due to the loss of

---

[44] Ronald B. Davies, *Tax Treaties and Foreign Direct Investment: Potential versus Performance*, 11 INT'L TAX & PUB. FIN. 775, 794 (2004), compares this option to the well-known Stopler-Samuelson effect, where the removal of protection against imports can affect relative wages. For the Stopler-Samuelson theorem, *see* BO SÖDERSTEN & GEOFFREY REED, INTERNATIONAL ECONOMICS 235 (3d ed. 1980).

foreign investments. First, the tax revenues collected from foreign investors would likely be lower than the gains labor could have reaped from an increased level of foreign investment (at least so long as residence and host countries split the tax revenues and refrain from such practices as tax sparing). The reason for this is that any tax on foreign investors inhibits the inflow of capital (and, consequently, the benefits to local labor). While it potentially increases the combined level of tax revenues collected by host and residence countries, the allocation of these revenues between the two types of countries, as well as their distribution within each individual country, is unclear. In other words, the distributive implications of the increased coordinated tax rates depend on how exactly the increased tax revenues are distributed between and within host and residence countries.

The allocation of these tax revenues could take many possible shapes since coordination would most likely be achieved through negotiations, which could result in any number of outcomes. Countries of residence could certainly – if they were to so desire – relinquish (at least part of) their tax revenues and agree to allocation mechanisms that benefit host countries (and their factors of production).[45] Assuming the revenues thus collected by developing countries are more than the deadweight loss from imposing the increased tax rate, this would result in redistribution from residence to host countries, potentially with gain funneled to labor in host countries. But if no effort were made to benefit poor countries, a harmonized tax regime would likely lead to host countries' collecting tax revenues that are lower than the gains labor could have amassed from greater foreign investment.

Could the taxes collected from a poor country's own capital owners under coordination compensate for the losses labor would incur due to the lower levels of foreign investment? Coordination could certainly enhance poor countries' ability to collect taxes from their mobile factors of

---

[45] Moreover, since residence countries benefit more than host countries from harmonization, it could be assumed that they would have to offer a generous allocation of revenues in order to secure cooperation. See Holzinger, *supra* note 38, at 497–98:

> In the asymmetric dilemma it is more difficult to find an agreement in the first place.
>   Thus, a negotiated solution to an asymmetric dilemma can take three forms: The first is full co-ordination of strategies (T,T). This requires compensation for those countries that prefer tax competition. The second solution is non-coordination of strategies (T;~T). This requires compensation for those countries that prefer co-operation. The third solution might be a compromise, which is neither full co-ordination, nor clearly non-coordination.

production. And yet the actual outcome depends on how tightly the coordinated regime restricts the ability of the wealthy residents of these (poor) countries to avoid taxes and on their inclination to continue to reside there despite the increased tax. Assuming that poor countries face greater challenges in providing collective goods and sustaining attractive residential environments, competition for residents may in fact intensify under a coordinated tax regime, causing poor states to lose their wealthier residents to richer states. In such an event, host countries would not be able to collect tax revenues from these expatriates. The actual benefits gained by host countries from a coordinated tax regime is, therefore, contingent on two factors: the (unfortunately unlikely) inclination of rich residence countries to transfer a larger part of the tax revenues to host countries, on the one hand, and poor countries' potential gain from their increased capacity to tax their own capital owners despite the latter's mobility and any remaining tax-avoidance opportunities. Moreover, even if host countries were, in fact, able to collect tax revenues from their own rich residents or to receive a larger share of tax revenues from foreign investors, there is still the matter of how these revenues would be distributed within these countries. In the case of countries with inferior (or even corrupt) governance, there could still be a risk that the host government will not efficiently redistribute the revenues to the needy and will instead channel the funds to other groups.[46]

If – as I suspect – poor countries are not very likely to collect enough tax revenues to compensate for the losses local labor incurs, the desirability of coordination for these countries as a whole and for labor in particular is doubtful. The most problematic aspect of this outcome is that labor is often precisely the group most in need of redistribution. Even if the government uses all of the tax revenues it collects for redistributive purposes, thereby transferring to labor the taxes it collected, labor as a group loses out because – in these conditions – it would have gained more had the government not levied the tax in the first place. Hence, while the end result could certainly be that by coordinating taxes, rich countries are able to increase their tax revenues and redistribute wealth among their own residents, there could be undesirable implications to this outcome in other countries. If labor in poor countries cannot be compensated for its losses

---

[46] For a suggestion for a more equitable regime that directly benefits labor in developing countries by endorsing tax incentives see Yoram Margalioth, *Tax Competition, Foreign Direct Investments and Growth: Using the Tax System To Promote Developing Countries*, 23 VA. TAX REV. 161, 189 (2003).

resulting from a lower capital inflow, the benefits of the redistribution in rich countries come at the expense of labor in poor countries.

In sum, then, there are clearly possible disadvantages to multilateral coordination, particularly for poor countries. To begin with, a higher tax rate might be imposed on countries for which lower taxes (and more investment) would be more beneficial. In the shift from competition to bargaining that coordination can be assumed to entail, stronger and more well-connected countries will enjoy a comparative advantage. Moreover, there is the troubling risk that a coordinated accord would benefit the poor in rich countries but at the expense of labor in poor countries. Although states could negotiate a more equalizing allocation of tax revenues, tax revenues might be regressively distributed among the participating countries if developed countries take advantage of their superior bargaining position to secure a bigger piece of the pie. Lastly, there is the related danger of inequitable allocation of transfer payments among the poor in developing countries.

c. The Efficiency Costs of Coordination

Doubts about the desirability of multilateral coordination of tax systems can also be raised from the perspective of efficiency. Section 1 presented some of the arguments regarding the inefficiencies of tax competition. Here, I consider the possible benefits of competition in light of the potential efficiency costs of coordination.

The first claim supporting competition as a more efficient mechanism for providing public goods is that it does a better job at matching public goods with individual preferences. Julie Roin has convincingly explained the benefits of tax competition in setting the optimal level of public goods. She contends that "the right tax" is not an axiom, and thus not every departure from noncompetitive tax levels is unduly low.[47] Tax competition, Roin claims, leads to "a diversity of governmental and tax regimes," which promotes locational efficiencies.[48] Faced with competition from

---

[47] Roin, *supra* note 24, at 553. But see Dietsch, *supra* note 17, arguing that the states should enjoy fiscal autonomy – the ability to determine the size of the public budget, and the level of redistribution in accordance with the preferences of their constituents.
[48] *Id.* at 561:

> In sum, advocates of tax harmonization overstate their case by implicitly assuming the fungibility of governments and jurisdictions. Countries are not like bushels of corn, indistinguishable from one another. Instead, they vary along many different

other countries, different countries will offer different services for different taxes based on what may appeal to the residents and investors they wish to attract. Since countries diverge in needs and preferences, competition has the benefit of channeling investments to the locations that value them most. Roin concludes that "tax competition is not a negative sum game, either from the perspective of participating countries or global welfare as a whole, when viewed from a strictly economic perspective."[49] Coordinating tax rates, in contrast, could narrow the spectrum of possibilities for taxpayers and countries alike, by imposing a "one size fits all" regime.[50]

The second, related, claim emphasizes competition's contribution to countering the inefficiencies of taxation. Under coordination, countries will have limited incentive to reduce their tax rates in order to limit governmental waste. Tax competition, in contrast, creates such an incentive and encourages countries to race governmental waste to the bottom. An extreme view would regard policymakers as inherently inclined to increase public revenues to advance their own interests rather than society's. If this is the case, tax competition serves a valuable social function in constraining these leviathans.[51] But even if the reality is less extreme, competition may assist in constraining the excesses of government. Without competition, governments have less of an incentive to restrict their size.[52] As Daniel Shaviro has put it,

> dimensions, some of which are quite important to investors. As a result, instead of leading to a pure "race to the bottom," tax competition has and is likely to continue to result in market segmentation, as investors and countries look for good partners. Just as we believe that society benefits from the availability of Chevy Cavaliers, Camrys, Lexuses, and Porches, so too can it benefit from the diversity of governmental and tax regimes encouraged by tax competition – benefits that would be lost under a strict form of harmonization. At least in an ideal world, then, tax competition can create locational efficiencies.

[49] *Id.* at 568.
[50] Theoretically, to enable locational efficiencies and allow states to set higher tax rates to compensate them for externalities and facilitate redistribution, a tax rate that equals the cost of public services could have been imposed, plus an agreed-upon uniform addition. Measuring the "correct" tax that should be paid for certain services, however, is impractical.
[51] *See, e.g.*, G. Brennan & J.M. Buchanan, The Power to Tax: Analytical Foundations of a Fiscal Constitution 186 (1980) (viewing tax competition as an objective to be sought in its own right).
[52] Brennan & Buchanan, *id.*, argue that tax competition improves welfare because the size of government would be excessive in its absence.

just as businesses need not please customers as assiduously if they can form cartels to limit supply, so governments use tax harmonization to loosen their competitive constraints. Once exit from the reach of their harmonized rules has become impossible, only internal political dynamics can limit their power to coerce and expropriate as they choose.[53]

A third efficiency argument in favor of tax competition over coordination highlights its role in overcoming political constraints that force governments to prefer the interests of certain groups in society. According to this view, competition operates (at least in theory) as a credible threat in the hands of policymakers when they refuse to meet the demands of local interest groups. It is important to note, however, that competition serves the interests of mobile residents and factors of production. Their power to leave incentivizes decision makers to promote the interests of mobile elements to the disadvantage of immobile factors of production and immobile residents. Hence, although competition may prevent policymakers from preferring certain groups among the immobile factors of production, as explained in Chapter 1, it also strengthens the mobile (e.g., capital) at the expense of the less mobile (e.g., labor).

The bottom line, then, is that tax competition can be more efficient than coordination in a number of important senses. It creates a diversity of governmental and tax regimes; it races governmental waste to the bottom; and it hinders (to some extent) the favoring of certain interest groups by policymakers. Tax competition does entail costs, the most serious of which is states' inability to collect taxes to fund public goods that involve spillovers. But there is no reason to decry the costs and downplay the benefits.[54] Moreover, regardless of how cumbersome the costs of tax competition might be, we must ask whether coordination is the appropriate way to deal with those costs, particularly in today's world, where the only way to achieve coordination is to shift from tax competition to multilateral negotiations.

4.3   Conclusion

The debate between supporters of tax competition and proponents of multilateral coordination is often portrayed as a struggle between the

---

[53] Daniel Shaviro, *Some Observations Concerning Multijurisdictional Tax Competition, in* REGULATORY COMPETITION AND ECONOMIC INTEGRATION: COMPARATIVE PERSPECTIVES 60 (Daniel C. Esty & Damien Geradin eds., 2001).

[54] Roin, *supra* note 25; Shaviro, *supra* note 53.

interest-based, self-serving market ideology, on the one hand, and the idea of promoting the public good, justice and cooperation on the other hand. The cooperative rhetoric suggests that if only policymakers were to try harder to put their narrow self-interests aside and cooperate toward building a multilateral regime, not only would we all be better off, but justice would be served as well. As this chapter has shown, however, this presumably Pareto-improving aspiration blurs the fact that despite being grounded on seemingly noble ideals of cooperation and distributive justice, coordination often advances the interests of specific groups and countries at the expense of others. The analysis in the chapter identified some of the winners and losers of cooperative policies in order to better evaluate such policies. It challenged the feasibility of establishing and sustaining a complex multilateral international tax regime that would coordinate basic tax mechanisms, mechanisms for alleviating double taxation, and tax rates among participating states. Collective-action problems, I argued, make such a regime unlikely, since the costs of defection, detection, and enforcement of sanctions seem prohibitive.

I further questioned the normative desirability of a comprehensive multilateral cooperative regime. While commonly held to be a universally beneficial strategy, the inefficiencies and potentially regressive outcomes of such a regime, both within and among states, casts doubts on whether it is necessarily or always desirable. Although coordination is certainly likely to improve participating states' ability to collect the taxes necessary for funding their public goods, there are important efficiency goals that tax competition supports. These include, among other things, the matching of public goods with individual preferences, the reduction of governmental waste, and the undercutting of political factors that lead policymakers to favor certain groups in distributing benefits.

In addition, the desirability of a coordinated tax regime was challenged on distributive grounds. The multilateral coordination of tax rates might, indeed, enable countries to tax mobile capital and thereby shift the tax burden back from less mobile labor to more mobile capital. However, restricting tax competition could have some very disturbing distributive effects for poor countries. The increase in taxation under a multilateral regime on cross-border investments could reduce the demand for labor in poorer countries, meaning lower wages. Poor countries may not be able to collect enough taxes to compensate labor for their lost wages, and the taxes they do collect may serve less needed goals. Thus, redistribution to the less mobile poor in developed countries could come at the expense of labor in poor countries.

As demonstrated in the previous chapters, ideas and initiatives commonly endorsed in the international tax arena often sound irrefutable. Upon closer scrutiny, however, it emerges that even very noble causes can yield ignoble results. This chapter has similarly demonstrated how cooperation, which is touted as a tool for saving the welfare state, can lead to outcomes that are not necessarily desirable. Most importantly, advocates of cooperation in international tax downplay the heterogeneity of the international community. In international tax, every policy chosen potentially affects different people, groups, and nations in different ways. Identifying the winners and losers from cooperative policies is therefore vital for evaluating the desirability of those polices. Cooperation should not be, and is not, the ultimate goal in international tax policy.

The next chapter will discuss cooperation in a more realistic setting. It will highlight some of the key cooperative efforts of the international tax community on a variety of issues asking the vital question of whether states' cooperation can be taken as proof of the desirability of the coordination regime for promoting their particular interests.

5

Cooperation and Its Discontents

Cooperation is touted as a universally beneficial strategy, presumed to be an important tool for promoting the collective good and building trust among a group of actors. Indeed, some notable international efforts have been possible solely due to cooperation. Thus, cooperation is, not surprisingly, enthusiastically advocated in international tax circles. The conventional rhetoric stresses the mutual benefits for actors who join the collective efforts and the net gain participants reap.[1] And yet, I have argued, contrary to this rhetoric, international tax cooperation would not necessarily serve the best interests of all parties involved. As I demonstrated in the previous chapters, cooperation could, in fact, yield inefficiencies as well as potentially regressive outcomes both among and within the cooperating states.

This chapter asks why some countries participate in efforts that do not serve their best interests. It reviews the key multilateral cooperative efforts in the area of international taxation: double-taxation prevention,

---

[1] *See, e.g.,* OECD, *Addressing Base Erosion and Profit Shifting* (2013), http://dx.doi.org/10 .1787/9789264192744-en:

> Though governments may have to provide unilateral solutions, there is value and necessity in providing an internationally co-ordinated approach. Collaboration and co-ordination will not only facilitate and reinforce domestic actions to protect tax bases, but will also be key to provide comprehensive international solutions that may satisfactorily respond to the issue. Co-ordination in that respect will also limit the need for individual jurisdictions' unilateral tax measures.

OECD, *Explanatory Statement, OECD/G20 Base Erosion and Profit Shifting Project* 4 (2015), https://www.oecd.org/ctp/beps-explanatory-statement-2015.pdf [hereinafter OECD, *Explanatory Statement*]:

> In a globalised economy, governments need to cooperate and refrain from harmful tax practices, to address tax avoidance effectively, and provide a more certain international environment to attract and sustain investment. Failure to achieve such cooperation would reduce the effectiveness of CIT as a tool for resource mobilisation, which would have a disproportionately harmful impact on developing countries.

the campaign against harmful tax competition, information-sharing initiatives, and efforts countering base erosion and profit-shifting. This review serves as the background for the theoretical analysis in the chapter, which attempts to explain the conundrum of why (some) countries cooperate against their best interests. The review will also be instrumental further on in the book, when I consider the design of a normatively desirable international tax regime.

The gap between the high hopes of cooperative arguments and its doubtful benefits emerges in three contexts of cooperative solutions. In Chapter 2, where I considered the potential of cooperative behavior in promoting global neutrality through unilateral alleviation of double taxation, I showed that cooperative behavior would not necessarily serve an individual country's best interests. Chapter 3, in examining bilateral cooperation in tax treaties for the prevention of double taxation, shed light on its potentially regressive results, that is, the harm it could cause to the interests of source countries. Lastly, Chapter 4's discussion of a hypothetical cooperative multilateral solution for preventing a race to the bottom in conditions of tax competition demonstrated not only the potential efficiency costs of harmonization but also its possible biases against labor in developing countries. Yet despite these controversial results, cooperation still seems to enjoy a positive reputation as an all-benefiting strategy, and countries are often encouraged to pursue cooperative strategies such as promoting neutrality, signing tax treaties, sharing information, and curtailing base erosion and profit shifting.

That cooperation can harm the interests of some actors is not, in itself, unexpected. Cooperation among a particular group of actors can clearly impair the interests of other parties. This is the classic case of cartels: market actors coordinate among themselves to increase their profits at the expense of noncooperating competitors or consumers in general. By constraining the competitive pressure, this kind of cooperation allows the cartel members to enjoy monopolistic gains at the expense of non-cartel competitors and consumers. One can think of a clear analogy in the international tax arena: when some countries cooperate in a way that is beneficial to them but imposes externalities on other states or even on their own taxpayers, this cooperation could undermine the efficiency of the international tax market as a whole. When this happens, cartelization can be criticized (as I have done in Chapter 4, for example). But the very existence of such cooperation should come as no surprise since all the cooperating parties benefit from cooperating and the costs are externalized to third parties who are not participants in the arrangement.

The cases of international tax cooperation that I focus on in this chapter differ from this in that they could potentially harm the interests of (some of) the actual parties to the cooperation. The question that I ask is why, if cooperation harms the interests of certain (mostly, developing) countries, do they join these efforts to begin with? If cooperation is not a good option for a potential participant, it should presumably refrain from joining. On the other hand, if participants are not coerced into cooperation, is their participation not clear indication of the desirability of the arrangement for them? Is the very fact that they endorse the cooperation by joining not proof in itself that it serves their interests? After all, why else would they cooperate? In other words, should we not rely on these actors to make the right choices for themselves?

Such claims are not uncommon. It has been asserted, for example, as noted in Chapter 3, that "[d]eveloping countries have benefited from the current bilateral tax treaty practice immensely, as their enthusiasm to conclude as many treaties as possible with developed countries proves. They have never been forced, nor have they claimed to have been forced, into concluding a bilateral treaty with a developed country."[2] In fact, goes the claim, it is actually developed countries that reject developing countries' requests to enter into such treaties and not vice versa.[3] This seems a reasonable approach; anything else would seem paternalistic. But as I argue here in this chapter, despite the absence of coercion when developing countries cooperate, cooperation does not necessarily serve their interests. Rather, their agreement *notwithstanding*, these actors could have been better off had cooperation not evolved in the first place, at least in some cases. In other words, their consent does not prove the desirability of the cooperative measure.

A well-known assertion made in collective-action contexts is that actors might defect even if the cooperation serves their own interests as well as the collective good. Less prevalent are the reverse arguments regarding why actors cooperate despite the fact that this may not serve their best interests. In this chapter, I argue that just as the decision to defect is often not proof that cooperation is not beneficial to the defecting party (as in a prisoner's dilemma scenario), the decision to cooperate is not evidence that cooperation is to the benefit of the cooperating parties. To show this, I will examine the path toward cooperation and explain the different ways in

---

[2] Yariv Brauner, *An International Tax Regime in Crystallization – Realities, Experiences and Opportunities*, 56 TAX L. REV. 259, 308 (2003).

[3] *Id.*

which the process producing bilateral and multilateral cooperation on tax matters can be constructed (whether deliberately or not) to manipulate the decisions of certain actors. I will expose why certain actors cooperate even though had they been given the choice ex ante, they would have preferred a different solution or even no solution altogether.

The chapter begins with a brief overview of the cooperative efforts orchestrated by developed countries in different multilateral forums. This brings to light the variety of issues for which cooperation has been sought as a solution and the degree to which states have endorsed the various cooperative initiatives. The tax treaties regime – its establishment, proliferation, and entrenchment – is analyzed not only as a platform for bilateral tax treaty negotiations but also as a model of an international tax system where domestic rules tend to converge. This is followed by a discussion of the less successful initiative to curtail harmful tax competition and its still-evolving successor: the campaign to increase transparency through information sharing. This overview concludes with the ambitious BEPS Project and its yet-to-be determined results.

The review demonstrates that cooperation has not always been successfully attained despite the significant multilateral efforts. Arguably, this finding supports the claim that when countries do not wish to cooperate, they simply can refuse to do so and that, given this assumption, when they do agree to cooperate, their consent can be taken as proof of the desirability of the cooperation for them. I will show, however, that the presumably voluntary nature of the cooperation is not, per se, proof that the regime benefits all of its participants, just as a single state's refusal to cooperate is not sweeping indication of the regime *not* being in participants' best interests. I support this claim through a discussion of the key potential flaws of the path toward cooperation: strategic interactions; substantial asymmetries between countries; network products and their inherent lock-in and cartelistic effects; and the problematics of agenda setting. In certain circumstances, these mechanisms put states (developing states in particular) in a position where they willingly cooperate even though, ex ante, they would rather cooperation not evolved. To explain the historic asymmetry of the international tax regime, in benefiting developed countries, I describe the unique position of OECD countries in international taxation, where they tend to have the upper hand in strategic situations. I elaborate on how these countries managed to capture this position and why other countries have difficulty challenging this reality. Finally, I explain why an opportunity to redesign the international tax game toward a better – more efficient and just – regime may be now emerging.

5.1   A Brief History of International Tax Cooperation

a.   The First Phase: The Tax Treaties Network

Perhaps the most extensive cooperative project in international taxation to date is the impressive network of bilateral treaties for preventing double taxation described in Chapter 3. Although seemingly a regime of bilateral interactions, the tax treaties network is in fact the product of a multi-state initiative. It has been dominated since 1977 by the OECD, which formulated the model tax convention and is responsible for updating it through its detailed commentary.

The story of the tax treaties network begins with the publication of the first model treaty by the League of Nations in 1928,[4] after which two additional models were developed by its fiscal committee, the 1943 Mexico Draft and 1946 London Draft.[5] The two latter models offered two alternative frameworks for dividing the tax base, in recognition of the fact that each approach favors a different set of countries.[6] The models led to the signing of more than seventy bilateral double-taxation-avoidance agreements between 1946 and 1955.[7] This occurred in parallel to the establishment of the OEEC[8] by countries seeking the harmonization of bilateral tax treaties to eliminate double taxation, as concern over the phenomenon increased with the post-war expansion of economic integration.[9]

---

[4] The issue was first addressed by the Commission on International Credits at the International Financial Conference of 1920. *See* MICHAEL KOBETSKY, INTERNATIONAL TAXATION OF PERMANENT ESTABLISHMENTS: PRINCIPLES AND POLICY 150 (2011). In 1928, the League of Nations first published the Draft Model Treaty on Double Taxation and Tax Evasion, LEAGUE OF NATIONS, DRAFT MODEL TREATY ON DOUBLE TAXATION AND TAX EVASION (1928), http://www.un.org/esa/ffd/wp-content/uploads/2014/09/DoubleTaxation.pdf. In 1929, it established the Fiscal Committee. For a full review, *see* KEVIN HOLMES, INTERNATIONAL TAX POLICY AND DOUBLE TAX TREATIES: AN INTRODUCTION TO PRINCIPLES AND APPLICATION 57 (2007); STEFANO SIMONTACCHI, TAXATION OF CAPITAL GAINS UNDER THE OECD MODEL CONVENTION: WITH SPECIAL REGARD TO IMMOVABLE PROPERTY (2007).

[5] LONDON AND MEXICO MODEL TAX CONVENTIONS COMMENTARY AND TEXT, C.88.M.88.1946.II.A (Geneva, Nov. 1946), http://biblio-archive.unog.ch/Dateien/CouncilMSD/C-88-M-88-1946-II-A_EN.pdf.

[6] THOMAS RIXEN, THE POLITICAL ECONOMY OF INTERNATIONAL TAX GOVERNANCE 96 (2008).

[7] Adrian A. Kragen, *Double Income Taxation Treaties: The OECD Draft*, 52 CAL. L. REV. 306, 307 (1964).

[8] The Organization for European Economic Cooperation, which became the Organization for Economic Cooperation and Development (OECD) in 1960.

[9] By the year 1961, four reports entitled *The Elimination of Double Taxation* had been released by the Committee. OEEC, THE ELIMINATION OF DOUBLE TAXATION, FOURTH REPORT OF THE FISCAL COMMITTEE (1961), http://setis.library.usyd.edu.au/pubotbin/toccer-new?id=oeectax.sgml&images=acdp/gifs&data=/usr/ot&tag=law&part=4&division=div1.

The 1977 OECD Model Tax Convention on Income and Capital ("the OECD Model") was the next step toward international tax cooperation, initiated to provide "a means of settling on a uniform basis the most common problems that arise in the field of international juridical double taxation."[10] The OECD Model has since dominated the international tax world[11] and generated an explosion of bilateral tax treaties. There are currently more than 3,000 such treaties crafted on the basis of the Model,[12] which serves as the framework for the negotiation of these treaties, highly similar in coverage and language.[13] The OECD Model has continued to evolve, through amendments recommended by the Committee on Fiscal Affairs.[14] The OECD also provides guidelines, commentaries, and best practices, which are often used to design and interpret treaties and laws and thus viewed as "soft laws."[15]

The OECD Model does more than simply serve as a manual for negotiations between countries.[16] It has essentially facilitated significant convergence of key elements of the tax systems of the states that comprise the network of bilateral tax treaties.[17] Reuven Avi-Yonah has described this process as amounting almost to international customary

[10] OECD COMMON FISCAL AFFAIRS, MODEL TAX CONVENTION ON INCOME AND ON CAPITAL, at I-1 (1997).

[11] Yariv Brauner & Pasquale Pistone, Introduction, in BRICS AND THE EMERGENCE OF INTERNATIONAL TAX COORDINATION 3 (Yariv Brauner & Pasquale Pistone eds., 2015).

[12] OECD, Developing a Multilateral Instrument to Modify Bilateral Tax Treaties 11(2014), http://www.oecd-ilibrary.org/taxation/developing-a-multilateral-instrument-to-modify-bilateral-tax-treaties_9789264219250-en.

[13] Yariv Brauner, Treaties in the Aftermath of BEPS, 41 BROOK. J. INT'L L. 973, 975 (2016).

[14] The Committee on Fiscal Affairs recommended several amendments to the model in subsequent years. Since 1991, the Committee has made periodic amendments, recognizing that the OECD Model should be revised more frequently. KOBETSKY, supra note 4. The latest version is OECD, MODEL TAX CONVENTION ON INCOME AND ON CAPITAL (FULL VERSION) (2014), http://dx.doi.org/10.1787/9789264239081-en.

[15] See Allison Christians, How Nations Share, 87 IND. L.J. 1407, 1411 (2012); A.P. Morriss & L. Moberg, Cartelizing Taxes: Understanding the OECD's Campaign against "Harmful Tax Competition," 4 COLUM. J. TAX L. 1, 21, 33 (2012).

[16] See, e.g., Itai Grinberg, Breaking BEPS: The New International Tax Diplomacy 38 (2015), https://ssrn.com/abstract=2652894 or http://dx.doi.org/10.2139/ssrn.2652894.

[17] Brauner, supra note 2, at 290: "In spite of some differences, most of the components of the current international tax regime are highly harmonized, and where they are not, they are within a tight margin of possible rules with which any international tax professional is fairly familiar." See also Brauner, supra note 13, at 977–78 ("The standardization of international tax law is not confined, however, to tax treaty law. Since (at least) the post-WWII period, international tax laws of essentially all countries have significantly converged."); Eduardo A. Baistrocchi, The International Tax Regime and the BRIC World: Elements for a Theory, 2013 OXFORD J. LEGAL STUD. 733 (describing the creeping convergence of BRICS countries into the international tax regime).

law.[18] The OECD has also made efforts to include in the process some nonmember countries, international organizations, and interested parties, allowing their input into what was once a closed group of developed countries[19] and thereby arguably increasing the legitimacy of its decisions.

Attempts to devise competing models, were far less successful than the OECD Model. In 1988, for example, the UN introduced a competing model for tax treaties, which was designed to accommodate the needs of developing countries. Based on the latter model and entitled "Model Double Taxation Convention between Developed and Developing Countries," it was devised by an ad hoc group that was formed for this purpose in 1968. The UN model reflects the fact that its membership included at the time both Soviet bloc and developing countries, whose tax systems differ significantly from the tax laws of Western, developed economies.[20] Despite such efforts, however, the OECD Model still rules the tax treaties sphere.

As detailed in Chapter 3, the conventional view on tax treaties focuses on their alleged indispensability for alleviating double taxation of cross-border transactions. The ubiquity of these treaties has led many to view them as the ultimate cooperative tool for facilitating trade and prosperity through the reduction of double taxation. However, as explained, treaties have been criticized for being biased against host countries (and, hence, developing countries) in their allocation of tax revenues and their failure to increase cross-border investments.[21] This criticism implies that what is usually regarded as a cooperative effort led by the OECD to prevent the harmful results of a collective-action problem (double taxation) is actually a mechanism that serves the interests of cooperating developed countries at the expense of other countries. Accordingly, although treaties do relieve some of the friction between national tax systems, this is likely at the expense of some (that is, developing) countries.

This recalls the cartel analogy referred to at the outset: developed countries presumably are simply imposing externalities on developing

---

[18] Reuven S. Avi-Yonah, *International Tax as International Law*, 57 TAX L. REV. 483 (2003); Reuven S. Avi-Yonah, *The Structure of International Taxation: A Proposal for Simplification*, 74 TEX. L. REV. 1301, 1303 (1996) ("[C]ontrary to a priori expectations, a coherent international tax regime exists that enjoys nearly universal support and that underlies the complexities of the international aspects of individual countries' tax systems.").

[19] OECD, *supra* note 10, I-3.

[20] *See* Morriss & Moberg, *supra* note 15, at 18. For more information on the UN model and a comparison between the UN and OECD models, *see* JENS WITTENDORFF, TRANSFER PRICING AND THE ARM'S LENGTH PRINCIPLE IN INTERNATIONAL TAX LAW 249–52 (2010).

[21] See Chapter 3 for the empirical debate over the link between treaties and increased investment.

countries. But as noted, what is puzzling is why countries (mainly host) that arguably lose out from signing tax treaties enter these agreements to begin with. On the other hand, is the fact that they sign these treaties not proof that these arrangements are good for them?[22] Later in this chapter, I will counter this intuition by suggesting that in joining the tax treaties club, host countries are not necessarily indicating the desirability of this regime from their perspective but, rather, strategic considerations may account for their decision to join. This may have more to do with the way that the process of treaty signing is structured than with the actual desirability of the treaties themselves: that is, the international tax game is set up in such a way so as to make joining the regime better than the other available alternatives.

b. *The Second Phase: Curtailing Tax Competition*

Double taxation was perhaps the first issue that led the international community to attempt cooperation in taxation, but certainly not the only one. Years after the successful launch of the treaty project, the international tax community shifted its focus to tax competition. The cooperative efforts began with a campaign against so-called "harmful tax competition."[23] Countries, in particular developed ones, were becoming increasingly concerned with the ability of their residents (both individuals and MNEs) to shift their activities and profits to more attractive jurisdictions.[24] At the same time, states began to realize they could not fight tax competition unilaterally.[25] The OECD therefore embarked on a widespread initiative to combat tax competition.[26] It was argued that this "harmful"

---

[22] As I explained, some interpret host countries' consent to sign these treaties as signaling that they serve their interests as well as the desirability of the cooperative mechanism in general. *See, e.g.*, Brauner, *supra* note 2, at 308.

[23] Morriss & Moberg, *supra* note 15, at 4 (describing the evolution of the OECD campaign against tax competition).

[24] *Yariv Brauner, What the BEPS?*, 16 FLA. TAX REV. 55, 61–67 (2014).

[25] *See* Morriss & Moberg, *supra* note 15, at 34–38 (describing generally how U.S., French, and German support for multilateral action grew when faced with the constraints of a more globalized economy).

[26] The OECD produced two 1987 reports on the issue: OECD, *Tax Havens: Measures to Prevent Abuse by Taxpayers, in* INTERNATIONAL TAX AVOIDANCE AND EVASION: FOUR RELATED STUDIES 19 (1987); OECD, *Taxation and the Abuse of Bank Secrecy, in* INTERNATIONAL TAX AVOIDANCE AND EVASION: FOUR RELATED STUDIES 107 (1987). For a detailed analysis of the process through which tax competition got onto the OECD agenda, the evolution of the global dialogue, and the steps that were ultimately taken, wee Diane M. Ring, *Who Is Making International Tax Policy? International Organizations as Power Players in a High Stakes World*, 33 FORDHAM INT'L L.J. 649, 703–15 (2010).

competition was eroding national tax bases, shifting tax burdens to immobile factors, and hampering redistributive goals.[27] The campaign against tax competition drew a lot of attention and signaled a serious attempt to initiate multilateral cooperation, which culminated in the 1998 OECD Report on Harmful Tax Competition.[28]

The report reflected not only a shift toward multilateral action but also a change in approach within the OECD "away from the past practice of articulating problems and recommending general solutions to pursuing a coordinated and active effort to counteract tax avoidance and evasion, to reduce financial privacy, and to influence states to end 'unfair' tax competition."[29] On the background of the rise of tax havens and tax evasion,[30] the initial strategy was to tackle the problem through the coordination of permissible and impermissible policies. As the Report notes, "countries should remain free to design their own tax systems ... as long as they abide by internationally accepted standards."[31] Specifically, the report condemned the use of tax policies to attract capital from other

---

[27] OECD, *Harmful Tax Competition: An Emerging Global Issue* 14 (1998), http://www.oecd.org/tax/transparency/44430243.pdf.

Globalization has, however, also had the negative effects of opening up new ways by which companies and individuals can minimize and avoid taxes and in which countries can exploit these new opportunities by developing tax policies aimed primarily at diverting financial and other geographically mobile capital. These actions induce potential distortions in the patterns of trade and investment and reduce global welfare. As discussed in detail below, these schemes can erode national tax bases of other countries, may alter the structure of taxation (by shifting part of the tax burden from mobile to relatively immobile factors and from income to consumption) and may hamper the application of progressive tax rates and the achievement of redistributive goals. Pressure of this sort can result in changes in tax structures in which all countries may be forced by spillover effects to modify their tax bases, even though a more desirable result could have been achieved through intensifying international co-operation. More generally, tax policies in one economy are now more likely to have repercussions on other economies.

The European Union also introduced a code of conduct aimed at tackling harmful tax competition and coordinating action on the European level. In 1996, the European Economic and Financial Affairs Council (ECOFIN) decided to seek a coordinated solution to contend with harmful tax competition. In 1997, the Code of Conduct for Business Taxation was adopted. 98/C 2/01 CONCLUSION OF THE COFFIN COUNCIL MEETING, 12/1/1997, http://eur-lex.europa.eu/legal-content/EN/ALL/?uri=OJ%3AC%3A1998%3A002%3ATOC.

[28] OECD, *supra* note 27.   [29] Morriss & Moberg, *supra* note 15, at 43.

[30] Allison Christians, *Avoidance, Evasion, and Taxpayer Morality*, 44 WASH. U. J.L. & POL'Y 39 (2014).

[31] OECD, *supra* note 27, at 15.

countries and set out a list of factors for determining whether a preferential regime is potentially harmful and four key criteria for defining tax
havens.[32] The OECD set-up a Harmful Tax Practices forum, which was
assigned the mission of blacklisting tax havens, including those involving non-OECD members.[33] A series of related reports followed, list-
ing harmful tax regimes and calling for sanctions against uncooperative
states.[34]

Some claimed that the OECD's list of harmful tax jurisdictions and
the agreements signed with some tax havens were "a visible sign of the
project's success."[35] This was hardly the case. Criticism was voiced by
off-shore jurisdictions,[36] while political pressure within the OECD and
participating countries[37] weakened support for the project;[38] by 2005, it
"was barely alive."[39] With this drop in support, the OECD set its sights on
another target, tax evasion, and focused its efforts on transparency. The
strategies of the Report on Harmful Tax Competition were, consequently,
replaced by the goals of information sharing and transparency.[40]

---

[32] Such factors included no tax or only nominal taxes, lack of effective exchange of information, lack of transparency, and no substantial activities. OECD, *supra* note 27, at 22:

> [The Chapter] discusses the factors to be used in identifying, within the context of this
> Report, tax-haven jurisdictions and harmful preferential tax regimes in non-haven
> jurisdictions. It focuses on identifying the factors that enable tax havens and harm-
> ful preferential tax regimes in OECD Member and non-member countries to attract
> highly mobile activities, such as financial and other service activities. The Chapter pro-
> vides practical guidelines to assist governments in identifying tax havens and in dis-
> tinguishing between acceptable and harmful preferential tax regimes.

[33] OECD, *Harmful Tax Competition*, http://ec.europa.eu/taxation_customs/taxation/
company_tax/harmful_tax_practices/index_en.htm.

[34] Allison Christians, *Sovereignty, Taxation, and Social Contract*, 18 MINN. J. INT'L L. 99, 127–
37 (2009); OECD, *Action Plan 5: Countering Harmful Tax Practices More Effectively* 17, 18
(2014).

[35] Morriss & Moberg, *supra* note 15, at 47. Steven A. Dean, *Philosopher Kings and International Tax*, 58 HASTINGS L. J., 911, 961. (2007) notes that tax haven's agreement is not
necessarily indication of their future compliance with the initial agreement.

[36] *Id.* at 50; OECD, *Tax Co-Operation: Towards a Level Playing Field* (2006), http://www.oecd
.org/tax/transparency/44430286.pdf.

[37] Christians, *supra* note 30, at 6; Ring, *supra* note 26, at 716–18 (describing the specific and
very strategic roles played by different international organizations in the process).

[38] OECD countries and the offshore financial centers began negotiating on a multilateral
basis, with the OECD agreeing to avoid targeted sanctions until OECD members complied
with the standards. *See* Morriss & Moberg, *supra* note 15, at 50.

[39] Morriss & Moberg, *supra* note 15, at 51.

[40] "A country would be removed from tax haven blacklists by having in place at least twelve tax
information exchange agreements (TIEAs) pursuant to OECD-drafted model language."
Christians, *supra* note 30, at 6.

Thus, the OECD's attempt to generate full-scale cooperation to contend with tax competition did not succeed. The failure of this project exemplifies the collective-action problems that hinder efforts to coordinate a large number of actors with a wide range of interests to promote. It can also, however, be seen as indication of the apparent "free will" of countries: presumably when a country believes that cooperation will not be to its benefit, it can – and does – refuse to cooperate. I do not underestimate the difficulties involved in achieving cooperation; nor do I deny the possibility that states that do not benefit from cooperation might refuse to participate in order to promote their self-interests. These are certainly major barriers to even the most desirable of cooperative initiatives. Yet the de facto failure of the harmful tax competition project does not imply that whenever states agree to cooperate, we can assume that cooperation serves them well. The strategic nature of the international tax game is such that states' decisions are constrained not only by their preferences but also by the strategies available to them. Consequently, just as a state's choice to defect is not necessarily proof that cooperation is *not* to its benefit, the choice to cooperate is not proof that cooperation *is* in its best interests. It is still possible – and, as we will see, quite probable in our context – that in some cases it would have been in that state's best interest if cooperation had not emerged as an option at all.

c. The Third Phase: Information Sharing and Transparency

Following the effective failure of its campaign against tax competition, the OECD redirected its efforts to the more modest goal of increasing transparency of tax systems and information sharing among countries. This third stage of international tax cooperation proved more successful. Rather than curtail tax competition, its central thrust was to assist states in collecting taxes on their residents' investments abroad when the latter attempt to evade taxes.

1. Bilateral Instruments

Treaties for the prevention of double taxation typically include clauses that obligate the signatory states to provide each other with information.[41]

---

[41] See the OECD's Model Tax Convention on Income and on Capital, OECD, *supra* note 10, I-11 § 26.

This arrangement tended to be limited in scope, however, as information was provided only upon specific request.[42] In 2002,[43] the OECD issued the model Tax Information Exchange Agreements (TIEAs), aimed at promoting international cooperation on tax matters through the exchange of information.[44] This instrument was a product of the OECD's harmful tax competition project, with the purpose of enabling countries to access information about their residents' investments in tax havens.[45] To be removed from the harmful tax haven blacklist, countries were required

---

[42] *Id*: "If information is requested by a Contracting State in accordance with this Article, the other Contracting State shall use its information gathering measures to obtain the requested information, even though that other State may not need such information for its own tax purposes."

[43] Efforts to promote the exchange of information actually date back to 1977, when the EU took some steps toward cooperation on enforcement and transparency of information. In 1977, the European Council approved a directive intended to facilitate mutual assistance between national tax authorities, Council Directive 77/799/EEC, Mutual Assistance by the Competent Authorities of the Member States in the Field of Direct Taxation, 1977 O.J. (L 336) 15. This was replaced in 2011 by Council Directive 2011/16/EU, which aligned standards for transparency and exchange of information on request with the international standards. The directive was amended in 2014, by Council Directive 2014/107/EU, which "extend[ed] cooperation between tax authorities to automatic exchange of financial account information." EU, *Enhanced Administrative Cooperation in the Field of (Direct) Taxation* (2011) (with amendments as adopted in 2014), http://ec.europa.eu/taxation_customs/taxation/tax_cooperation/mutual_assistance/direct_tax_directive/index_en.htm. It was amended again in 2016 Council Directive 2011/16/EU, Administrative Cooperation in the Field of taxation and repealing Directive 77/799/EEC, 2016 O.J. (L 64) 1–12.

In 2003, the EU endorsed Council Directive 2003/48, Taxation of Savings Income in the Form of Interest Payments, 2003 O.J. (L 157) 38 [hereinafter Savings Directive], which "mandates ... that member states *either* exchange information with one another *or* impose a withholding tax to be deducted from interest income." Itai Grinberg, *Beyond FATCA: An Evolutionary Moment for the International Tax System* 13 (2012) https://papers.ssrn.com/sol3/papers.cfm?abstract_id=1996752. notes that "Most countries within the EU adopted the information exchange regime. The three EU member bank secrecy states adopted the withholding tax system, as did many of the ten dependent territories of the UK and the Netherlands, including the Channel Islands." *Id.* at 20.

[44] OECD, Exchange of Information, Tax Information Exchange Agreements (TIEAs) (2002), http://www.oecd.org/ctp/exchange-of-tax-information/taxinformationexchangeagreementstieas.htm. The Convention was developed by the OECD and the Council of Europe and was based on a first draft prepared by the Committee on Fiscal Affairs. OECD, *supra* note 10, I-11; OECD Convention on Mutual Administrative Assistance in Tax Matters (1988) (with amendments as adopted in 2010), http://www.keepeek.com/Digital-Asset-Management/oecd/taxation/the-multilateral-convention-on-mutual-administrative-assistance-in-tax-matters_9789264115606-en#.WF0lRvl95nI.

[45] Miranda Stewart, *International Tax, the G20 and Asia Pacific*, 1 ASIA & PAC. POL'Y STUD. 484, 490 (2014).

INTERNATIONAL TAX POLICY

to sign twelve TIEAs.[46] Endorsed by many countries,[47] the model is not a binding instrument but, rather, provides the "basis for an integrated bundle of bilateral treaties."[48] A party to the multilateral TIEAs is bound by their terms only with respect to the specific parties with which it has signed the treaties.[49] Concerns raised by tax haven countries, which sought a voice in the coercive process of the blacklisting and TIEAs requirement, led to the establishment of the Global Forum on Transparency and Tax Information Exchange.[50] At first designed only to track the signing of TIEAs, the forum subsequently evolved into an "unprecedented in scale and depth"[51] process of peer review of domestic laws to facilitate the practical implementation of the agreements.

The 2008 financial crisis led to an intensified wave of cooperation over transparency standards and exchange of information. Countries were encouraged anew by the Global Forum to sign bilateral TIEAs.[52] Article 26 of the OECD Model Tax Convention, which sets standards for exchange of information on request, was also updated in 2012, expanding states' ability to demand information regarding a group of taxpayers by removing the need to name the specific taxpayers targeted in the request.[53]

---

[46] Christians, *supra* note 30, at 6; Stewart, *supra* note 45.

[47] For a complete list, *see* http://www.oecd.org/ctp/harmful/43775845.pdf.

[48] OECD, Agreement on Exchange of Information on Tax Matters, Introduction § 5 (2002), http://www.oecd.org/ctp/exchange-of-tax-information/2082215.pdf.

[49] *Id.* For a list of the bilateral treaties signed, *see* http://www.oecd.org/tax/transparency/exchangeoftaxinformationagreements.htm.

[50] On the Global Forum, *see* www.oecd.org/tax/transparency. Stewart, *supra* note 45, at 490, describes the forum as follows:

> The Global Forum was restructured at its meeting in Mexico in 2009 to give all country members an equal vote, even though technically it remains a program initiated by the OECD. Member countries contribute to administrative costs, with the bulk of funding coming from OECD member countries. The Forum is open to all and now has a membership of 121 countries, plus the EU and numerous international organizations as observers. The TIEA process and the Global Forum directly engage national tax agencies with each other. However, the Forum is a "soft" institution in the sense that it has no rule-making or administrative power of its own and is not supported by any multilateral treaty or other delegated legal authority.

[51] Stewart, *supra* note 45.

[52] Between 2008 and 2011, 700 TIEA treaties were signed. The background to this surge was not only the global financial crisis but also the UBS bank and other tax haven scandals. *See* T.A. Van Kampen & L.J. Rijke, *The Kredietbank Luxembourg and the Liechtenstein Tax Affairs: Notes on the Balance between the Exchange of Information between States and the Protection of Fundamental Rights*, 5 Econ. Tax Rev. 221 (2008).

[53] OECD, *Tax: OECD Updates OECD Model Tax Convention to Extend Information Requests to Groups* (July 18, 2012), http://www.oecd.org/ctp/taxoecdupdatesoecdmodeltaxconventiontoextendinformationrequeststogroups.htm.

Another interesting development that began as a unilateral initiative but has since produced considerable similar mechanisms is the United States' unilateral adoption of the FATCA[54] in 2010. Under FATCA, foreign financial institutions are required to report identifying information and documents for U.S. account holders, account numbers and balances, and any income paid to those accounts, as well as required to withhold 30 percent on certain payments to anyone not in compliance with FATCA requirements. Interestingly, the unilateral move represented by FATCA has enhanced multilateral cooperation. Peer countries have developed and signed agreements with the United States in order to reduce compliance costs and legal friction for foreign financial institutions (in particular, client-confidentiality obligations).[55] Even more significant, however, is the adoption of FATCA-like mechanisms by other jurisdictions.[56] This unilateral initiative thus evolved into a full-fledged multilateral accord, when the Common Reporting Standard under the Standard for Automatic Exchange of Financial Account Information in Tax Matters (described in Section 3) adopted a standard that "draws extensively on the intergovernmental approach to implementing FATCA."[57]

2. The (Multilateral) Convention on Mutual Administrative Assistance in Tax Matters

In 2010, the G-20 called on the Global Forum to amend the OECD Convention on Mutual Administrative Assistance in Tax Matters.[58] Originally developed in 1988 to set an international standard on exchange of

---

[54] Hiring Incentives to Restore Employment Act, Pub. L. No. 111–147, § 501, 124 Stat. 71 (2010).

[55] For a detailed description of the process see Joshua D. Blank & Ruth Mason, *Exporting FATCA*, 142 TAX NOTES 1245 (Mar. 17, 2014).

[56] *Id.*

[57] OECD, *Standard for Automatic Exchange of Financial Account Information in Tax Matters* 5 (2014). For a timeline of the process see Ricardo García Antón, The 21st Century Multilateralism in International Taxation: The Emperor's New Clothes?, 8 WORLD TAX J. 147, 168 (2016); Alessandro Turina, *Visible, Though Not Visible in Itself: Transparency at the Crossroads of International Financial Regulation and International Taxation*, 8 WORLD TAX J. 378 (2016).

[58] The 1988 OECD Convention on Mutual Administrative Assistance in Tax Matters was amended with a new protocol, and countries were expected to sign it. OECD & Council of Europe, Protocol Amending the Convention on Mutual Administrative Assistance in Tax Matters (2011), http://www.oecd.org/ctp/exchange-of-tax-information/ENG-Amended-Convention.pdf.

information on request and open it to all countries, the convention had little impact until its 2010 amendment. Since then, more than sixty countries have signed it.[59] Recognition of the convention has continued to grow with the support of the G-20, which recently called on all countries to sign it without delay.[60]

An interesting development in this context has been the attempt to formulate a standard requiring automatic exchange of information. Under the TIEAs regime, information is provided "on demand"; that is, a country is in compliance when it properly responds to a request for information by a treaty partner for specific information.[61] Current efforts are being directed at pushing states to actively collect specific information and share it with other states. For example, the multilateral convention provides for on-demand exchange of information and expands cooperation to allow (should states so choose) for spontaneous and automatic exchanges as well as "all possible forms of administrative co-operation between States in the assessment and collection of taxes, in particular with a view to combating tax avoidance and evasion. This co-operation ranges from exchange of information to the recovery of foreign tax claims."[62]

3. Automatic Exchange of Information

Since 2012, various attempts have been made to establish a uniform automatic system for information exchange that goes beyond the elective, passive compliance, "upon demand" system and imposes affirmative duties on states to collect and transfer information. France, Germany, Italy, Spain, the United Kingdom, and the United States have been joined by

---

[59] For a complete list of participating jurisdictions, see http://www.oecd.org/ctp/exchange-of-tax-information/Status_of_convention.pdf.

[60] Morriss & Moberg, *supra* note 15, at 55, stress the unique multilateral nature of the Convention:

> Because it is multilateral, jurisdictions do not negotiate over adapting the provisions to the particulars of their circumstances but can only alter their obligations by making reservations, which can be withdrawn later. Moreover, as a country enters the convention, it enters an agreement with all prior signatories. . . . The updated Convention may be limited to issues of disclosure and transparency, but it is a large step towards reaching the goal of a tax agreement including all countries of the world.

> Miranda Stewart, *supra* note 45, at 491–92, notes the establishment of a coordinating body of representatives of national revenue agencies and argues that "this coordinating body has the potential to develop greater powers and institutional character."

[61] OECD, *supra* note 47.

[62] OECD & Council of Europe, *Text of the Revised Explanatory Report to the Convention on Mutual Administrative Assistance in Tax Matters as Amended by the Protocol* (2010).

COOPERATION AND ITS DISCONTENTS

the rest of the G-20 members in an initiative to develop an automatic multilateral tax-information-exchange standard[63] that would require states to periodically share bulk taxpayer information.[64] The support for automatic exchange of information was behind the OECD 2013 report "A Step Change in Tax Transparency,"[65] which laid out practical steps toward applying an information-exchange standard and formed the basis for the 2014 Standard for Automatic Exchange of Financial Account Information in Tax Matters.[66] The G-20 finance ministers endorsed a Common Reporting Standard for automatic exchange of tax information, as did thirty-four OECD member countries and several nonmember countries. The standard requires states to obtain specific financial account information from their financial institutions and automatically share it with other states on an annual basis. In addition, more than 101 jurisdictions have publicly committed to implementing an automatic information exchange, with more than fifty-five of them[67] committing to an ambitious timetable beginning in 2017 (early adopters).[68]

The idea of exchange of information emerged also as part of the BEPS Project in the context of transfer pricing.[69] Action Plan 13 and its deliverables recommended the development of a common pool of information, to be called "Country by Country Reporting" (CbCR). Under this proposed system, reporting regarding transfer-pricing mechanisms are to be submitted in the jurisdiction where the ultimate parent company

---

[63] OECD, *Standard for Automatic Exchange of Financial Account Information in Tax Matters* (2014).

[64] Another global initiative for knowledge sharing and tax cooperation is the International Tax Dialogue (ITD), a joint initiative launched by the European Commission, Inter-American Development Bank, International Monetary Fund, OECD, World Bank Group, and Inter-American Center of Tax Administrations.

[65] See OECD, *A Step Change in Tax Transparency* (2013), http://www.oecd.org/ctp/exchange-of-tax-information/taxtransparency_G8report.pdf.

[66] OECD, *supra* note 63, at 10.

[67] Interestingly, the United States did not commit to this. It has indicated – perhaps instead – that it has entered into intergovernmental agreements (IGAs) with other jurisdictions to meet its FATCA requirements. The Model 1A IGAs entered into by the United States acknowledge the need for the United States to attain equivalent levels of reciprocal automatic information exchange with partner jurisdictions. They also include a political commitment to pursue the adoption of regulations and to advocate and support relevant legislation to achieve these levels of reciprocal automatic exchange. For the U.S.'s long-standing unilateral position on information sharing see e.g., Steven A. Dean, *Neither Rules nor Standards*, 87 NOTRE DAME L. REV. 537, 568 (2012).

[68] For a complete list, see http://www.oecd.org/tax/transparency/AEOI-commitments.pdf.

[69] Ana Paula Dourado, *May You Live in Interesting Times*, 44 INTERTAX 2, 5 (2016) (supporting the exchange of information under the various BEPS actions).

resides and shared automatically between jurisdictions. This proposal was criticized for being tailored specifically to the needs of OECD countries, as the MNEs that would be subject to its automatic exchange system would be the largest ones and, accordingly, likely residents of OECD countries.[70] Moreover, the mechanism endorsed in the recommendations would be costly for poor countries, which lack the enforcement agencies, computing capacities, and administrative capabilities necessary for implementation.[71] The automatic exchange of information was also endorsed in the recommendations in BEPS Action Plan 5, entitled "Countering Harmful Tax Practices More Effectively,"[72] with the focus on the exchange of different types of ruling information between tax authorities to curtail the taxpayers' ability to tax plan and thereby limit their tax liability.

Increased transparency – as I argue in Chapter 7 – likely improves overall global welfare, since it reduces a market failure (i.e., information asymmetry). But is it in the best interests of developing countries to cooperate with such transparency-enhancing processes given the extra costs and lower benefits they must consequently bear?[73] The underlying point of the discussion below will be that the adoption of an information-sharing agreement, like other cooperative measures, is not *necessarily* indicative of its being beneficial for the cooperating state any more than initial reluctance to cooperate is indicative of the inadequacy of cooperation; hence, such desirability requires independent substantiation. As Section 2 will

---

[70] For a criticism of this tool, see Reuven S. Avi-Yonah & Haiyan Xu, *Evaluating BEPS* 18 (Michigan Law, Public Law & Legal Theory Research Paper Series No. 493, Jan. 16, 2016), http://papers.ssrn.com/sol3/papers.cfm?abstract_id=2716125.

[71] The BEPS Monitoring Group, *OECD BEPS Scorecard*, 76 TAX NOTES INT'L 243, 251 (Oct. 20, 2014) ("At present, corporate data, even if they originate from state legal requirements, e.g. for publication of company accounts, are in practice extremely difficult to access. Hence, both researchers and even government bodies such as tax authorities are dependent on private providers of data-bases. This is particularly damaging to developing countries, both because of the high cost of subscriptions and because the coverage of developing countries in such databases is poor.").

[72] OECD, *Countering Harmful Tax Practices More Effectively, Taking into Account Transparency and Substance*, OECD/G20 BASE EROSION AND PROFIT SHIFTING PROJECT (2015), http://www.oecd.org/ctp/countering-harmful-tax-practices-more-effectively-taking-into-account-transparency-and-substance-action-5-2015-final-report-9789264241190-en .htm.

[73] *See* Ana Paula Dourado, International Standards, Base Erosion and Developing Countries, *in* TAX DESIGN ISSUES WORLDWIDE 179 (Geerten M.M. Michielse & Victor Thuronyi eds., 2015). But *see* Itai Grinberg, *Taxing Capital Income in Emerging Countries: Will FATCA Open the Door?*, 5 WORLD TAX J. 325 (2013) (describing the benefits of a uniform reporting standard for emerging economies as well as for financial institutions).

explain, the strategic nature of the international tax game can facilitate either cooperation or defection and not necessarily in relation to any inherent desirability of the cooperative measure. The insight that cooperation is not an indicator of desirability is just as relevant (perhaps even more so) with regard to the BEPS, which is currently a prominent cooperative framework in international taxation.

d. The BEPS Project

The latest – some claim, most ambitious – multilateral initiative to date set out at the end of 2015 when the OECD released the highly anticipated deliverables of the Base Erosion and Profits Shifting (BEPS) project. This project is specifically aimed at preventing tax planning of various kinds so as to help states restore their eroding tax bases. On the background of the 2008 financial crisis and Lichtenstein disclosure, along with the demands of NGOs and protests by citizens[74] the G-20 finance ministers waged a coordinated fight against base erosion and profit shifting, concurring that multilateralism is vital for resolving the global economy's difficulties.[75] These efforts came in response to significant changes in the formerly prevailing international tax regime that "lead[] some to suspect its demise."[76] The BEPS Action Plan summarized the situation nicely:

> Taxation is at the core of countries' sovereignty, but the interaction of domestic tax rules in some cases leads to gaps and frictions. When designing their domestic tax rules, sovereign states may not sufficiently take into account the effect of other countries' rules. The interaction of independent sets of rules enforced by sovereign countries creates frictions, including potential double taxation for corporations operating in several countries. It also creates gaps, in cases where corporate income is not taxed at all, either by the country of source or the country of residence, or is only taxed at nominal rates. . . .
>
> Inaction in this area would likely result in some governments losing corporate tax revenue, the emergence of competing sets of international standards, and the replacement of the current consensus-based framework

---

[74] Lee Seppard, *Saint-Amans Takes a BEPS Victory Lap*, 80 TAX NOTES INT'L 212 (Oct. 19, 2015) also notes the "unwillingness of Europe's bank masters to monetize the bad loans except in ways limited to bank recapitalization."

[75] G20, *G20 Leaders Declaration* 48 (June 18–19, 2012); Brauner, *supra* note 24, at 57.

[76] Yariv Brauner notes two primary developments through which such a demise manifests itself. One is the active role taken by emerging economies in the reversal of the trend toward maximizing residence taxation and thereby reducing the level of convergence and standardization within the international tax regime. Second is the increasing ability of MNEs to avoid states' regulatory powers, which the international tax regime was unable to prevent. Brauner, *supra* note 24, at 63–64.

by unilateral measures, which could lead to global tax chaos marked by the massive re-emergence of double taxation. In fact, if the Action Plan fails to develop effective solutions in a timely manner, some countries may be persuaded to take unilateral action for protecting their tax base, resulting in avoidable uncertainty and unrelieved double taxation.[77]

The OECD was quick to take up this challenge with the speedy production of an initial report and fifteen action plans on central subjects of concern for international tax policymakers. Action 15 in particular raises the intriguing option of developing a multilateral hard law instrument to update bilateral tax treaties.[78] This project generated high hopes and expectations. As the 2013 BEPS Action Plan stated, "The BEPS project marks a turning point in the history of international co-operation on taxation"[79] for it promises to "develop a new set of standards to prevent BEPS issues such as double non-taxation through hybrid mismatch arrangements, base erosion via interest deductions, or artificial profit shifting through transfer pricing."[80] Even prior to the release of the deliverables, some urged the OECD to deliver a meaningful reform through the BEPS Project[81] and to pursue a collaborative effort that offers a

---

[77] OECD, *Action Plan on Base Erosion and Profit Shifting* 11 (2013), http://www.oecd.org/ctp/BEPSActionPlan.pdf.

[78] *See* OECD, *supra* note 12, at 10:

Action 15 of the BEPS Action Plan provides for an analysis of the tax and public international law issues related to the development of a multilateral instrument to enable countries that wish to do so to implement measures developed in the course of the work on BEPS and amend bilateral tax treaties. On the basis of this analysis, interested countries will develop a multilateral instrument designed to provide an innovative approach to international tax matters, reflecting the rapidly evolving nature of the global economy and the need to adapt quickly to this evolution. The goal of Action 15 is to streamline the implementation of the tax treaty-related BEPS measures. This is an innovative approach with no exact precedent in the tax world, but precedents for modifying bilateral treaties with a multilateral instrument exist in various other areas of public international law. Drawing on the expertise of public international law and tax experts, the present report explores the technical feasibility of a multilateral hard law approach and its consequences on the current tax treaty system. The report identifies the issues arising from the development of such an instrument and provides an analysis of the international tax, public international law, and political issues that arise from such an approach. It concludes that a multilateral instrument is desirable and feasible, and that negotiations for such an instrument should be convened quickly.

[79] OECD, *supra* note 77, at 25, 29–40.

[80] OECD/G20, *Base Erosion and Profit Shifting Project Information Brief* 4 (2014), http://www.oecd.org/ctp/beps-2014-deliverables-information-brief.pdf.

[81] *See, e.g.,* Yariv Brauner, *BEPS: An Interim Evaluation*, 6 WORLD TAX J. 31 (Feb. 4, 2014), http://online.ibfd.org/kbase/#topic=doc&url=/collections/wtj/html/wtj_2014_01_int_3.html&WT.z_nav=Navigation&colid=4948; Philip Baker, *Is There a Cure for BEPS?*, 5 BRIT. TAX REV. 605 (2013).

holistic, rather than ad hoc, approach and innovative solutions to the new challenges of international taxation.[82]

The BEPS deliverables were met with mixed reviews.[83] On the one hand, they were criticized for being insufficiently innovative and holistic for the modern global economy and for failing to engage in a meaningful discourse about the principles underlying the international tax regime[84]and, in their absence, likely to fail.[85] The deliverables, it was claimed, did not generate the revolutionary changes and more radical solutions[86] the current regime required.[87] On the other hand, there were those who wondered whether the BEPS reports were trying to achieve too much at once.[88] They claimed that the application of the report's recommendations could have overly harsh consequences for cross-border economic activity and bemoaned the costs of implementation for businesses and law enforcement. These critics further noted the risk of increased taxpayer uncertainty and the potential jeopardizing of companies' confidential information.[89] But whether the deliverables were too ambitious or did not go far enough, "virtually all agree that rules proposed in the final

---

[82] Brauner, *supra* note 24, at 55.

[83] For a review of the various criticisms, *see* Mindy Herzfeld, *Coordination or Competition? A BEPS Score Card*, 83 Tax Notes Int'l 1093 (Sept. 26, 2016).

[84] *See* Jeffery M. Kadet, *BEPS: A Primer on Where It Came from and Where It's Going*, 150 Tax Notes 793, 804 (Feb. 15, 2016).

[85] Brauner, *supra* note 24; Dourado, *supra* note 69.

[86] Avi-Yonah & Xu, *supra* note 70, at 12 (doubting the relevance of the independent entity principle in the modern business reality and suggesting replacing it with the single unitary entity principle); Kadet, *supra* note 84, 804 (suggesting the formulary system and the full-inclusion system as two efficient approaches that can replace the independent entity approach); Brauner, *supra* note 2 (describing and criticizing the limited vision of the various actions).

[87] Avi-Yonah & Xu, *supra* note 70; Ryan Finley, *The Year in BEPS: Phase 1 Completed*, 80 Tax Notes Int'l 983 (Dec. 21, 2015):

> some tax justice groups and nongovernmental organizations have argued that the BEPS project remains wedded to a failed system based on the arm's-length principle and the separate-entity approach. Despite the OECD's forceful arguments to the contrary, these groups also said that developing countries weren't given a meaningful role in the project.

[88] Dourado, *supra* note 69, at 4, points to the complexity of the coordination under the BEPS Project, wondering whether "it would not have been preferable to continue working on increased international transparency and allow each jurisdiction or group of associated jurisdictions to find the adequate national tax policy."

[89] *See* Finley, *supra* note 87 ("business groups and their professional advisers, have complained that the final recommendations will increase taxpayer uncertainty, subject more companies to double taxation, drive up compliance costs, and put companies' confidential information at risk"); Kadet, *supra* note 84, at 805.

BEPS report are unnecessarily vague."[90] Further criticism was directed at the deliverables for not being strict enough and settling for soft recommendations for states instead of more stringent obligations and for failing to coordinate minimal standards to limit competition.[91] The plan, it was argued, left too much to domestic legislation, which would be bound to generate internal opposition as well as lobbying efforts to undermine its effectiveness.[92] The unilateral reaction of some states has raised doubts as to the prospects of the BEPS Project: U.S. officials recently raised some concerns about the project,[93] while the EU has revived its CCCTB, leading some to wonder whether it is getting cold feet.[94]

Thus, the initial excitement notwithstanding,[95] it remains to be seen whether the BEPS project signals a new phase in international cooperation on tax matters. The recommendations of the various actions have yet to be adopted by participating states. Only time will tell how quickly and to what degree they will be incorporated into domestic legislation,[96] given the possibility of domestic opposition,[97] and whether and to what degree its technical procedures are actually implemented.

There is still a long way to go before the recommended measures become operative, if ever. Even if the BEPS Accord is fully adopted by participating states, it is hard to predict whether the result will simply be a tweaking of old concepts of international taxation (e.g., transfer pricing and the arm's length principle, treaty shopping, CFC rules, interest deductions, and PE status[98]) or, instead, the advent of a new phase in

---

[90] Herzfeld, *supra* note 83.

[91] Brauner, *supra* note 81, at 31–32. In particular, the relative laxity of the CFC rules in Action Plan 3 raised significant disapproval. *See, e.g.,* Avi-Yonah & Xu, *supra* note 70, at 11 ("it is difficult to expect that action 3 will effectively reduce and deter the motivation of MNEs to abuse the system of exemption or deferral of tax on foreign income"); Kadet, *supra* note 84, at 799 (strong CFC rules can discourage profit-shifting and result in higher tax collection in both source countries and home countries).

[92] Avi-Yonah & Xu, *supra* note 70, at 31; Kadet, *supra* note 84, at 806 (predicting pushback by MNEs).

[93] See, for example, the criticism expressed by Robert Stack at the June 10–11, 2015, International Tax Conference in Washington, D.C., in Stuart Gibson, *BEPS Approaches the Finish Line - Or Does It?*, 78 TAX NOTES INT'L 965 (June 15, 2015) [hereinafter Gibson, *BEPS Approaches the Finish Line*]. *See also* Stuart Gibson, *Is the EU out to Scuttle BEPS?*, 78 TAX NOTES INT'L 1065 (June 22, 2015) [hereinafter Gibson, *Is the EU out to Scuttle BEPS*].

[94] Gibson, *Is the EU out to Scuttle BEPS*, *supra* note 93.

[95] *See* Brauner, *supra* note 24; Sheppard, *supra* note 74.

[96] *See, e.g.,* Kadet, *supra* note Kadet, *supra* note 84, at 804.

[97] *Id.* at 806; Ryan Finley, *The Year in BEPS: Phase 1 Completed*, 80 TAX NOTES INT'L 983, 984 (Dec. 21, 2015), http://pdfs.taxnotes.com/tnipdf/2015/80ti0983.pdf (noting that the implementation phase will face a "tough road" in the United States).

[98] *See* Brauner, *supra* note 2.

international taxation: a serious effort to transform international taxation into an operating (and unbiased[99]) multilateral regime that is to the benefit of the entire international community.[100] This unpredictability as to the eventual shape of the post-BEPS international tax regime is because most of the substantial BEPS actions provide only soft-law recommendations, with considerable flexibility allowed to the adopting states,[101] while only some imply a somewhat stronger consensus (e.g., Action 4's treatment of interest payments). Regardless, the actions that could have the greatest impact are the deliverables dealing with procedures. This may be where real change is achieved: the recommendations for rules targeting international tax schemes via the duty of disclosure of aggressive tax planning and the Mandatory Disclosure Rules in Action

---

[99] Mindy Herzfeld, for example, argues that

> Stead [a senior economic justice adviser at Christian Aid] noted an important point rarely raised in global tax policy debates: the extent to which equality, or a lack of it, should affect the allocation of international tax rights. The BEPS project was designed to strengthen the tax-collecting abilities of countries that already had claims on MNE profits under existing rules. While stronger, emerging economies such as China and India saw the project as a chance to shift the allocation of tax rights to their own jurisdictions, any changes like those were unlikely to help less-developed countries.

Mindy Herzfeld, *BEPS 2.0: The OECD Takes on New Territory*, 81 Tax Notes Int'l 987, 990 (Mar. 21, 2016), http://www.taxnotes.com/tax-notes-international/base-erosion-and-profit-shifting-beps/news-analysis-beps-20-oecd-takes-new-territory/2016/03/21/18293691?highlight=beps.

[100] For an excellent review of the potential for such a multilateral accord, see Brauner, *supra* note 81, at 13, who argues that

> current rules are based on tax base allocation rules that are primarily all-or-nothing (source or residence) norms, they do not solve the difficult conflict cases, and provide little, although increasingly more, guidance on implementation issues. This paradigm has failed. What does that mean? It means that primary reliance on domestic law rules – primarily of the anti-abuse variety – alone is clearly inconsistent with this insight. It means that mere "soft law", best practices guidance with no implementation mechanisms is insufficient. It means that an unsophisticated all-or-nothing allocation rules are not sustainable. A paradigm shift would require more sophisticated allocation rules, active collaboration between tax authorities, departure from the bilateral-only structure of the international tax regime, and some form of implementation assuring mechanisms, to name a few. The introduction of such paradigm shift would be the primary test for the success of the BEPS project.

[101] For example, Action Plan 2 (neutralizing the effects of hybrid mismatch arrangements), Action Plan 3 (designing effective CFC rules), and Action Plan 5 (countering harmful tax practices more effectively) are all considered soft because they are merely recommendations on how to design domestic rules. They therefore depend on countries' consent to adopt them and do not serve as a minimum standard. *See* Brauner, *supra* note 24, at 79–96; Avi-Yonah & Xu, *supra* note 70, at 10–13; Kadet, *supra* note 84, at 798–800.

Plan 12;[102] the country-by-country reporting requirement in Action Plan 13 to standardize reporting and simplify audits of transfer-pricing issues;[103] the tool kit for evaluating the fiscal effects of BEPS countermeasures offered by the BEPS data analysis set out in Action Plan 11;[104] the dispute resolution mechanism set in Action Plan 14;[105] and, most significantly, Action Plan 15's recommendations for future cooperation under a multilateral instrument to be developed with the participation of all countries.[106] Unfortunately, the last instrument is (even) vaguer than the other recommended instruments. Thus it is hard to estimate how significant the multilateral instrument would become.

The conclusion of the BEPS project was celebrated as a success.[107] The G-20 leaders recently reconfirmed the group's support of the project, indicating that it still enjoys political support.[108] And yet, skeptics doubt its success. Michael Graetz recently offered the following evaluation:

---

[102] OECD, *Mandatory Disclosure Rules, Action 12 – 2015 Final Report*, OECD/G20 BASE EROSION AND PROFIT SHIFTING PROJECT (2015).

[103] OECD, *Transfer Pricing Documentation and Country-by-Country Reporting, Action 13 – 2015 Final Report*, OECD/G20 BASE EROSION AND PROFIT SHIFTING PROJECT (2015).

[104] OECD, *Measuring and Monitoring BEPS, Action 11 – 2015 Final Report*, OECD/G20 BASE EROSION AND PROFIT SHIFTING PROJECT (2015).

[105] OECD, *Making Dispute Resolution Mechanisms More Effective, Action 14 – 2015 Final Report*, OECD/G20 BASE EROSION AND PROFIT SHIFTING PROJECT (2015).

[106] OECD, *Developing a Multilateral Instrument to Modify Bilateral Tax Treaties, Action 15 – 2015 Final Report*, OECD/G20 BASE EROSION AND PROFIT SHIFTING PROJECT (2015), http://dx.doi.org/10.1787/9789264241688-en. The Multilateral Convention to Implement Tax Treaty Related Measures to Prevent Base Erosion and Profit Shifting was signed, June 7th 2017. The multilateral instrument transposes results from the BEPS Project into bilateral tax treaties worldwide. It modifies the application of thousands of bilateral tax treaties, by implementing agreed minimum standards to counter treaty abuse and to improve dispute resolution mechanisms while allowing flexibility to accommodate specific tax treaties. For the text of the Convention http://www.oecd.org/tax/treaties/multilateral-convention-to-implement-tax-treaty-related-measures-to-prevent-BEPS.pdf; for the explanatory statement accompanying it see http://www.oecd.org/tax/treaties/explanatory-statement-multilateral-convention-to-implement-tax-treaty-related-measures-to-prevent-BEPS.pdf

[107] *See* Brauner, *supra* note 24; Sheppard, *supra* note 74.

[108] At its 2016 Hangzhou Summit, the G20 leaders re committed to the BEPS Project as well as the information-exchange efforts:

> We will continue our support for international tax cooperation to achieve a globally fair and modern international tax system and to foster growth, including advancing on-going cooperation on base erosion and profits shifting (BEPS), exchange of tax information, tax capacity-building of developing countries and tax policies to promote growth and tax certainty. We welcome the establishment of the G20/OECD Inclusive

OECD's BEPS effort may reverse that trend [of states' competition] with regard to information production and sharing, but not, I believe, with respect to the fundamental substantive rules governing international income taxation. . . . BEPS will not usher in a new era of international cooperation, rather than competition, in international taxation. Nations will continue to compete – especially for good jobs – and will offer low rates and special tax breaks in an effort to get them.[109]

The bottom line is that despite the strong rhetoric, the support of high-level political figures, and the rapid pace of current changes, it is difficult to predict whether and to what degree the BEPS project will actually make a difference in international tax cooperation.

The various initiatives aimed at promoting multilateral cooperation in international taxation share the common premise that such cooperation benefits all states involved. Accordingly, they implicitly assume that all states should be equally interested in alleviating double taxation, sharing information, preventing harmful tax competition, and coordinating their policies to curtail tax avoidance (although states do not all share the same problems, and – more importantly – the solutions advocated do not work equally well for all of the participants). The cooperation of specific actors is often interpreted as indicating that the solution is indeed good for them. Why else, would states sign on to a cooperative accord absent coersion? The next section argues that the dynamics of cooperation may drive some states to cooperate against their best interest.

Framework on BEPS, and its first meeting in Kyoto. We support a timely, consistent and widespread implementation of the BEPS package and call upon all relevant and interested countries and jurisdictions that have not yet committed to the BEPS package to do so and join the framework on an equal footing. We also welcome the progress made on effective and widespread implementation of the internationally agreed standards on tax transparency and reiterate our call on all relevant countries including all financial centers and jurisdictions, which have not yet done so to commit without delay to implementing the standard of automatic exchange of information by 2018 at the latest and to sign and ratify the Multilateral Convention on Mutual Administrative Assistance in Tax Matters. We endorse the proposals made by the OECD working with G20 members on the objective criteria to identify non-cooperative jurisdictions with respect to tax transparency.

G20 Leaders' Communique Hangzhou Summit (2106), file:///C:/Users/user/Dropbox/ Bbook%20International%20Tax%20Policy%20(nonshare)/chapter%207–%20Perfecting %20Tax%20Competition/G20%20recommit%20to%20beps.pdf.

[109] *See* Michael Graetz, *Bringing International Tax Policy into the 21st Century*, 83 TAX NOTES INT'L 315 (July 25, 2016).

5.2   Why (Some) Actors Cooperate Against Their Better Interests

Cooperation certainly sounds like an indisputable good. After all, how can one resist an endeavor to which all of its participants agree? In the international taxation game, cooperation can, indeed, prove to be a particularly effective strategy where noncooperative strategies produce suboptimal results. This raises one of the classic problems of collective action, namely, that in the absence of cooperation, actors are driven to adopt suboptimal unilateral strategies even though there would have been superior outcomes for all had everyone cooperated. In other words, when state-actors defect, they are not necessarily indicating that cooperation would not yield superior results for them had they been able to coordinate and enforce effective cooperation. In fact, a prominent assumption is that international taxation is a noncooperative game that could benefit from cooperation.[110] In the previous chapters, I discussed the difficulty, sometimes implausibility, of achieving and maintaining cooperation even if and when we assume it to be desirable, due to coordination, strategic, and monitoring hurdles. But just as a lack of cooperation is no proof of the undesirability of cooperation for the actors, so is cooperation not necessarily proof of its desirability. This section now attempts to explain why this is so in today's international tax policy world, focusing on features of cooperation that, although beneficial to some state-actors, are harmful to others relative to the noncooperative alternative. These relate primarily to strategic factors, the asymmetrical power of developed and developing countries, the network effects of the treaty system, and the agenda-setting influence of developed countries.

a.   Strategic Considerations

At its core, the international tax game is noncooperative. As explained already, the decentralized nature of international taxation – where every

---

[110] Reuven S. Avi-Yonah, *Globalization, Tax Competition and the Fiscal Crisis of the Welfare State*, 113 HARV. L. REV. 7 1573, 1583 (2000), argues that

> [t]he current situation resembles a multiple-player assurance ("stag hunt") game: all developed countries would benefit if all re-introduced the withholding tax on interest because they would gain revenue without the risk that the capital would be shifted to another developed country. However, no country is willing to attempt to spark cooperation by imposing a withholding tax unilaterally; thus, they all "defect" (that is, refrain from imposing the tax) to the detriment of all.

But *see* C.M. Radaelli, *Game Theory and Institutional Entrepreneurship: Transfer Pricing and the Search for Coordination International Tax Policy*, 26 POL'Y STUD. J 603 (1998) (rejecting the view that cooperation is impossible due to states' prisoner's dilemma).

state designs its own tax rules independently – mandates competition among states. The strategies states adopt, however, are interdependent, for the consequences of the actions of one state depend on the actions of other states. Even when two state-actors cooperate, as in the tax treaties scenario, the bilateral cooperation does not alter the competitive nature of the interaction between them and their peers (e.g., other host countries or other residence countries), which, in turn, can impact the payoffs for the two cooperating states from signing a treaty.

   This dynamic can explain the strategic considerations that drive developing countries to sign tax treaties even though it is costly in tax revenues for them and, arguably, not particularly effective in preventing double taxation. Eduardo Baistrocchi has convincingly explained the strategic dilemma faced by developing countries in contending with competition from peer countries, which alters their payoffs.[111] In these conditions of competition, developing countries do not simply have a choice between a treaty regime and a non-treaty regime but face the conditions of the availability of an existing treaty regime for other states. Hence, their choice is in fact between joining the "treaty club" and staying out of it given that their competitors, other developing states, are likely to join. In the latter scenario, they are likely to lose to those other states in the competition for foreign investments. As Chapter 3 explained at some length, being part of the treaty club signals to foreign investors the respectability of the signatory state as well as its compatibility with the treaty regime, albeit not necessarily better in terms of preventing double taxation. Hence, all other things being equal, foreign investors are likely to prefer the familiar and relatively simple tax treaties regime to investing considerable effort and resources in becoming acquainted with the specific rules of an unfamiliar foreign regime, which can require adaptation even if the actual degree of prevention of double taxation is similar under both regimes. Unlike the reduction of double taxation (which, as explained in Chapter 3, is likely to occur even in the absence of a treaty), the compatibility advantage emerges only under treaties. Which is why it can help developed countries use it as a payoff in playing hosts states against each other in their treaty negotiations. The strategic outcome is that developing countries face a prisoner's dilemma: although the treaty regime is costlier for them in tax revenues than the alternative, they join it so as to benefit from the competitive edge

[111] Eduardo A. Baistrocchi, *The Structure of the Asymmetric Tax Treaty Network: Theory and Implications* (Bepress Legal Series Working Paper 1991, Feb. 8, 2007), http://law.bepress .com/expresso/eps/1991.

it offers or, alternatively, out of fear that their competitors will join and have that advantage.[112]

This analysis implies that it is the strategic interaction between competing states, rather than the superiority of the treaty regime as such, that drives developing states to join.[113] Accordingly, one reason why developing countries might sign treaties that are costly for them is the structure of the game that positions them in a prisoner's dilemma in relation to competing developing countries. It is intriguing, however, that Baistrocchi assumes (what seems intuitively plausible) that only developing countries find themselves in such a strategic dilemma and that developed countries, namely, countries of residence, face no parallel competition from their peer residence countries – competition that could potentially mitigate the costs of the strategic interaction for developing countries. The next section points to the asymmetries between developed and developing countries as a possible explanation for this asymmetry.

b. Asymmetric Capabilities to Cooperate

An interesting phenomenon that the analysis in this chapter exposes is the dominant position the OECD and the developed countries it represents occupied in the international tax arena. In addition to bolstering the economic and political power of developed countries in the negotiation of international accords, this chapter suggests that by effectively combining their power as a group, OECD countries were able to entrench their market power and dominance and reap disproportionate benefits from multilateral cooperation. Thus, the current international tax arena was designed to serve the OECD's interests. It targeted the issues that are most important to developed countries and adopted solutions that are tilted in their favor in terms of tax-revenue allocation, the income tax base, and information-sharing standards.[114]

It seems fairly obvious that the OECD would seek to advance the interests of developed countries rather than providing benefits for all; naturally, wherever the OECD initiates a multilateral accord, it will promote

---

[112] As in a classic prisoner's dilemma, if all hosts end up joining in, the compatibility effect is not likely to increase investment because all hosts will share the same level of cross-border investment.

[113] Yariv Brauner, *The Future of Tax Incentives for Developing Countries, in* THE FUTURE OF TAX INCENTIVES FOR DEVELOPING COUNTRIES 25 (Yariv Brauner & Miranda Stewart eds., 2013) describes a similar situation between certain developing countries that are providing tax incentives that do not benefit them out of fear of losing the tax competition to other developing countries.

[114] This dominance may be wavering now. See the discussion in Section 3 below.

its members' interests. However, what remains puzzling is that other groups of countries have not joined forces to renegotiate the terms of the current regime or to introduce an alternative system that better serves their own interests. The answer may be in the asymmetries between developed and developing countries in terms of ability to cooperate.

Two factors might explain developing countries' inferior ability to form a cooperative bloc. First, OECD countries have a longer tradition of cooperation with one another in general and therefore already share the platforms and interrelations necessary for successful cooperation. Furthermore, the long-standing relationships among OECD members mean they risk greater reputation costs if they defect (which is likely what enabled them to create effective cooperation to begin with). Moreover, their governments generally seem more transparent than those of developing countries, which makes defection easier to detect.

Second, developing countries compete almost exclusively for capital, in particular, foreign direct investments. Developed countries, in contrast, compete more for residents, which are a far less mobile resource than capital. As a consequence, the tax competition among developing countries can be expected to be fiercer and the costs of cooperation higher. When the resource competed for is highly mobile, and thus responsive to slight changes in the taxes of each of the countries, it puts greater pressure on states to offer attractive "deals." When, on the other hand, the costs of shifting to a competitor are higher, the original state has more leeway to impose taxes that are higher than those of its competitor. Since residents are much less likely than capital to move, they can be taxed more effectively than capital (through residence-based taxation), and since their costs of moving away are higher, the taxes residence countries can impose should be higher too. When the stakes are not as high, it should be easier to agree on cooperative measures, such that would apply pressure on another group of states (host-developing states) to reduce their own taxes.

Add to this the fact that developing states probably had less motivation to cooperate in the first place. Since cooperation serves to limit competition, it is only natural that developed-residence countries may have greater incentives to invest in it. Cooperation originally served the interest of its developed initiators in curtailing competition so as to protect their tax bases and welfare states. Developing countries, in contrast, may have preferred the uncoordinated international tax regime that enabled them to attract more foreign investment. All other things being equal, this in itself would have made it more likely for developed countries to make the first move toward cooperation.

When only one group of countries joins forces and negotiates as a group while the rest of the countries operate individually, it is easy to see why the former may enjoy superior political and economic power to promote its interests in multilateral bargaining with the latter. The following sections further explain how this collective power can be effectively translated into gains even when states compete with one another in the international tax market and must independently decide whether to adopt a specific international tax instrument or sign bilateral tax treaties.

c. Network Effects

Despite the bilateral nature of tax treaties, they are not isolated strategic events initiated independently by the pair of negotiating states. Rather, they are based on a common standard that becomes more attractive the greater the number of users that apply it. Tax treaties, in other words, are a network, and the model they adhere to is a network product.[115] In what follows, I will use tax treaties as my main example, but my analysis is equally applicable to other – both existing and future – multilateral instruments. These include the model for Tax Information Exchange Agreements (TIEAs), the Multilateral Convention on Mutual Administrative Assistance, FATCA and the Standard for Automatic Exchange of Financial Account Information in Tax Matters and even the BEPS project, but in particular, the multilateral Instrument to Modify Bilateral Tax Treaties it included. All of these are standards that can form a network around a common instrument.[116] Like in other networks (e.g., telecommunications

---

[115] For a general analysis of law as a network industry and the costs and benefits associated with it see Talia Fisher, *Separation of Law and State*, 43 U. MICH. J.L. REFORM 435 (2010). In the tax context see Eduardo A. Baistrocchi, *The International Tax Regime and the BRIC World: Elements for a Theory*, 33 OXFORD J. LEGAL STUD. 733 (2013) (applying a dynamic theory to explain what he describes as the "the creeping convergence of the BRIC world" with the international tax regime using a two-sided platform network theory). *See* also Miranda Stewart, *Transnational Tax Information Exchange Networks: Steps towards a Globalized, Legitimate Tax Administration*, 4 WORLD TAX J. 152 (May 30, 2012) (describing the tax information-exchange networks as a new technology of regulation that extends beyond national borders, as part of the somewhat different tradition of the global governance network, where government units work across borders to create a new transnational order and emphasizing the separate legitimation fact that these networks require).

[116] Some of them are even advertised as such. For an interesting example, see the flyer advertising the Multilateral Convention on Mutual Administrative Assistance in Tax Matters, http://www.oecd.org/ctp/exchange-of-tax-information/ENG_Convention_Flyer.pdf, which suggests that states become parties to the convention:

> The Convention covers a much wider range of taxes than bilateral treaties (e.g., it covers VAT/GST and social security contributions). In addition, the Convention provides

networks or ATMs), the value of the instrument to its users increases with every user who joins the network.[117] More than mere cooperation to promote mutual interests, a network product entails an inherent incentive for users to join and stay in the network. To illustrate, if other consumers are using a certain word-processing software or a system of automated bank machines, there is greater incentive for new users to use the same software or bank machines. Likewise, when other users are using a certain format for collecting and disseminating tax information, it makes sense for new users to use similar formatting so as to save on the costs of processing the information being exchanged;[118] when other states are using the model tax treaty standard, it makes sense to adopt a similar standard. By joining and staying in a network, users benefit from their compatibility with other users. This is known as the "network effect."

The benefits of joining the network – the network effect – support membership in the network even if the costs of adopting the standard would prevent states from adopting similar rules had there not been a network product available. The standard set by the OECD Model has been the basis of the successful tax treaties network and offers a strong incentive for potential users to join and stay in the network.[119] Thus, states have been incentivized to join and remain in the tax treaty network by the very fact that other states are increasingly adopting the standardized version of tax treaties and despite the costs involved in adopting the standard. Thus, although the OECD Model pushes source countries to relinquish tax revenues without the benefit of an increased incentive for inbound investment, the network-like advantages of the tax treaties system seem nonetheless to incentivize them to join the system.[120]

a single legal basis for multilateral country co-operation in tax matters and sets up a body that can, at the request of a Party, furnish opinions on the interpretation and application of the Convention. Further, it specifies uniform procedures for various forms of mutual assistance such as service of documents, simultaneous tax examinations and tax examinations abroad.

[117] Michael L. Katz & Carl Shapiro, *Network Externalities, Competition, and Compatibility*, 75 AM. ECON. REV. 424 (1985).

[118] Grinberg, *supra* note 73 describes the benefits of a uniform reporting standard for emerging economies as well as for financial institutions as opposed to a fragmented international reporting regime. Emerging economies would benefit from the reduction in the administrative and political costs of taxing income from capital. Financial institutions would benefit from the reduction in compliance costs.

[119] *See* Baistrocchi, *supra* note 115.

[120] Note that there could also be benefits for countries that decide to operate outside the network, particularly those that offer tax-haven specifications. I will discuss this in

Both the costs and benefits involved in the tax treaties system are characteristic of a network structure. The *benefits* are typical network externalities: the accessibility, familiarity, and extensive shared corpus of interpretations provided by the OECD generate recognition and reputation that characterize membership in the network. In other words, the use of a similar structure, shared tax terms (e.g., the arm's-length mechanism[121] and the concept of permanent establishment[122]), agreed-upon tie-breaking rules (e.g., for determining the residency of dual-residence taxpayers), and common standards for alleviating double taxation renders investing in foreign jurisdictions easier (and less costly) for taxpayers and increases the network's appeal.[123] The standard also saves on the costs of designing tax systems for states.[124] Remaining outside the network, in contrast, could mean that foreign investors will bypass the nonjoiners in favor of network countries because the latter offer the simplicity and security of the compatible standard. Hence, the network structure of tax treaties can encourage adherence to a unified standard where countries would

Chapter 7. *See also* Omri Marian, *The State Administration of International Tax Avoidance*, 7 Harv. Bus. L. Rev (forthcoming 2017) Available at SSRN: https://ssrn.com/abstract=2685642.

[121] Baistrocchi, *supra* note 115, at 759 (arguing that the application of American law's arm's length principle has expanded to the rest of the world, mainly through the tax-treaty network).

[122] Reuven S. Avi-Yonah, *Tax Competition, Tax Arbitrage, and the International Tax Regime* 7 (Univ. Michigan Public Law Working Paper No. 73, Jan. 2007) (using South Korea to exemplify the claim that even before entering any tax treaties, the freedom of most countries to adopt international tax rules is severely constrained by the need to adapt to generally accepted principles of international taxation).

[123] Michael Lang & Jeffrey Owens, *The Role of Tax Treaties in Facilitating Development and Protecting the Tax Base* 36, 39 (WU Int'l Taxation Research Paper Series No. 2014–03, 2014), http://ssrn.com/abstract=2398438, highlight the specific details of the treaty that could make a difference in terms of its desirability for MNEs and, therefore, for countries seeking their business activity. They argue more generally that

> [s]urveys of business suggest that MNEs look at whether there is a treaty and examine its provisions when deciding where to locate. Other things being equal, MNEs will favor a country with a good treaty network. How important this is will depend on the economic structure in each country, the relationship between treaty and domestic law and the attitudes of the administration and the courts in the application of the treaty.

[124] Treaties also often serve as a bridge between countries that are not direct partners to the treaty. However, this feature of the treaty regime is currently under attack in the fight against base erosion and profit shifting, which urges states to adopt LOB rules that would prevent nonresidents to use treaty benefits. OECD, *Preventing the Granting of Treaty Benefits in Inappropriate Circumstances*, Action 6 - 2015 Final Report, OECD/G20 Base Erosion and Profit Shifting Project 94–95 (2015), http://dx.doi.org/10.1787/9789264241695-en.

otherwise have little or no incentive to do so. Even if a country prefers different terms, mechanisms, or interpretations to those offered by the network's standard, the fact that many other countries use that standard will often be determinative in its decision as to whether to join the network. In short, one reason for why states join a network – in this case, the tax treaty network – is that the positive network externalities they gain from the standard outweigh the costs.

Just like the benefits, the *costs* of the tax treaty network are also typical of networks in general. First, the initiators of a network standard that dominates the market could exploit the network to extract cartelistic gains from potential competitors and monopolistic rents from its own users. Second, once a network is established, even if the standard is less than optimal, it will survive since it is very difficult for users to shift to a different one, even if superior. Subsections (1) and (2) will consider these two issues, the (perhaps surprising) benefits of operating outside the network will be separately discussed in Chapter 7.

1.   Excessive Prices: Cartelistic Behavior

One of the greatest assets of network structures is their stability due to the incentives they create for members to cooperate. Yet it is also one of their central flaws, as the enhanced incentive for cooperation could lead to the emergence of cartels and the extraction of monopolistic rents.[125] A network's amenability to cartel-building can both explain the extra benefits enjoyed by developed countries from the tax treaty system as well as provide a plausible account for why developing countries join and remain in the network despite the limited benefits they derive.

The tax treaties regime allows developed residence countries – the network's initiators – to extract cartelistic profits. This is a manifestation of the first-mover advantage characteristic of networks.[126] The fact that the tax treaties model was designed by and for developed countries gave them this advantage. Regardless of whether the standard was purposely thus designed or simply emerged as such, once the path of lowering host countries' tax revenues at source was chosen, there was little chance of turning

---

[125] T. Cowen, *Law as a Public Good – The Economics of Anarchy*, 8 ECON. & PHIL. 249, 253–59 (1992) ("The same factors that allow anarchy to be stable may also allow the ... agencies to exercise monopoly power to collude ... [C]ompeting legal systems are either unstable or collapse into a monopoly agency or network.").

[126] M.A. Lemley & D. McGowan, *Legal Implications of Network Economic Effects*, 86 CAL. L. REV. 479, 495 (1998).

back. The first (developed) countries to join the network enjoyed individual gains from the simplification and reduction of transaction costs. The uniform standard they created offered network externalities for all users of the standard by further reducing the transaction costs for cross-border transactions. Once the network dominated the international tax market and the costs of staying outside the network increased, developed countries could extract monopolistic rents from developing countries joining the system. The excessive price paid by developing countries does not, however, reflect any inherent superiority to the treaty system's mechanisms in terms of eliminating double taxation but, rather, the market power of the network's initiators. In other words, in designing the treaty mechanism to favor countries of residence in the allocation of tax revenues, the network initiators were able to extract monopolistic rents at the expense of late-coming developing (host) countries.

2. Inferior "Products": The Lock-In Effect

Tax treaties are far from flawless: their scope is incomplete, solutions only partial, and distributive results problematic. In particular, they are biased against developing countries. The question that arises is why a competing standard has yet to evolve if a different solution is preferable for some (developing) countries. One would expect that these flaws would be readily addressed either by updating the model and revising existing treaties accordingly or by initiating a competing – improved – standard. Although either is a viable solution, neither has arisen (although, the hopes are that the recently signed Multilateral Instrument may facilitate exactly such a change). A partial explanation is developing states' inferior ability to cooperate among themselves (as discussed in Section b); this puts them at a built-in disadvantage relative to developed countries in any attempt to negotiate or initiate a more balanced standard.

This asymmetry is exacerbated by the network structure of the treaties regime, with its inherent barriers to such change. In particular, the lock-in effect of networks makes a spontaneous shift to an alternative standard unlikely.[127] The existence of a compatible standard significantly changes the relevant market, as competition among standards is typically a case of

---

[127] In fact, competing standards that were proposed in the past failed to gain the support enjoyed by the OECD standard. The most famous of these, of course, is the UN model treaty, which is very similar to the OECD Model in general structure and terminology but diverges in its specific terms and treats developing countries more favorably than the OECD Model does.

"winner takes all," where the dominant standard tends to "take over" the market.[128] Once such a winning standard is established, other compatible standards, even if superior, have lower chances of infiltrating the market, let alone dominating it. The benefits users will derive from compatibility with the dominant system's users facilitate conversion, as these benefits may outweigh preferences for the features of other, non-compatible systems. Establishing a competing network, anchored, for example, on a fairer distribution of tax revenues or lower overhaul taxation, is therefore doubly problematic due to the tendency of successful networks to crowd out new (even if better) standards. Even if a group of countries could initiate a standard that better serves their interests, other countries may be reluctant to join since rational investors might be less inclined to invest in their jurisdictions.

The treaty network may be particularly subject to the lock-in effect, since treaties set a standard for not only negotiating tax treaties but also for structuring what some refer to as the international tax regime.[129] Many of the tax systems around the world have corresponding systems for classifying income from different sources and for classifying income sources. They also share a similar distinction between business and non-business income and a similar concept of permanent establishment; they apply the same practice of withholding taxes at source and often the same double-taxation relief in the country of residence.[130] And, perhaps more significantly, the treaty network has entrenched the traditional distinction between source and residence countries; it has entrenched the idea that income must have some geographical source and that individuals and corporations must be residing in some geographical location. It conforms to the premise that the challenges of international taxation can be overcome by refining the traditional definitions and rectifying the gaps and overlaps between systems, even where applying the conventional concepts is clearly

---

[128] Stanley M. Besen & Joseph Farrell, *Choosing How to Compete: Strategies and Tactics in Standardization*, 8 J. Econ. Persp. 117 (1994).

[129] *See* Brauner, *supra* note 2 (arguing that the standardization of international tax law is not confined to tax treaty law and that the international tax laws of essentially all countries have significantly converged); Avi-Yonah, *supra* note 122 (claiming that "a coherent international tax regime exists, embodied in both the tax treaty network and in domestic laws, and that it forms a significant part of international law (both treaty-based and customary)"); Eduardo A. Baistrocchi, *The Use and Interpretation of Tax Treaties in the Emerging World: Theory and Implications*, 4 Brit. Tax Rev. 352, 353 (2008), http://ssrn.com/abstract=1273089 ("Both the asymmetric and symmetric tax treaty networks constitute the core structure of the international tax system.").

[130] Brauner, *supra* note 2, at 269. For a more detailed account, see *id.* at 285–90.

inappropriate. Hence, the standards of the tax treaties network are deeply embedded in states' domestic legislation and might be difficult to amend. To illustrate this lock-in effect, imagine a competing standard that completely revises the system for international taxation and sets a formulary apportionment of income among countries based on sales, workforce, and production location.[131] Even assuming that such a standard is superior to the existing regime, the initiators of this standard might have a hard time recruiting other states to join the network. Such a standard requires that investors subscribe to a new system of reporting their income worldwide and could – potentially – entail additional planning and reporting costs and additional tax liability due to conflicts between the old and new standards.[132] Again, the lock-in effect will make it extremely hard for a competing standard to gain a foothold: the general inclination is to prefer an existing dominant network over less dominant emerging networks, at least until a critical mass of users has joined the latter. Consequently, even if certain countries are unhappy with the established standard (that is, even if the product offered by the dominant network is unsatisfactory) and even if a superior product exists, they may be unable to shift standards.

The bottom line is that under a network regime, certain countries might be paying too high a price for an inferior "product." The positive externalities created by the network can sway countries to join it despite the high costs and inferior mechanisms it may offer. And though they might have preferred a different solution – one that promotes cross-border investments or more fairly distributes tax revenues or rethinks the system altogether – when a network is successful, like the tax treaty network, it is extremely difficult for a single country or even a group of countries to reduce their costs or improve the technology such a network offers. Hence, countries are likely to compromise and use the network product, even though they would have preferred a different mechanism.

[131] See, e.g., Reuven S. Avi-Yonah & Ilan Benshalom, Formulary Apportionment–Myths and Prospects, 2011 WORLD TAX J. 371, 373, 378; Reuven S. Avi-Yonah, Kimberly A. Clausing & Michael C. Durst, Allocating Business Profits for Tax Purposes: A Proposal to Adopt a Formulary Profit Split, 9 FLA. TAX REV. 497, 500, 501–07, 510–13 (2009); Julie Roin, Can the Income Tax Be Saved? The Promises and Pitfalls of Adopting Worldwide Formulary Apportionment, 61 TAX L. REV. 169, 172–73 (2008). But see J. Clifton Fleming, Robert J. Peroni & Stephen E. Shay, Formulary Apportionment in the U.S. International Income Tax System: Putting Lipstick on a Pig?, 36 MICH. J. INT'L L. 1 (2014).

[132] Lemley & McGowan, supra note 126, at 497 ("[T]he rational consumer might well choose to wait until an alternative had been adopted by others who incurred the costs of shifting to the new standard but reaped fewer benefits relative to later adopters.").

d. Agenda-Setting

Another factor that enabled developed countries to gain dominance in the international tax arena was their agenda-setting power: their control of the order in which issues were brought up for discussion and decisions made in the international tax community.[133] This has allowed them to unravel the complex set of potential disputes among countries and separate them into isolated stages of deliberation, to be raised at their convenience. Thus, for example, states first contended with the question of how to distribute tax revenues among source and residence countries in the context of treaties for the prevention of double taxation, and only once this was settled did they turn to other issues. The treaty regime therefore not only opened up the sphere of international taxation to a cooperative alternative but also represented the first move in a sequential game where players can move at different times and more than once. In such a game, the order in which players take their turn at making their decisions matters, as one player's choice impacts the choices available to the other players in the next round of the game. Through the tax treaties project, the OECD has systematically determined the choice-making agenda for states' choices in international taxation.

To illustrate, consider the issues of double taxation and tax competition, which were contended with at two separate stages in the history of international taxation. Bilateral treaties began with tackling double taxation, and only with the consolidation of the tax treaties regime was the campaign against tax competition initiated. Interestingly, despite the failure of the latter effort, calls to establish a single-tax international tax regime remain strong.[134] From the perspective of the traditional discourse, this dual-stage process makes perfect sense, as the issues are seemingly not interrelated. One can support the alleviation of double taxation to facilitate capital mobility, while being wary of taxes being driven down to suboptimal levels due to this same mobility. Yet, this process has set source countries

---

[133] For the crucially important role of agenda setting in international tax organizations, see Ring, *supra* note 26, at 669–73.

[134] Thus, one of the key purposes of the BEPS project was to limit "double non-taxation." OECD, *supra* note 1, at 22:

> Beyond securing revenues by realigning taxation with economic activities and value creation, the OECD/G20 BEPS Project aims to create a single set of consensus-based international tax rules to address BEPS, and hence to protect tax bases while offering increased certainty and predictability to taxpayers. A key focus of this work is to eliminate double non-taxation.

at a disadvantage. The first stage alleviated double taxation through tax treaties and, at the same time, structured the distribution of tax revenues to the advantage of residence countries. The second, supposedly unrelated, stage of curtailment of tax competition has operated in tandem with the biased distribution of tax revenues to produce the worst of both worlds for source countries. In other words, the solutions raised for both problems work to the disadvantage of source countries. The cost that each mechanism entails for source countries might be reasonable in itself. In combination, however, they produce a regime that is highly burdensome for source countries, on the one hand, and asymmetrically beneficial for developed states, on the other. Recall that developing countries are usually host countries for investments, and relatively fewer of their residents invest overseas. Hence, they stand to lose from the lowering of taxation at source under tax treaties, while they could benefit from increased foreign investment under tax competition. Accordingly, the combination of the current tax treaty regime and the efforts to limit tax competition works to their double disadvantage. Source countries would have been better-off under a regime that curbs competition by imposing a higher harmonized tax level but allocates them a larger share of the tax revenues or, alternatively, a regime under which they do not collect more taxes but can benefit from increased foreign investment generated by tax competition. Instead, they disproportionately bear the costs of a regime that both restricts competition *and* allocates tax revenues in favor of countries of residence. Countries of residence, in contrast, benefit from this regime.

The other contexts in which cooperation has been advocated – namely, information-sharing, improved enforcement, and combatting tax avoidance through the BEPS project – also have yielded asymmetrical outcomes for developed and developing countries. The dual-staged negotiation process – setting tax treaties (and their allocation of tax revenues in favor of countries of residence) first and leaving the rest for later – prevented the consideration of a reallocation of tax revenues at the later stage of discussions. Political powers aside, had negotiations on all matters been conducted simultaneously, (developing) states would have been in a better position to demand a more favorable allocation of tax revenues in light of the costs they would incur in the information-exchange and enforcement contexts. Again, information sharing and enforcement sound like measures that should benefit all countries involved, and the issue of double-taxation prevention sounds unrelated. In practice, however, enforcement and information collection are also asymmetrical in their results.[135] The reason is that the enforcement and information-collection systems in developing countries lag far behind those of developed countries[136] *as well as* the fact that developing countries, which are generally host countries, reap fewer gains from cooperation than residence countries, which emerge as the prime beneficiaries of the curtailment of tax planning opportunities and improvement of tax collection.

Agenda-setting power is commonly acknowledged as one of the key factors in strategic planning. A party with the power to determine the issues raised for discussion and the order in which they are discussed enjoys a considerable advantage in the sequential strategic game.[137] Even if not as part of a predetermined strategy, the fact that OECD countries were able to move first and set the international taxation agenda served their interests well. Once the treaty format – with its tax revenues distribution

---

[135] *See*, for example, criticism of the recent Action Plan 13 in Avi-Yonah & Xu, *supra* note 70, at 42 (developing countries "do not have the necessary resources and expertise to administer the revised version of TPG"); Kadet, *supra* note 84, at 803 (noting that beyond the need to gain the knowledge, tax authorities will need considerable resources to have more than a minor effect on BEPS behavior).

[136] I.J. Mosquera Valderrama, *Legitimacy and the Making of International Tax Law: The Challenges of Multilateralism*, 7 WORLD TAX J. (Oct. 6, 2015), http://ssrn.com/abstract=2528044 (arguing that developed countries will benefit more from an exchange of information since they have the necessary administrative capacity, knowledge, and computing capabilities to make use of the information).

[137] *See generally* Saul Levmore, *Parliamentary Law, Majority Decisionmaking, and the Voting Paradox*, 75 VA. L. REV. 971 (1989). On the importance of the first move in setting the agenda and promoting the agenda of powerful states, *see* Eyal Benvenisti & George W. Downs, *The Empire's New Clothes: Political Economy and the Fragmentation of International Law*, 60 STAN. L. REV. 595, 607–08 (2007):

> Weingast's stylized game possesses two features that correspond to important aspects of the contemporary international system – and its impact on international law – as well as the domestic context of an earlier era. The first is that the sovereign possesses a notable first-mover advantage. This corresponds to the agenda-setting power that hegemons and coalitions of powerful states frequently enjoy at the international level, where the final outcome of multilateral negotiations is usually strongly anchored to their initial bargaining position.

The first move made by developed countries puts developing countries at a strategic disadvantage. A successful strategy on the latter's part would be to cooperate among themselves and to shift to a repeated game. For a coherent explanation of this in international law contexts, *see id.* at 608:

> For our purposes the primary significance of Weingast's game lies in its message that a hegemon (or small group of powerful states) interested in preventing weaker states from cooperating can do so by using its first-mover advantage to 1) limit the perception of weaker parties that they are involved in a repeated game, and 2) limit the opportunities that weaker states have to resolve the differences in their preferences.

arrangement – had been set, individual countries could either join the regime or remain outsiders.[138] Current discussions of further cooperation in international taxation generally takes the existing allocation of taxing rights as a given, and pursuant subjects are considered as separate issues.[139] This discourages non-OECD countries from revisiting the distribution of tax revenues and demanding a more balanced allocation as part of an overall better deal, thereby entrenching the bias against them.

5.3   Game-Makers and Game-Changers

A particularly prominent point that has arisen from the analysis in this chapter is the dominant role played by the OECD in facilitating international cooperation accords. Over the past ninety years or so, OECD countries have taken the lead in almost all of the major cooperative initiatives on international tax issues.[140] This dominance has allowed the OECD to set – whether intentionally or not – the rules of the international tax game in ways that benefit its own members. The OECD has consistently pushed nonmember countries to join these initiatives, using powerful pro-cooperation rhetoric that invokes the classic strategy for overcoming collective-action problems – that it is to the benefit of all actors involved. As described, the OECD has consistently set the agenda. This began with its model tax treaty, followed by the campaign it led against harmful tax competition and information-sharing initiatives, and, now, most recently, manifested in the BEPS project.[141] Sometimes made explicitly and sometimes implicitly, the claim has always been that cooperation under the OECD's guidance will be beneficial to all countries involved.[142] The justification for cooperation is often asserted as self-evident, and countries are simply expected to conform. I have argued in

---

[138] *See* E.A. Baistrocchi, *The International Tax Regime and the BRIC World: Elements for a Theory*, 33 OXFORD J. LEGAL STUD. 733 (2013) (describing the delayed stage at which BRICS join the international tax regime).

[139] *See* Brauner, *supra* note 13, at 1035 ("The single tax principle ignores the key issue of tax base division that is at the core of the BEPS project. The BEPS solutions do not support a claim by source countries to tax, and sometimes they do not support their claim not to tax.").

[140] *See* Brauner & Pistone, *supra* note 11, at 3, 3–4 (noting that the general criticism of the OECD's dominance became more focused as some of the developing countries gained economic and political power and joined the OECD); Garcia, *supra* note 57, at 175–179.

[141] Although the OECD has made a concrete effort to include developing countries in the process, "there have been concerns that the needs of developing countries have not always been appreciated or sufficiently reflected in the various discussion drafts and final reports." Kadet, *supra* note Kadet, *supra* note 84, at 797.

[142] *See* OECD, *supra* note 1, at 4:

this chapter, however, that contrary to this predominant rhetoric, cooperation is not inherently desirable since it can, and often does, promote the interests of a narrow group of actors. The obvious case is cartelistic cooperation, which serves the cooperating actors but not their competitors or the market at large. I have also highlighted some of the subtler ways in which the cooperative process is tilted in favor of some (that is, developed) state-actors. Moreover, but all too often, the structure of the game forces states to cooperate against their best interests. In other words, joining a cooperative initiative can create beneficial opportunities for some states, while others will find that even though cooperation works to their disadvantage, it is their best available option.

But times are changing. Over the course of the last decade, the developed countries that were represented by the OECD have been losing some of their clout as a group. The rise of emerging economies such as the BRICS countries could signal a shift in not only economic power but also political power and, therefore, in developed states' dominance of agenda-setting and rule-making in the international tax game. Yariv Brauner and Pasquale Pistone have described the changing landscape of international taxation as follows:

> The remodeling of the power structure shaping the global economy and global economic governance more generally is possibly being paralleled by a corresponding reformatting of international taxation. The dominance of the richest countries in the world over the international tax regime ... is being defied. ... Emerging economies – most vocally, China and India – are challenging this dominance, effectively asserting some of their newly found power in various forums. Even within the OECD, most of the new members (and some less recent additions) share more tax policy challenges with emerging economies than with their richest co-members at the OECD.[143]

Developed states are also having to contend with a significant shrinkage of their tax bases. They are facing considerable challenge from multinational

---

Estimates of the impact of BEPS on developing countries, as a percentage of tax revenues, are higher than in developed countries given developing countries' greater reliance on CIT revenues. In a globalised economy, governments need to cooperate and refrain from harmful tax practices, to address tax avoidance effectively, and provide a more certain international environment to attract and sustain investment. Failure to achieve such cooperation would reduce the effectiveness of CIT as a tool for resource mobilisation, which would have a disproportionately harmful impact on developing countries.

But see Brauner, *supra* note 13, at 979 (arguing that the international tax regime evolved with the apparently sole aim of perfecting competition rather than curbing it).

[143] Brauner & Pistone, *supra* note 11, at 3–4.

enterprises, in addition to the rivalry of competing countries, which has made them far more dependent on source countries' cooperation. Perhaps in anticipation of these developments, some of the emerging economies have become observers in the OECD[144] and have taken on important, more effective roles in the G-20, which has become a key player in international taxation in recent years.[145] The success of the multilateral taxation project is, to a significant extent, contingent on the continuous political commitment of the G-20 states and their financial support.[146] The support of developing countries has also become more significant, since the more states that join the cooperative regime, the greater its prospects.[147]

The increasing dependence of developed countries on the cooperation of developing and emerging economies in their struggle against the erosion of their tax bases could be a sign that the time is ripe for a shift in the rules of the game. This will mean the adoption of rules and procedures that will enable developed, developing, and emerging countries alike to renegotiate the terms of the international taxation regime. The recent amendment to the OECD Model that allowed for non-OECD countries to contribute to the Model's orientation could well constitute such a shift. The participation of developing countries and their signing the Multilateral Instrument could further their inclusion. However, turning around the huge and stable ship that is the treaties network to pursue new goals is a formidable task, especially given that the dominant members will fight

---

[144] Brauner, *supra* note 13, at 982–83, notes that

> [t]he OECD had anticipated the importance of communicating with non-member states long before these developments and launched an observation program for such countries. Yet, the power to observe proceedings was not sufficient for countries that started viewing themselves as world leaders, especially when, for most purposes, their participation did not result in significant enough changes (subjectively) in the division of tax bases and other norms. The demand for more source taxation conflicted with the opposite trend to eliminate source taxation in favor of residence based taxation that has always been the hallmark of OECD tax policy and a consequence of the competition framework of the international tax regime. Some countries have unilaterally departed from some of the prior universal norms of the international tax regime to assert their tax jurisdiction and views of appropriate division of tax bases.

[145] *See id.* at 984.
[146] Kadet, *supra* note 84, at 806 ("The first test will be the commitment of countries to the effort to develop the action 15 multilateral agreement").
[147] Michael P. Devereux & John Vella, *Are We Heading towards a Corporate Tax System Fit for the 21st Century?*, 35 FISCAL STUD. 449, 467 (2014) (arguing that because the project is not truly global, its efforts to prevent harmful competition will fail).

to safeguard their privileged position. Exemplifying this challenge is the clarification made in the 2013 BEPS Action Plan:

> In the changing international tax environment, a number of countries have expressed a concern about how international standards on which bilateral tax treaties are based allocate taxing rights between source and residence States. This Action Plan is focused on addressing BEPS. While actions to address BEPS will restore both source and residence taxation in a number of cases where cross-border income would otherwise go untaxed or would be taxed at very low rates, these actions are not directly aimed at changing the existing international standards on the allocation of taxing rights on cross-border income.[148]

5.4 Conclusion

For almost a century, the impressive multinational cooperative campaigns in the international tax arena have been led primarily by OECD countries, some more successfully than others. In this period, OECD countries have relentlessly advanced cooperative initiatives, in line with the premise (or at least rhetoric) that cooperation is beneficial for all of its participants. This assertion is consistent with the classic collective-action rationale that everyone stands to lose if every state-actor promotes its own self-interests and rejects cooperation. We see here the problematic strategic dynamics of the game that cause some state-actors to choose an action (defection) that conflicts with their best interests. However, the pro-cooperation narrative misses the converse alternative: that for some states, the fact that they cooperate does not necessarily mean that this is their best option. As I have sought to show in this chapter, sometimes states cooperate *despite* this not being in their best interests. That is not to say, of course, that *any* cooperation is bad but, rather, that instead of assuming that a country's cooperation is proof per se that the initiative is beneficial to it, we must look more closely at the interests at stake.

The cooperative accords discussed in this chapter are a mixed bag of goods. Some have had greater success in enlisting the cooperation of non-OECD countries; some have better served the interests of developing and emerging countries. Some are thriving, while others have failed dismally, and with others, it is too soon to tell what outcomes they will yield. The central point here was that success in convincing developing states to join a multilateral initiative is no indication of its inherent desirability for those

---

[148] OECD, *supra* note 77.

states. Each initiative should be evaluated according to its concrete results and not the number of states that endorse it, given that the cooperation could be strategically structured to benefit only some of the participants.

The chapter illuminated the mechanisms on which the international tax game can be constructed to benefit some (that is, developed) countries at the expense of other (that is, developing) states. I would not go so far as to suggest that developed countries cooperated in a premeditated manner so as to deliberately create negative externalities for developing countries. But even assuming the current international tax system was not intentionally designed to impose these externalities on developing countries, by pursuing the interests of OECD countries in limiting tax competition and increasing their tax revenues while disregarding the interests of developing countries, it has de facto led to a reality in which the latter face a very narrow range of choices.

Is it too late at this stage of the game to consider establishing a different international tax regime, one that aspires to worthy normative goals shared by all states? Could this be the stage where considerations of global justice are considered and inter-nation equity plays a greater part? Can different game rules be adopted to ensure the emergence of such a regime? And can this be accomplished in the framework of the BEPS project? These questions will be discussed in Chapters 6 and 7.

6

International Tax and Global Justice

The previous chapters focused on international taxation as a competitive game played by independent sovereign states, where market forces increasingly determine not only investment flows but also relocation decisions and states' ability to collect taxes. I argued that the competitive and decentralized structure of this game shapes the strategies available to these state-actors to promote their interests and evaluated the consequences of each potential strategy: to act unilaterally, anticipating or reacting to other states' strategies; to cooperate bilaterally; or to pursue multilateral accords in an effort to improve gains from the international tax game. The choice of policy, I explained, is a matter of which strategy can most effectively promote the given state's interests.

My analysis did not, however, pose the normative question of what is the right thing to do. I did not relate to the issue of whether considerations of justice *should* in any way constrain states' decisions, and if so, justice for whom. I also did not take a normatively critical view of the institutional design of international taxation nor have I considered what the rules of the international tax game should be. Instead, the discussion in the first chapters of this book simply described what sovereign states and what they can do regarding taxation in the global economy; I then moved directly to how states can best promote their-presumably desirable-goals. This chapter takes up the normative challenge and considers the right thing to do in terms of global justice. In other words, what goals *should* international taxation pursue? Specifically, I focus on the normative challenges globalization poses for distributive justice in the context of inter-state interaction.

As stressed in the preceding chapters, income taxation has traditionally and conventionally been regarded as a key tool (if not *the* tool) for redistribution, and the state has been the key sphere in which considerations of justice have been discussed. In creating both new links between states as well as competition among them for residents, investments, and tax revenues, globalization forces us to consider issues of justice that go beyond the state level. And yet, cooperative efforts in the international tax arena rarely consider global justice. International taxation policymakers have engaged substantially in the practicalities of income taxation in a globalized world, paying close attention to the erosion of states' income tax bases and potential solutions. However, despite the focus on international cooperation in this context, global justice has rarely been at the forefront.

Political philosophers vigorously debate the scope of applicability of the duty of justice: Does it apply exclusively at the state level, or should it transcend state boundaries? Yet, until recently, these thinkers rarely delved into the actual mechanisms of income taxation, while international tax experts, for their part, rarely engage in the normative questions of global justice.[1] This chapter seeks to contribute to this important discourse by considering international tax policy from the perspective of global justice.

Globalization has seriously challenged state tax policies. It has intensified tax competition by allowing individuals and businesses more leeway in tax planning and thereby critically undermining states' ability to pursue domestic redistribution. At the same time, globalization and global inequality have led political philosophers to consider the application of distributive justice duties beyond national borders, with their debate centered on the appropriate level of redistribution. Whereas proponents of cosmopolitan justice argue that justice should be upheld between individuals irrespective of their national affiliation, institutionalists assert justice to be a duty that is a derivative of political institutions. Statists, for

---

[1] For some notable exceptions, see Ilan Benshalom, *The New Poor at Our Gates: Global Justice Implications for International Trade and Tax Law*, 85 N.Y.U. L. REV. 1 (2010); Gillian Brock, GLOBAL JUSTICE: A COSMOPOLITAN ACCOUNT (2009); Kim Brooks, *Inter-Nation Equity: The Development of an Important but Underappreciated International Tax Value*, in TAX REFORM IN THE 21ST CENTURY 1 (Richard Krever & John G. Head eds., 2008); Allison Christians, *Sovereignty, Taxation and Social Contract*, 18 MINN. J. INT'L L. 99 (2009); Allison Christians, *How Nations Share*, 87 IND. L.J. 1407 (2012); Alexander Cappelen, *National and International Distributive Justice in Bilateral Tax Treaties*, 56 FINANZARCHIV N.F. 424 (1999); Peter Dietsch & Thomas Rixen, *Tax Competition and Global Background Justice*, 22 J. POL. PHIL. 150 (2014); PETER DIETSCH, CATCHING CAPITAL: THE ETHICS OF TAX COMPETITION (2015); D. Paolini, P. Pistone, G. Pulina & M. Zagler, *Tax Treaties with Developing Countries and the Allocation of Taxing Rights*, 39 EUR. J. L. & ECON. 1 (2015); Diane Ring, *Democracy, Sovereignty and Tax Competition: The Role of Tax Sovereignty in Shaping Tax Cooperation*, 9 FLA. TAX REV. 555 (2008); Miriam Ronzoni, *Global Tax Governance: The Bullets Internationalists Must Bite–and Those They Must Not*, 1 MORAL PHIL. & POL. 37 (2014).

their part, focus specifically on the state as the primary forum in which duties of redistribution apply. Thomas Nagel in particular has taken a strong statist position, arguing for a sharp distinction between the domestic arena, where the distinctive convergence of the state's coercive power and its constituents' coauthorship gives rise to exceptional duties of justice, and the international arena, beyond the state, where no duty of justice other than humanitarianism exists. While Nagel, like others, is deeply troubled by global inequality, he asserts that a distributive duty cannot be legitimately extended beyond the coauthored, coercive institution of the state. Many have criticized this position, supporting instead a broader duty of justice in the international arena. Cosmopolitans object to this political conception of justice;[2] others, albeit conceding a special duty to redistribute within the state, challenge the lack of any duty of justice beyond the state.[3] I make no attempt here to settle this philosophical debate regarding the appropriate level of redistribution. Rather, I seek to show that state competition reframes this debate: that it represents a new world order that is challenging existing political institutions and mandates a reevaluation of the duties of justice under the emerging arrangements. State competition goes to the heart of the social contract and possibly requires its renegotiation. The reason for this, in a nutshell, is that competition undermines the ability of states (rich as well as poor) to maintain the domestic background conditions necessary to sustain their legitimacy and that make the state a uniquely appropriate candidate for promoting justice. Under tax competition, I argue, the state can no longer unilaterally provide the assurances required for social cooperation. At the same time, its constituents are no longer independent in jointly coauthoring their collective will. Both coercion and coauthorship are now contingent on conditions that transcend state boundaries.

In the international tax market, where states compete for residents, investments, and tax revenues, their sovereignty has become fragmented. As chapter 1 has explained, many residents can now unbundle their state's sovereignty and pick and choose from among the public goods other states offer. In these conditions of unbundled sovereignty, a state cannot unilaterally ensure the cooperation of its citizens without either imposing illiberal restrictions on them or else cooperating with other states. Thus, as far as tax and redistribution are concerned, in the era of globalization,

---

[2] *See* text accompanying *infra* notes 7-11 and references therein.
[3] *See* text accompanying *infra* notes 16-29 and references therein.

the state can no longer be considered a sovereign with monopolistic coercive power. Moreover, as explained in the previous chapters, as states become market players, redistribution is, to a large extent, becoming a price that is set by the forces of supply and demand in the global market for sovereign goods. As a result, market rules are increasingly replacing citizens' coauthorship in determining states' redistributive capabilities and, consequently, their tax policies as well. Instead of equally engaging in a deliberative process with their fellow citizens, (some) taxpayers simply exercise their exit power when (redistributive) prices become too high.[4] Thus, the level of redistribution that states can afford under global tax competition – and not what is arrived at through the collective coauthorship of their citizenry – is what determines their redistribution policies.

In short, states' monopoly on coercive power and their representation of the collective will of their constituents have been undermined. The more fragmented sovereignty becomes, the less it is able to enforce its policies. The more marketized sovereignty becomes, the less voice it allows its citizens. Thus, in conditions of tax competition, justice is under constant threat.

Given the state's fading coercive power in taxation and the decreasing power of its citizenry to coauthor its collective will due to global competition, we can no longer assume that justice can be realized within the parameters of the state. If the state can no longer ensure justice, what entity can? The available option for promoting justice may be to move beyond the state level to the international sphere. More than mere bargaining between states to secure their goals and interests, cooperation may serve as a means for allowing states to regain their legitimacy by enabling them to ensure collective action among their citizenry and to treat them with equal respect and concern.

The traditional discourse in international taxation seems to endorse a statist position in its implicit assumption that when states bargain for a multilateral deal, justice is completely mediated by the states' consent. However, I contend, if such a multilateral regime is to provide the state with fundamental legitimacy, independent justification, beyond the participants' consent, is necessary. The duty of justice cannot be presumed to be entirely mediated through the cooperating states. Thus, contrary to the conventional statist position, that the contents of multilateral

---

[4] Dietsch *supra* note 1, at 19 refers to the mobility of capital and describes it as "de-democratization of capitalism," as "the mobility of capital in an environment of deregulated markets has allowed capital to extricate itself from the implicit social contract."

duties are exhausted by the agreements between states as "the relations themselves do not trigger norms, only the agreements do,"[5] I maintain that cooperating states have a duty to ensure that the constituents of all cooperating states are not treated unjustly as a result of the agreement. The statist approach holds that bargaining between states must conform only to duties of humanitarianism; I argue that not only cosmopolitanism but also political justice (statism) mandates that for a multilateral regime established through cooperation to be justified it must improve (or at least not worsen) the welfare of the least well-off citizens in all the cooperating states. I explain that cooperation alone is no guarantee of improved welfare for all and that certain transfer payments between rich and poor countries might be required to ensure this.

In the face of intensifying domestic inequalities and dwindling tax bases, states are struggling to figure out their next step. The newest G-20/OECD project described in Chapter 5 (combatting base erosion and profit-shifting) is engaged in extensive efforts to devise workable solutions for states to sustain their tax bases. Justice does not seem to be a key concern for either the G-20 or OECD. Both are sticking to the conventional pro-cooperation rhetoric that these efforts – allegedly – benefit all cooperating states. This phase of international taxation does, however, represent a unique opportunity to reevaluate the notion of the duties of justice in the international arena, which is the aim of this chapter.

6.1 The Global Justice Debate in Political Philosophy

Political philosophers have devoted considerable attention to the question of international distributive justice and have raised a wide range of conceptions of global justice. The central point of controversy has been the scope of redistribution. Should distributive justice be pursued solely on the national level or on a global scale as well? Cosmopolitans and proponents of political justice represent the two polar ends on the spectrum of ideas supporting global justice.[6]

---

[5] Joshua Cohen & Charles Sabel, *Extram Republicam Nulla Justitia?*, 34 PHIL. & PUB. AFF. 147, 149, 162 (2006).

[6] There are other variants of the conceptions of global distributive justice. *See, e.g.*, Simon Caney, *International Distributive Justice*, 49 POL. STUD. 974 (2001). Caney divides the varying approaches into four categories: cosmopolitan, nationalist (political), society of states, and realists. Realists (or skepticists) view global justice as an unattainable ideal and, hence, leave distributive justice to the only arena capable of promoting it – the state. The society-of-states approach rejects this skepticism and holds that although states are,

Cosmopolitans (such as Brian Barry, Charles Beitz, and Thomas Pogge) argue that principles of distributive justice should be applied universally: to all human beings across the entire globe.[7] Their thinking, as Simon Caney summarizes it, is that "given the reasons we give to defend the distribution of resources and given our convictions about the irrelevance of people's cultural identity to their entitlements, it follows that the scope of distributive justice should be global."[8] Cosmopolitans (or left institutionalists, as Michael Blake and Patrick Smith refer to them[9]) who follow Rawls' concepts of justice tend to criticize his distinction between domestic and international duties of justice. Pogge, for example, regards nationality as just another deep contingency (similar to race, social class, and gender) that is "inescapable from birth."[10] Thus, following Rawls' conception, Pogge argues, international institutions can be justified only "if the inequalities they produce optimize (against the backdrop of feasible alternative global regimes) the worst social position."[11]

indeed, responsible for their residents' welfare, the global community bears responsibility for ensuring adequate conditions for states to be able to achieve distributive justice. Under this view, outsiders to the state have a duty to contribute only in special circumstances. See Charles R. Beitz, *International Liberalism and Distributive Justice: A Survey of Recent Thought*, 51 WORLD POL. 269, 272–73 (1999):

> David Miller, John Rawls, and John Vincent, among others, have set forth views of this kind. Although these views differ in important respects, they have two central elements in common. First, they hold that all societies should respect basic human rights, conceived as universal minimum standards for domestic social institutions that apply across variations in cultures and conceptions of social justice. (There is some disagreement, however, about which rights count as "human" rights.) Second, they contend that the primary responsibility for satisfying these rights rests with a society's own government and people. Outsiders have a responsibility to contribute only under special circumstances. As Miller puts it, for example, that occurs when there are extreme levels of deprivation which the local government is in no position to relieve and when foreign governments or other international actors can do so effectively without a morally significant sacrifice.

7   There are many strands to the cosmopolitan view. Caney, *supra* note 6, at 975–76, distinguishes between radical cosmopolitanism (principles of distributive justice apply only on the global level and not on the national level) and mild cosmopolitan (distributive principles apply on the global and national levels), institutional global justice (i.e., justice within institutions) and interactive institutionalism (in the context of individuals), and distribution among individuals and distribution among states. Moreover, the measures of distribution vary from one approach to another.

8   Caney, *supra* note 6, at 977.

9   Michael Blake & Patrick Taylor Smith, *International Distributive Justice*, *in* THE STANFORD ENCYCLOPEDIA OF PHILOSOPHY (Edward N. Zalta ed., 2013), http://plato.stanford.edu/archives/win2013/entries/international-justice.

10 THOMAS POGGE, REALIZING RAWLS 247 (1989).   11 *Id.*

Proponents of political justice, in contrast, assert the duality of a justice regime and firmly distinguish between the national and global levels.[12] Under this approach, justice is a good provided by social institutions. As Nagel explains,

> On the political conception, sovereign states are not merely instruments for realizing the pre-institutional value of justice among human beings. Instead, their existence is precisely what gives the value of justice its application, by putting the fellow citizens of a sovereign state into a relation that they do not have with the rest of humanity, an institutional relation which must then be evaluated by the special standards of fairness and equality that fill out the content of justice.[13]

Strong statists, like Nagel, insist not only that special duties of justice exist within the state but that "[j]ustice is something we owe through our shared institutions *only* to those with whom we stand in a strong political relation. It is, in the standard terminology, an associative obligation."[14] Outside the framework of the state, in the absence of such unique relations and, in particular, of the state's coercive power, justice does not impose distributive duties, for "[m]ere economic interaction does not trigger the heightened standards of socioeconomic justice."[15] In the international arena, Nagel argues, only duties deriving from simple humanitarianism are binding.

Unlike classic proponents of cosmopolitanism, contemporary left institutionalists generally concur that the state gives rise to especially stringent demands of distributive justice. However, they reject the bifurcated distinction between national and international institutions and argue for more robust distributive obligations on the international level than those imposed by humanitarianism.[16] They also reject the statist emphasis on coercive power as activating claims of distributive justice and identify, instead, various reasons for supporting a less dichotomous rendition of global justice. Joshua Cohen and Charles Sabel, for example, argue that "a political morality can be political in a capacious sense, that is, sensitive to the circumstances and associative conditions, to the 'different cases or types of relation' for which it is formulated, without being statist."[17] In lieu of Nagel's strong statist position, according to which normative

---

[12] Proponents of the national approach emphasize the moral relevance of membership in a nation. Again, national approaches vary. For a survey of these approaches, see Caney, *supra* note 6, at 980–83.

[13] Thomas Nagel, *The Problem of Global Justice*, 33 PHIL. & PUB. AFF. 113, 120 (2005).

[14] *Id.* at 121 (emphasis added and omitted).   [15] *Id.* at 138.

[16] Blake & Smith, *supra* note 9, at 11–12/22.   [17] Cohen & Sabel, *supra* note 2, at 149.

requirements beyond humanitarianism emerge only in the framework of the state, Cohen and Sabel advocate a more flexible conception of justice.[18]

> We think that global politics does implicate more demanding norms, and think that the rationale lies in a mix of the factors suggested by Strong Interdependence,[19] Cooperativism,[20] and Institutionalism,[21] as well as a degree of involvement of will on the global scale that is more extensive than Nagel's argument suggests.[22]

Andrea Sangiovanni, for his part, downplays Nagel's reliance on coercion.[23] Instead of on how the state "engages, constrains or thwarts the will," Sangiovanni suggests focusing on "what the state does – on the object of our authorization." He argues that "because states provide the goods necessary for acting on a plan of life, we have special obligations to our fellow-citizens." This does not imply that we have *no* obligations of distributive justice at the global level, only that these are different in both form and content from those we have at the domestic level.[24]

Darrel Moellendorf agrees that duties of justice are owed only to comembers of institutions and not universally to all, but disagrees with the assertion that citizenry is the only kind of comembership that generates duties of social justice. He argues that "the inherent dignity of persons

---

18   The concern that Cohen & Sabel, *id.* at 154, have with Nagel "is not distinctively egalitarian: not that some people are better off than others, nor that some improvements are larger than others; nor is there any assumption that all inequality requires an especially compelling justification." Instead, they stress *inclusion*: "Some people are treated by consequential rule-making processes as if, beyond the humanitarian minimum owed even in the absence of any cooperation, they count for nothing." *Id.* at 154. Their concept of inclusion corresponds with the kind of respect and concern (*e.g.*, human rights, standards of fair governance, and norms of fair distribution) "that is owed by the variety of agencies, organizations, and institutions (including states) that operate on the terrain of global politics." *Id.* at 149.

19   Whenever the fate of people in one place depends substantially on the collective decisions made by people in another place, and vice versa.

20   The existence of a consequential scheme of organized, mutually beneficial cooperation governed by rules.

21   The existence of an institution with responsibilities for distributing a particular good.

22   Cohen & Sabel, *supra* note 2, at 164 (footnotes added).

23   Andrea Sangiovanni, *Global Justice, Reciprocity, and the State*, 35 PHIL. & PUB. AFF. 3, 15 (2007): "[A]lthough Nagel often speaks of coercion . . . all that is required is that the system of societal rules be nonvoluntary for those subject to it." Sangiovanni further suggests that while with voluntary associations (*e.g.*, tennis clubs) one has a viable option to leave, nonvoluntary organizations allow for no such option and hence require more stringent justification. The state "must give each of us special reason to accept its laws strong enough to rebut any objection we might have to them. The justification, in turn must show that the law could reasonably be seen as acceptable from within each person's individual point of view, although no one consents to it." *Id.* at 18.

24   *Id.* at 4.

constrains institutional power. Institutions express respect[25] for persons only if they are such that persons whose lives are lived within the institutions could reasonably endorse."[26] Thus, the positions of these left institutionalists are less egalitarian on the global level than the stance of early cosmopolitans, ranging from "reciprocity,"[27] to "inclusion,"[28] to support for equal sharing only of the public goods supplied by the international system.[29]

Without undermining the importance of these distinctions, I focus on states, arguing that the competition among them in the era of globalization has stripped them of their status as a unique forum in which duties of justice arise. Specifically, states can no longer unilaterally enforce justice-promoting cooperation, nor are they a unique locus of independent coauthorship for their citizens. This reality undermines the ability of states (rich and poor alike) to sustain the domestic background conditions necessary for their legitimacy and which make them an exceptional candidate for promoting justice. Section 6.2 will now expand on this perceived uniqueness of the state and explain why, in the marketized and fragmented competitive market of states, this distinctiveness is eroding.

6.2 The Lost State

a. Why the State?

The key challenge for statists like Nagel is to explain their dichotomization of duties of justice into expansive duties at the state level and minimal humanitarian duties at the supranational/international level. According to Nagel, justice should be national because "[t]he state makes unique demands on the will of its members . . . and those exceptional demands bring with them exceptional obligations, the positive obligations of justice."[30] But what produces these exceptional obligations? Nagel contends that the complex combination of coercively enforced, co-authorized rules are the source of the transcendence above simple humanitarianism. As Cohen and Sabel explain, "Nagel argues that a normative order

---

[25] Moellendorf refers to this as "justificatory respect." Darrel Moellendorf, *Cosmopolitanism and Compatriot Duties*, 94 THE MONIST 535, 537 (2011).

[26] *Id.* at 537. Social justice, Moellendorf argues, exists between persons if they are co-members in an association that is "(1) relatively strong, (2) largely (individually) non-voluntary, (3) constitutive of a significant part of the background rules for the various relationships of their public lives, and (4) governed by norms that can be subject to (collective) human control."

[27] *Id.* at 537.   [28] Cohen & Sabel, *supra* note 5, at 148.   [29] Sangiovanni, *supra* note 23.

[30] Nagel, *supra* note 10, at 130.

beyond humanitarianism's moral minimum emerges only within states whose central authority coercively enforces rules made in the name of everyone subject to those rules: only, that is, when individuals are both subjects in law's empire and citizens in law's republic."[31]

Nagel offers two answers to the question of what can "move us past humanitarianism."[32] The first is social cooperation, for which the state functions as a third-party enforcer.[33] Assurance of this cooperation is necessary, according to him, as an "enabling condition of sovereignty to confer stability on just institutions."[34] The only way to provide that assurance, Nagel argues,

> is through some form of law, with centralized authority to determine the rules and a centralized monopoly of the power of enforcement. This is needed...both in order to provide terms of coordination and because it doesn't take many defectors to make such a system unravel. The kind of all-encompassing collective practice or institutions that is capable of being just in the primary sense can exist only under sovereign government.[35]

Coercion is, of course, a fundamental component of the state. It both ensures cooperation and, at the same time, requires legitimation. In Nagel's words,

> adherence to...[political institutions] is not voluntary: Emigration aside, one is not permitted to declare oneself not a member of one's society and hence not subject to its rules, and other members may coerce one's compliance if one tries to refuse. An institution that one has no choice about joining must offer terms of membership that meet a higher standard.[36]

Nagel's second explanation for limiting expanded duties of justice to the sphere of the state is "that states not only foster cooperation by coercively enforcing rules but implicate the will of those subject to their coercive authority by making, in the name of all, regulations that apply to them all."[37] According to Cohen and Sabel, will-implication is significant

---

[31] Cohen & Sabel, *supra* note 5, at 154.   [32] *Id.* at 160.
[33] Nagel, *supra* note 10, at 116, extends the Hobbesian idea of the sovereign as the entity that provides assurances of cooperation with the non-self-interested motives of justice: "[E]ven if justice is taken to include not only collective self-interest but also the elimination of morally arbitrary inequalities,... the existence of a just order still depends on consistent patterns of conduct and persisting institutions that have a pervasive effect on the shape of people's lives."
[34] *Id.*   [35] *Id.*   [36] *Id.* at 133.   [37] Cohen & Sabel, *supra* note 5, at 160.

since "it is impermissible to speak in someone's name ... unless that person ... is ... given equal consideration in making the regulations."[38] Regulations made by the state must therefore be justified to their co-authors. "And not just any justification will do ... the justification must treat each person ... in whose name the coercion is exercised – as an equal."[39]

In contrast to the state, Nagel claims, the international system does not embody such a complex combination of coauthorship and coercive implication of will. The relationship of individuals to the supranational bodies, he maintains, is completely mediated by governments. Hence, as Cohen and Sabel clarify,

> Intergovernmental agreements or other forms of supra-national arrangement can give rise to new normative requirements but the content of those requirements is exhausted by the agreements or conventions: the relations themselves do not trigger norms, only the agreements do ... even with these newer forms of governance, the relationship of individuals to the supranational bodies is completely mediated by governments ... those bodies do not speak in the name of all, their conduct is not authorized by individuals, and the wills of those individuals are not implicated.[40]

Nagel explains that "[i]f the default really is basic humanitarianism, permitting voluntary interaction for the pursuit of common interests, then something more is needed to move us up toward the higher standard of equal consideration. It will not emerge merely from cooperation and the conventions that make cooperation possible."[41] Since global regulation does not speak in the name of individuals, it can settle for humanitarian obligations only and is not obliged to apply the standard of equality. Cooperation alone and the voluntary conventions signed by the countries that make such cooperation possible are not enough to move us up to the high standard of equal consideration.

Nagel's critics focus on his claim that duties on the international level do not exceed humanitarianism. Even if the international duties do not amount to full duties of justice, they are more than humanitarianism, argue critics. Blake and Smith query whether left institutionalists are in fact begging the question by assuming that the international system is "indeed coercive, will remain coercive even if reformed, and is coercive in precisely [the] way needed to generate obligations of distributive justice."[42] They contend that "left institutionalists, therefore, are quite adept at identifying injustices in the international arena, but they are less

---

[38] *Id.* at 160. [39] *Id.* [40] *Id.* at 162. [41] Nagel, *supra* note 10, at 142–43.
[42] Blake & Smith, *supra* note 9, at 13/22.

persuasive at showing that the appropriate normative response to these wrongs is to have the international system be governed by principles of distributive justice."[43] Yet even these critics admit that duties of justice (should) exist within the state. Cosmopolitans posit that states should uphold pre-political rights for justice. Institutionalists, in turn, hold that the legitimacy of the state's use of its coercive powers is contingent on its treating its subjects-citizens with equal concern and respect, but some nonetheless assert that, for a variety of reasons, duties of justice should apply beyond the state.

In what follows, I focus on the state and argue that globalization is undermining the underlying conditions not only for the feasibility of the state's cooperative efforts but also its very legitimacy. Under globalization, I will contend, both coercion and co-authorship are dependent on what happens beyond state boundaries. The state's coercive power is reliant on other states' cooperation, and the design of its tax rules is increasingly being determined by global supply and demand rather than the coauthored collective will of its constituents. Thus, for those seeking to sustain states' legitimacy (and for those interested in promoting justice), the international arena may be the only viable recourse.[44]

b. A Fragmented and Marketized (Tax) Sovereignty

For Nagel, sovereignty is key: "The kind of all-encompassing collective practice or institutions that is capable of being just in the primary sense can exist only under sovereign government."[45] To Nagel, who stresses the coercive nature of the state and the coauthorship of its constituents, sovereignty would seem nothing like a consumer good.[46] However, as

---

[43] Id.

[44] Ronzoni, *supra* note 1, makes a forceful case for the need for an international tax governance to sustain states' self-determination, based on an anti-cosmopolitan (though not strictly statist) position. She suggests that the occurrence of tax competition mandates an enhanced obligation of states toward one another. She argues that competition challenges states' fiscal self-determination (since it decreases the budget and curtails redistribution) and thereby impairs their capacity to be just. Thus, she argues, even non-cosmopolitans are bound to agree to an international regime that would constrain sovereign power in order to enable states to regain their self-determination and justice-providing capabilities.

[45] Nagel, *supra* note 13, at 116.

[46] The State is not conceptualized as merely a supplier of public goods, nor are its subjects conceptualized as mere consumers. Rather, the state is regarded as a sovereign, and its subjects conceived of according to their civic personhood. *See* Michael Sandel, *What Money Can't Buy: The Moral Limits of Markets, in* 21 THE TANNER LECTURES ON HUMAN VALUES 89,

described in Chapter 1, globalization is significantly transforming the nature of sovereignty. Competition with other sovereigns for capital and residents is increasingly turning states into market players that offer their goods and services to potential "customers." This competition percolates into the relations between sovereigns and their subjects and alters the traditional roles of sovereigns and constituents alike. It impacts the kinds and quantities of public goods and privileges offered by the state to its constituents;[47] it affects the meanings and values underlying the sovereign-subject interaction; and most relevant to our purposes, it transforms modes of political participation and schemes of distribution.

As I explained above, this market is steered by two main forces. First and foremost is the mobility of residents and capital; second is the ability of stakeholders (often with the encouragement of governments) to unbundle the "packages" of sovereignty. Let us consider mobility first. Taxpayers, both individuals and businesses, are becoming increasingly mobile. This enables them to select from a range of alternative jurisdictions to relocate their places of residence, investments, business activities, and even citizenship. States often foster such mobility by offering certain privileges and incentives to desirable potential residents.[48] In-demand residents relocate to more appealing jurisdictions, lured by states seeking to benefit from their positive spillovers.[49] This has put states in an unfamiliar position. In this competitive setting, they no longer strictly impose compulsory tax and regulatory requirements on their subjects; they are instead increasingly operating as recruiters of mobile investments and residents from other states while striving to retain their own residents and investors. Tax rules and rates have become, to a large extent, the currency of state competition, pushing states to lower their taxes and curtail

---

94–96 (Grethe B. Peterson ed., 2000); MICHAEL WALZER, SPHERES OF JUSTICE: A DEFENSE OF PLURALISM AND EQUALITY (1983).

[47] See Tsilly Dagan, The Tragic of Choices of Tax Policy in a Globalized Economy, in TAX AND DEVELOPMENT 57 (Yariv Brauner & Miranda Stewart eds., 2013).

[48] See Tsilly Dagan & Talia Fisher, State Inc., 28 Cornell J.L. & Pub. Pol'y (forthcoming 2018) and references there.

[49] Ayelet Shachar, The Race for Talent: Highly Skilled Migrants and Competitive Immigration Regimes, 81 N.Y.U. L. REV. 148 (2006); Ayelet Shachar, Picking Winners: Olympic Citizenship and Global Race for Talent, 120 YALE L.J. 2098 (2011). Multinational enterprises are also mobile, of course. They can incorporate and sometimes reincorporate in their jurisdiction of choice and move their production, marketing, and R&D activities to more favorable locations. see Tsilly Dagan, The Future of Corporate Residency, available at https://papers.ssrn.com/sol3/papers.cfm?abstract_id=3045134, and references there.

redistribution, as explained in Chapter 1. There are, of course, several factors that counterbalance competition's downward pressure on redistribution.[50] One central factor is the fact that the mobility of residents and even of investments is not entirely elastic. People and businesses alike bear costs – economic and otherwise – in shifting their residences. Similarly, states might find altering their tax policies costly. Yet given mobility, states – even those that traditionally support redistribution – are seriously constrained in setting their redistributive policies.

In addition, the divergences in taxpayers' mobility make it more difficult for states to treat their constituents equally. Mobility increases the market power of certain individuals. The opportunities open to them in other jurisdictions pressure their present jurisdiction to treat them favorably in order to retain them and thereby maximize the collective welfare pie. Thus, even if policymakers were to focus solely on the interests of the poorer segments of society, ensuring those interests entails a trade-off between treating them equally and increasing the collective welfare. If a state taxes immobile and mobile taxpayers equally, it risks the exit of the latter, which could reduce the welfare of those left behind.

The ability of individuals and businesses to relocate and opt for better packages of public goods and services at a better price is only part of the story. No less significant and too often overlooked is the ability of (certain) individuals and businesses to unbundle and then reassemble packages tailored to their specific needs. As elaborated on in Chapter 1, the current market of states enables individuals and businesses not only to shop for their jurisdiction of choice but also to buy à la carte fractions of such regimes under different state sovereignties. This fragmentation of sovereignty occurs in many areas of state regulation, but tax seems particularly amenable to such tailoring by expert tax planners. Sophisticated and well-advised taxpayers can assemble different components into a tax regime that is preferable to them and does not necessarily overlap with any of the regimes governing their other affairs.[51] Constructing such a tax package may or may not involve actually relocating resources, for tax

---

[50] *See* Sijbren Cnossen, *Tax Policy in the European Union* (CESifo Working Paper No. 758, Aug. 2002); Thomas Plümper, Vera E. Troeger & Hannes Winner, *Why Is There No Race to the Bottom in Capital Taxation? Tax Competition among Countries of Unequal Size, Different Levels of Budget Rigidities and Heterogeneous Fairness Norms*, 53 INT'L STUD. Q. 761, 764 (2009): "No doubt, the prediction of zero capital tax rates was not in line with reality when it was first formulated and it did not come true since." *See also* Vivek H. Dehejia & Philipp Genschel, *Tax Competition in the European Union*, 27 POL. & SOC'Y 403, 409 (1999).

[51] For a more detailed analysis, see Chapter 1, Section 1.II.b.

matters are well known for being planned and conducted through "paper-shifting."[52] The end result is that citizens and residents do not necessarily have to leave their home country in order to avoid paying its taxes. Skillful tax planning enables them to pay lower taxes than they would have otherwise paid in their home jurisdiction. It is important to note that this is not merely an enforcement issue, nor is it a matter of states' being unaware of their tax system's vulnerabilities. States commonly knowingly allow for the use of instruments by residents (and, obviously, investors) to lower their tax rates. Exotic tax shelters may be infamous for the generous tax benefits they offer and creative tax planning they facilitate,[53] but the distinction between these tax havens and (presumably) legitimate countries providing tax benefits to attract or retain economic resources is certainly hazy. Moreover, even when states do not use tax policies as competitive tools, uncoordinated rules could give rise to arbitrage opportunities. Thus, innocent rules such as allowable deductions, unique forms of incorporation (such as LLCs), conflicting source rules, and differing interpretations of certain types of transactions (e.g., a lease versus a loan) all open up the path to tax planning seeking to profit from inconsistencies across jurisdictions. Thus, rather than a pathology requiring stricter enforcement, fragmentation – and the planning opportunities it breeds – is a natural outcome of the decentralized nature of international taxation.

In any event, the reality of tax competition is that income taxation is no longer an archetypical example of a sphere where states exercise coercive power. Instead, it has come to more closely resemble a menu of options for (mostly wealthy and well-advised) taxpayers to select from. When tax policies are competitive and elective rather than the product of political deliberation coerced by state power, they reflect a very different vision of the state as a locus for the duties of justice than what political philosophers traditionally conceived. The next section will discuss this transformed role of the state.

c. The Market of States as Undermining States' Legitimacy

State competition for residents and mobile factors of production and the fragmentation of state sovereignty both challenge the conception of the state as the key forum in which duties of justice apply. If the state can no

---

[52] See Chapter 1 for a more detailed description of tax planning techniques.
[53] See, e.g., Omri Marian, *The State Administration of International Tax Avoidance*, 7 HARV. BUS. L. REV. (forthcoming 2016).

longer use its coercive power to assure its constituents' mutual responsibility, can it still legitimately impose duties of justice? If it no longer equally implicates the will of its constituents in a political dialogue among themselves, but rather caters to their relative market value (most significantly their mobility), can it genuinely speak in the name of them all? And if the state allows (some of) them to pick and choose among its various functions, does it still constitute the political institution envisioned by statists when they designate it *the exclusive* political institution where socioeconomic justice can and should prevail?

The decline in the power of states to provide and enforce assurances for the collective action of their constituents undermines the legitimacy of their use of coercive power. The shift away from political participation and toward market norms in formulating regulation calls into question the state's ability to give equal consideration to all its constituents in the regulation. Treating some constituents (those with other available options) more favorably than others, I argue, undermines the state's unique position as speaking in the name of all. With its lack of ability to ensure justice and diminishing capacity to equally pronounce its constituents' collective will, the state's ability to provide justice and thus its legitimacy in applying its coercive power wanes.

To clarify this, recall Nagel's first explanation for "why the state": "[t]he state makes unique demands on the will of its members . . . and those exceptional demands bring with them exceptional obligations, the positive obligations of justice."[54] In conditions of tax competition, however, the state's demands of its constituents are asymmetrical and potentially regressive – that is, inherently unjust. Whereas some taxpayers can pick and choose among their duties, others enjoy less leeway and must comply strictly with the state's coercive authority, meaning that this coercion is effective only in relation to some of the state's members. Some taxpayers – those who are more mobile or who can more effectively opt out of the state's jurisdiction – are able to escape its coercive power. Hence, the state does not equally impose demands (including the duty to pay taxes) on all taxpayers. In these circumstances, then, is it still legitimate for the state to make such demands?

Furthermore, as explained, the state's ability to assure justice is critically diminished if the stronger segments of society are able to opt out of its tax system. Consequently, while the state's demands on taxpayers with lesser tax-planning opportunities capacity are still sound, its demands on

---

54 Nagel, *supra* note 10, at 130.

taxpayers who can plan must be adjusted to the elasticity of their planning opportunities. The rules of the market dictate that the more elastic constituents will get what they pay for, whereas the others – albeit bound to comply with the state's demands – will trail behind. The bottom line is that states make coercive demands on their less-elastic constituents without being able to ensure them the justice they deserve, namely: the justice that legitimates the coercive demands. Making demands without conferring the benefits of state duties undercuts state legitimacy as conceived by Nagel.[55] The state is thus able to uphold only a very thin conception of justice: one that is based on people's goodwill and sense of loyalty and not on the coercive coauthored nature of the state.

To better understand this, recall Nagel's two rationales for the unique duties borne by the state: both become debatable in conditions of state competition. First is the state's ability to assure social cooperation. The state's centralized monopolization of the power of enforcement is crucial, Nagel explains, for ensuring the terms of coordination, because it doesn't take too many defectors for such a system to unravel. Although it would be inaccurate to claim that states' authority has completely collapsed, their inability to enforce taxation equally due to competition certainly undercuts their ability to enforce a redistributive scheme. Whereas immobile taxpayers, low-demand taxpayers, and taxpayers with little or no tax-planning leeway are "stuck" with the state's coercive power, the better-off taxpayers (i.e., those who could actually support the state's duties of justice were they to bear their full tax burdens) can often evade their domestic tax duties. Thus, states can de facto enforce their tax laws predominantly on the immobile segments of society and on those segments that are incapable of effectively tax planning. Coercion of this kind cannot provide the necessary assurances for redistribution and is therefore flawed in terms of legitimacy.

Nagel's second justification for "why the state" is will-implication, namely, that the state "mak[es], in the name of all, regulations that apply to them all."[56] Since it is illegitimate to speak in someone's name without according her equal consideration, regulations made by the state must be justified to their coauthors as equals.[57] As explained, however, under

---

[55] Moreover, since the better-off segments of society are often those that are less coerced *and* enjoy more effective voice in coauthoring the collective will, the competitive state regime is really a mixture of the political and market spheres, whereby state coercion and constituents' voices are adjusted to their ability to opt out of the system.
[56] Cohen & Sabel, *supra* note 2, at 160.   [57] *See supra* text to notes 37–39.

competition, state regulation does not apply equally to all. When – especially in the tax context – (some) people can choose between their loyalties and their tax liabilities and when states are increasingly under pressure to recruit desirable constituents, the norms controlling the state-citizen relations inevitably change. Competition between states introduces market valuation into the state-citizen relationship. The competitive context emphasizes the level of a taxpayer's attractiveness to the state, as well as his or her degree of mobility. In highlighting attractiveness and mobility, competition also brings to the forefront the exit power and use-value of taxpayers. These market features infuse the relationship between individuals and their state with the qualities of market relations, thereby reshaping both individuals and the national valuation schemes. As opposed to the political sphere's scale of valuation, whereby all individuals (at least ideally) enjoy equal respect and concern, market valuation accords some citizens – those with effective exit power – greater value than others (i.e., more than those who enjoy voice but not exit). Instead of a tax system based on principles of distributive justice, the market setting imposes a price-based taxing system. The market-based criteria clash with the idea of what it means to be an equal and viable part of the community. Potential as well as existing residents are evaluated according to whether or not they are beneficial to the state, and their provisional status is focused on and rewarded. The more in-demand and impermanent taxpayers are, the better deal they can expect in terms of their tax liability and the public benefits they enjoy. As is often the case, in this context too, the market tends to push aside other scales of valuation. Global competition for residents and resources drives the state to consider the relative market value and elasticities of its constituents and to prioritize those who are in high demand rather than adhere to the requirements of justice. Market value, in highlighting constituents' use value and exit, crowds out equal respect and concern for constituents. Hence, the state can no longer claim to genuinely implicate the will of all of its constituents, nor, accordingly, to legitimately speak on their behalf.

If states' coercive power is diminishing due to competition and if they now find it difficult to treat their citizens justly, what, if anything, can be done to promote justice? Can we still expect states to uphold principles of justice even if they can no longer do so unilaterally? Can we expect them to cooperate to ensure justice? And if they have to rely on the cooperation of other states in order to sustain their sovereign power, does this give rise to a new level of justice duties that transcends state boundaries? Section 6.3 will discuss some possible responses to these questions.

6.3   Where Are We Headed?

The shrinking capacity of sovereign states to collect tax revenues has led many to view global cooperation among states as a way of restoring state sovereignty and, hopefully, promoting justice. As Chapter 4 described, tax competition has been blamed for the decline of the state's tax-collecting ability and the welfare state.[58] Many have asserted that cooperation and/or coordination among states are crucial for countries to preserve their tax bases and attain the traditional goals of tax policy, most significantly redistribution. The idea of multilateral cooperation has not been restricted to the sphere of theoretical debate. In Chapter 5, I explained that much of the international efforts in recent years have been directed at enhancing such cooperation, most recently manifested in the G-20 call for coordinated action to strengthen international tax standards (which resulted in the OECD's BEPS project). These efforts, however, have not centered on considerations of justice but, rather, on ways to improve states' ability to collect taxes in conditions of intensifying tax competition. The question I now ask is whether, and on what terms, multilateral cooperation is just.

a.   Is Cooperation the Solution for Achieving Justice?

As explained, tax competition has eroded states' legitimacy by undermining their coercive power, their ability to equally implicate the will of their constituents, and, consequently, their ability to treat their constituents justly. It therefore seems to make sense for states to cooperate to jointly structure an enforceable regime beyond the state. As Miriam Ronzoni has claimed, "[t]o restore the capacity of state institutions to tax 'as they see fit' (or, better still, as their citizens see fit), a structured institutional response is required."[59] Yet, I argue, mere cooperation is not enough to ensure justice. A multilateral regime established through cooperation is just, I

---

[58] *See, e.g.*, Reuven S. Avi-Yonah, *Globalization, Tax Competition, and the Fiscal Crisis of the Welfare State*, 113 HARV. L. REV. 1573, 1575–1603 (2000).

[59] Ronzoni, *supra* note 1, at 13. Nagel, *supra* note 13, at 143, also qualifies his uncompromising statist position, where "there are good reasons, not deriving from global socioeconomic justice, to be concerned about the consequences of economic relations with [other] states." One is where the cooperation supports an internally egregiously unjust regime. The other is considerations of humanity demanding that we "allow poor societies to benefit from their comparative advantage in labor costs to become competitors in world markets... for example, when subsidies by wealthy nations to their own farmers cripple the market for agricultural products from developing countries, both for export and domestically."

contend, if and only if it improves (or at least does not worsen) the welfare of the least-well-off of the constituents in all the cooperating states.

As discussed at some length in Chapters 4 and 5, a variety of proposals for international cooperation have been raised within international organizations and in the scholarly literature. These include schemes for increasing transparency by facilitating exchanges of information between states (in order to prevent tax evasion); proposals for harmonizing taxing mechanisms (to avoid tax arbitrage and double taxation); and a (highly hypothetical) notion of a coordinated effort initiative engaged in by all states to preserve a certain level of taxation (to prevent "harmful" tax competition).[60] Proposals for promoting justice are less common among policy-makers.[61] In fact, justice is rarely, if ever, referred to as a key feature in international tax frameworks, which seem to implicitly take as an axiom the inherent justice of cooperative efforts and of enabling states to collect taxes.

If successful, such cooperative regimes might optimally restore states' coercive power as well as their ability to uphold justice for their

---

Nagel would probably see even tax cooperation as not demanding political justice (*id.* at 140):

> Justice applies, in other words, only to a form of organization that claims political legitimacy and the right to impose decisions by force, and not to a voluntary association or contract among independent parties concerned to advance their common interests. I believe this holds even if the natural incentives to join such an association, and the costs of exit, are substantial, as is true of some international organizations and agreements. There is a difference between voluntary association, however strongly motivated, and coercively imposed collective authority.

[60] Despite the use of the term "harmful" in relation to tax competition, proposals rarely suggest actually coordinating tax rates across countries and instead settle for tackling tax rates that are "too low" and other policies (such as ring fencing) that are perceived as harmful. OECD, HARMFUL TAX COMPETITION AN EMERGING GLOBAL ISSUE 14 (1998), http://www.oecd.org/tax/transparency/44430243.pdf.

[61] Political philosophers have recently proposed justice-based international tax mechanisms. *See* Brock, *supra* note 1, at 131–41, suggesting the imposition of non-income based global taxes (*e.g.*, carbon tax, Tobin taxes, air ticket, and e-mail taxes) that would be collected by states, of which a progressive amount (higher for developing countries) could be saved by the collecting states and the rest deposited in a global justice fund managed by an international tax organization. *See also* Ronzoni, *supra* note 1, supporting an international regime based on the damage tax competition inflicts on states' self-determination by limiting their budgets as well as ability to redistribute. Dietsch & Rixen, *supra* note 1, propose an international tax organization that would enable national polities regain the capacity to make collective fiscal choices about the size of the budget and the level of domestic redistribution. For an extended argument supporting this proposal, DIETSCH, *supra* note 1.

constituents. However, this seemingly commendable convergence of state efforts is not free of either justice or legitimacy concerns. Although absent cooperation, the state loses its unique status as a locus for justice, a multilateral regime does not necessarily replace it as such. The reason for this, I hold, is that although coercive power is leveraged through this mechanism, coauthorship is not. Thus, if Nagel is correct in his assertion that the unique combination of coercive and coauthored power in a political institution both demands justification and imposes a duty of justice on that institution, then both the state and the multilateral regime each lack some crucial ingredient. Without multilateral cooperation, the state lacks coercive force: it is incapable of providing its coauthoring constituents with assurances of justice without deferring to a multilateral regime.[62] The multilateral regime, for its part, although capable of providing enforcement if successful, lacks collective coauthorship. Despite some recent efforts to include non-OECD countries in the decision-making process, the international arena seems to suffer from a lack of representation, accountability, and political membership. Although the G-20 and OECD have sought to include BRICS and developing countries in the process of designing the current BEPS Accord, it is unclear whether this would become part of an exhaustive effort to be inclusive and representative.[63] As in many other international arenas, many countries (not to mention individuals within such countries) are not well-represented in the international tax forums, and even for those that are represented, the processes do not fully include them or allow them, let alone their constituents, an equal say.

Hence, at least in the tax context, there seems to be no "natural" locus for pursuing justice under Nagel's political conception – that is, where coercion and coauthorship converge. For those seeking the promotion of justice (or sustainability of the state as a legitimate institution), the question then is, which is the right way to go?

One possible avenue is to increase the responsiveness of the international regime to the point where it is considered coauthored. The extreme path for facilitating coauthorship on a larger scale in the name of justice would be to establish a global state and to impose the duties of justice on the multilateral level. Such a regime could presumably respond well to the

---

[62] It might also be lacking in terms of equal treatment of its constituents, assuming competition causes it to treat mobile taxpayers better than the non-mobile. *See* Ronzoni, *supra* note 1.

[63] Jeffery M. Kadet, *BEPS: A Primer on Where It Came from and Where It's Going*, 150 Tax Notes 793, 804 (Feb. 15, 2016).

justice concerns of cosmopolitans and statists alike. However, it is not only an unfeasible solution but probably also an unwarranted one.[64] A global state would likely not be particularly responsive to its constituents' preferences; it would suffer from an excessive concentration of power and lack of accountability;[65] and it would be plagued by serious efficiency problems.

Another possible way to overcome the justice deficiency is to use the multilateral cooperation as a framework for re-empowering states to domestically pursue justice within their borders.[66] This is a solution often advocated in international tax discussions. However, would this hybrid bi-level model for implementing duties of justice be in itself justified and, if so, under what terms?

b. Justice for All (States)

Perhaps to answer this question, we should return to Nagel's basic inquiry: Should we view cooperation as essentially a matter of "bargaining," or has "a leap . . . been made to the creation of collectively authorized sovereign authority"?[67] The former option seems to infer that cooperation is justified per se (at least so long as it is not coerced). The latter implies that an autonomous duty of justice exists beyond state boundaries, but on the condition that a sovereign authority has emerged on the multinational level. The conventional discourse in international taxation implicitly takes the former view, namely, that these are sovereign states bargaining for

---

[64] See e.g., Dietsch, *supra* note 1, describing proposals to "enlarge the democratic tent and . . . go for global democracy" as utopian if not counterproductive.

[65] See Ronzoni, *supra* note 1, at 14, noting the potential of the "despotic dangers of a global fiscal authority."

[66] Dietsch, *supra* note 1, for example, supports reforms that would bring all stakeholders of capitalism under the control of democratic decision making; Ronzoni, *supra* note 1, argues that even non-cosmopolitans are bound to agree to an international regime that would constrain sovereign power in order for states to regain their self-determination and justice-providing capabilities. See also Yariv Brauner, *What the BEPS?*, 16 FLA. TAX REV. 55, 59 (2014):

> The BEPS project's most fundamental insight to date has been noting the failure of this paradigm. Countries, even those with the strongest economies, are not powerful enough to satisfactorily enforce their tax laws pursuant to the current regime. By definition, unilateral action, regardless of its substance, cannot succeed, and consequently, international coordination of tax policies is required as a condition for any chance to implement substantial reform.

[67] Nagel, *supra* note 10, at 141.

cooperation – and, hence, presumably unencumbered by any duty of justice that transcends state duties. Under this approach, the proposed cooperative regime seems like the perfect statist solution: each of the states is responsible for justice among its own constituents, and they all cooperate to achieve the mutually beneficial goals of domestic redistribution. They do not owe one another or the constituents of other states anything beyond the express agreement reached through the bargaining.

This seems to be fully consistent with Nagel's position on international institutions:

> [International institutions] are not collectively enacted and coercively imposed in the name of all the individuals whose lives they affect; and they do not ask for the kind of authorization by individuals that carries with it a responsibility to treat all those individuals in some sense equally. Instead, they are set up by bargaining among mutually self-interested sovereign parties. International institutions act not in the name of individuals, but in the name of the states or state instruments and agencies that have created them. Hence, the responsibility of those institutions toward individuals is filtered through the states that represent and bear primary responsibility for those individuals.[68]

By taking a statist-like position, the rhetoric of international tax cooperation obviates the desirability of cooperation, endorsing it as an unequivocally right thing to do in terms of justice (since it presumably promotes domestic justice), and treats lack of cooperation by any single state as opportunism. This rhetoric frames states' refusal to cooperate as taking a hardball bargaining position rather than a principled call for justice among states. After all, it is claimed, if a state has an option to increase its tax collection (and thereby presumably afford domestic redistribution) by cooperating with other states, why would it pass up this opportunity? Distributive disparities among states or among their constituents are taken as irrelevant in this discussion, since states bear a duty of justice only toward their own constituents – not toward other countries or their constituents. Hence, demands for a more level playing field between developed and developing countries, for example, are not seriously addressed or are instead treated like a plea for charitable treatment rather than a duty of justice.

This statist position could hold were every state to wield independent legitimacy in imposing its tax system – that is to say, could successfully provide assurances for its collectively coauthored regime. However, as has

---

[68] *Id.* at 138.

been explained, this is not the case under tax competition, where individual states struggle to enforce their own tax systems and the rules of taxation are, to a large degree, determined by market conditions.

To conclude this chapter's discussion, I challenge this conventional view, arguing that a multilateral regime that enables states to retain their legitimacy requires its own independent legitimation. Specifically, such a regime will be legitimate only if it ensures domestic justice for the constituents of all the cooperating states. To comply with this requirement of justice, the multilateral regime must set terms that ensure the welfare of the weakest segments in poor countries that might otherwise be harmed by the cooperative arrangement.

We can return to Nagel and the traditional view to better understand this claim. Nagel asserts that a supranational duty of justice arises only if the multilateral cooperation leads to the creation of a collectively authorized sovereign authority. The cooperative regime derives its legitimacy from the legitimacy of the cooperating states. As Nagel puts it,

> a global or regional network does not have a similar responsibility of social justice for the combined citizenry of all the states involved, a responsibility that if it existed would have to be exercised collectively by the representatives of the member states. Rather, the aim of such institutions is to find ways in which the member states, or state-parts, can cooperate to better advance their separate aims, which will presumably include the pursuit of domestic social justice in some form. Very importantly, they rely for enforcement on the power of the separate sovereign states, not of a supranational force responsible to all.[69]

Recall, however, that states have lost a significant extent of their coercive power, in particular, their ability to unilaterally ensure equal treatment of their constituents at least insofar as tax is concerned. Hence, their legitimacy in imposing taxation has been undermined as well. In many cases, it will be *only* through the cooperative accord that they could regain these powers.[70] Cooperation in these circumstances is more than a matter of

---

[69] *Id.* at 138–40: "even the coercive authority of the security council is primarily a form of collective self-defense exercised by traditional sovereign powers, although there is some erosion of sovereignty in the move toward intervention to prevent domestic genocide." Here, the erosion of sovereignty is that of the state where genocide occurs. International tax, however, is different in the sense that sovereign power is eroding in the absence of intervention, and it is intervention that is required to sustain sovereign power. In other words, without international collective action that imposes duties on individuals in other states, the state cannot impose its sovereign power to ensure justice for its own subjects.

[70] *See* Ronzoni, *supra* note 1; Dietsch, *supra* note 1.

sheer preference on the part of the cooperating states or a framework for promoting their goals through bargaining. Rather, the cooperation goes to the heart of state legitimacy. Without the ability to ensure the collective action of its citizenry and to treat them with equal respect and concern, the state can no longer legitimately make use of its coercive powers. Furthermore, cooperation with other states is vital for the state's ability to enforce its powers. In such cases, I argue, the question of the legitimacy of the multilateral regime itself arises: Can a regime intended to provide a state with fundamental legitimacy base its own legitimacy solely on the – in itself deficient – legitimacy of another state? And if the answer is yes, does such a regime – which transcends the state in order to preserve the cooperating states' legitimacy – require independent justification?

When states initiate multilateral cooperation to restore their legitimacy, they entrust the multilateral regime with the authority to coordinate their acts so as to enable them to provide their constituents with justice. This is the *sine qua non* for their legitimacy. They combine their impaired individual taxing power into a collective regime that encompasses more power than the sum of its components' power. Hence – arguably – each state can treat its own citizens justly.

But what if the agreement undermines justice within some of the countries? Presumably, under the statist rationale, the states that reacquire power should not even consider whether the agreement produces injustice in another state so long as all cooperating states have consented to the multilateral agreement.[71] Recall that according to the statist position, justice is completely mediated by the cooperating states, and the agreement between them generates no independent duty of justice beyond humanitarianism.

Absent the ability to ensure justice for their constituents, states lack the legitimacy to apply coercive power. And since use of power requires justification, I contend that states cannot entrust the multilateral regime with anything more than the power to enable them to treat their constituents justly. In the absence of justice for their own constituents, the very ability of states to act as sovereigns – for our purposes – is undermined. Hence,

---

[71] *cf.* Mathias Risse & Marco Meyer, Catching Capital: The Ethics of Tax Competition NOTRE DAME PHIL. REVS. (Mar. 19, 2016), http://ndpr.nd.edu/news/catching-capital-the-ethics-of-tax-competition: "But why would it be the concern of inhabitants of B that inhabitants of A live in a just state? How much exactly do they have to do for inhabitants of A to make sure they can do so? The difference between the domestic case and the international case is substantial. Domestically we are talking about obligations among the inhabitants of the same state, whereas internationally we are talking about obligations across states."

states cannot be trusted to mediate justice when contracting with other states. Even assuming that states do not bear an independent duty of justice toward the citizens of other countries (that is, they are under no duty to treat such constituents with equal concern), I hold that they cannot hide – in the name of justice – behind their unjust (and thus illegitimate) partners as mediators of justice. Unlike other agreements between legitimate sovereigns, a multilateral arrangement that provides legitimacy to one country by increasing the illegitimacy of another does not offer the necessary justification for the use of coercive power. Although the arrangement is officially based on the consent of the two countries, that consent is no guarantee for justice. For justice to prevail and for states to be able to legitimately agree to a multilateral accord, I argue, the cooperative regime should be duty-bound to ensure the ability of each state to provide domestic justice.

As explained in Chapter 4, cooperation may produce injustice in some states, in particular the poorer ones. Not all states are cut of the same cloth. Hence, cooperation that may be unquestionably justice-promoting for some states could have completely different outcomes for others. To demonstrate this, the discussion in Chapter 4 analyzed a hypothetical version of harmonization, where states agree to impose a unified tax of x percent above the value of the public goods provided by each state in order to facilitate redistribution (that is, that the x percent collected by each state will be progressively distributed among its constituents). We saw that while in some countries, the government will, indeed, be better able to collect taxes from capital owners (and, therefore, to redistribute wealth), this will not be the case in other (usually developing) countries. In the latter, local factors of production could lose out due to the reduction in cross-border investment as a result of the increase in taxation. Accordingly, such a regime comes at a cost to local labor, for example. Although a harmonized tax regime could enable host countries to collect more tax revenues from incoming investments and to collect taxes from their own capital owners investing overseas, those revenues will not necessarily compensate local factors of production for the lost inbound investments. Moreover, in some of these countries, the government may be corrupt or captured and hence less inclined to use the funds for redistribution. If host countries are, indeed, unable to collect enough taxes to compensate labor for their lost wages, cooperation might not be a good idea from a distributive perspective. Residence countries might be better able to tax capital owners in order to redistribute wealth to labor, but in host countries, labor could be harmed by the coordinated regime because it would pay for the redistribution to labor in residence countries.

Of course, residence countries could hand over a larger share of the increased revenues to host countries and thereby balance the gains and losses across national borders. But should they? Assuming the residence countries wish to do the right thing, is there a duty of justice for them to (re)distribute these benefits? This, of course, is the question that lies at the heart of this chapter: Does the cooperation in itself impose a duty of justice on the cooperating states? Contemporary left institutionalists as well as Cosmopolitans will surely support such duty of justice between states. In fact, Cosmopolitans would likely recommend have the multilateral mechanism directly redistribute wealth among the people of all countries. But strong statists too, I believe, would not (or at least should not) argue that such a multilateral regime is no more than a bargaining move. When the regime promotes domestic justice within some of the states but produces injustice in others, the cooperating states cannot rely on the claim that the will of the people in those states is completely mediated by their state. An international regime would not be legitimate if it brings justice to some states and injustice to others.[72] My reasoning suggests that when (rich) states need the cooperation of other (poor) states to promote domestic justice, their bargaining position is constrained by the requirement that justice not be compromised within their cooperating state partners. It is – I argue – unjust for a state to promote its own domestic justice at the expense of domestic justice in other states.

Thus, a regime built on injustice in some states cannot resort to the theory of bargaining to claim that the agreement is completely mediated by sovereign states. The states that operate unjustly are making illegitimate use of their sovereign powers (i.e., their coercive and bargaining powers). Rich states cannot legitimize their justice-based domestic coercive power on an agreement that creates domestic injustice in their cooperating states. A multilateral regime established through cooperation is justified in promoting justice *if and only if* it improves (or at least does not worsen) the welfare of the least well-off in all cooperating states. Consequently, a multilateral agreement that pursues harmonization will be valid only if it ensures domestic justice in all states involved.

Although in theory, states could cooperate to maximize global welfare and justly distribute it by transferring wealth from richer to poorer countries, the prevailing decentralized nature of international taxation creates some

[72] Nagel, *supra* note 13, considers a similar arrangement – i.e., allowing poor countries to preserve their comparative advantage in low-cost labor in trade agreements – to be humanitarian in nature rather than a duty of justice.

serious coordination problems. Assuming transfer payments between states to be utopian and that promoting redistribution in rich countries at the expense of the poor in poor countries (without such transfer payments) to be unjust, the next chapter explores a third option – namely, to perfect, rather than curtail, tax competition. Under this scheme, countries would work together in an effort to perfect tax competition by targeting market failures such as free riding, transaction costs, information asymmetries, and barriers to competition. These classic inhibitors of competition translate, in international taxation, into issues of tax avoidance, tax arbitrage, tax evasion, and governmental cartels. Some of these issues (particularly tax evasion and avoidance) are currently being seriously addressed in international tax policy circles (notably, in the BEPS report); other issues (cartels) are receiving less (if any) attention.

Perfecting the International Tax Market

The chapters of this book have painted a fairly grim picture of the current international taxation regime. The decentralized and competitive structure of the field yields inefficiencies and unjust results on both the domestic and global levels. Tax competition creates intense pressure for states to reduce their tax rates in general but in particular for mobile resources and residents, which jeopardizes the very endurance of the welfare state. Tax planning and tax avoidance thrive due to discrepancies between the different tax systems; tax evasion abounds with the lack of transparency; and inter-state injustice persists at troubling levels despite initiatives on the multilateral level. In this complex reality, income tax, once the quintessential tool for financing public goods and promoting distributive justice, has significantly lost its capacity to collect public funds justly and efficiently. And with the waning of taxation, states are increasingly losing their legitimacy to act on tax matters.

For almost a century, the international community has struggled with the project of international taxation. There have been continuous shifts in the targets of international tax policy, and the proposed solutions have varied with the challenges. As described in the book, efforts were initially focused on preventing double taxation. They then turned to "harmful" tax competition, attempting to distinguish good from bad taxation regimes and, subsequently, to transparency as a key goal of multilateral cooperation. More recently, the BEPS reports zoomed in on "gaps and frictions" between tax systems, targeting key tax-planning strategies by providing governments with more effective tools for synchronizing their actions against such planning but not wholesale re-writing of the international tax rules.[1] The latest development has arisen on the international

---

[1] *See* Mindy Herzfeld, *News Analysis: BEPS Alternatives: Evaluating Other Reform Proposals*, 83 Tax Notes Int'l 253 (2016) (describing the BEPS Project as nothing more than a Band-Aid); Yariv Brauner, *Treaties in the Aftermath of BEPS*, 41 Brook. J. Int'l L. 973, 975 (2016)

tax front, with the EU Commission's decision on competition in relation to Apple's Ireland operations. This decision added another dimension to the efforts to overcome the challenges of international taxation, by requiring that states collect *enough* taxes from MNEs under the EU state aid mechanism. However, all this notwithstanding, it seems that the struggle to save income taxation in the global economy still has a long way to go.

Looking across time, the efforts in the international sphere seem to lack coherency and are in need of a focused vision. Improving international taxation is a highly intricate task on both the normative and institutional levels. As the discussion in this book has sought to show, the multiplicity of regimes and the decentralization of the decision-making process are key factors in this complexity. Not only do they set significant technical obstacles to synchronizing international tax policies, but they also require that a fundamental decision be made as to the appropriate level for determining the normative issues of international taxation – that is, should this occur at the domestic level or global level? For those ultimately seeking justice, the question – raised in Chapter 6 – is whether cosmopolitan or political justice should prevail (and, of course, what kind of duties of justice each entails). For those seeking efficiency, the question – again – is what would generate better overall results, competition among states or a central, harmonized regime (discussed in Chapter 4) and whether any kind of neutrality is feasible (a claim I reject in Chapter 2). For those focusing on the political sphere, the issues at hand are the optimal size, level, and power of political institutions and how to shield the political sphere from the market realm, elaborated on in Chapter 1.

The multilateral efforts have thus far pushed in the direction of cooperation. Implicit in this approach is the presumably indisputable correctness of the goals pursued by the collective efforts and the inevitability of the need for a greater degree of coordination. However, as this book has explored in detail, these initiatives have been undercut by collective-action problems and tainted by the biases (about both the issues being targeted and the solutions adopted) and self-interests of those initiating and leading the efforts, which have historically been developed countries

(arguing that despite all the accompanying fanfare, the outcome of the BEPS Projects is unlikely to be dramatic); Michael Graetz, *Bringing International Tax Policy Into the 21st Century*, 83 TAX NOTES INT'L 315, 317 (July 25, 2016) (criticizing the efforts to solve twenty-first-century problems with a twentieth-century international tax system and predicting that the BEPS will "not usher in a new era of international cooperation").

by and large. Moreover, these initiatives have been constrained by the lock-in effects of what I describe in Chapter 5 as an outdated and inferior standard, including obsolete concepts of source and residence, impractical sharing of information, and wide gaps between participating jurisdictions.

This is not an unexpected outcome. The decentralized, competitive structure of the international tax regime is based on a network of states engaged in a strategic interaction with one another. This structure almost begs solutions that are haphazard. The states struggle on a number of fronts simultaneously, contending with problems (and, hence, solutions) that are, in some cases, systematic and common to all, but in other cases, unique to the individual states. States – the key actors and policymakers in this arena – are fighting the battle against tax planners, most prominently MNEs that use international tax policies as leverage in their efforts to minimize their worldwide tax liability. The multiplicity and fragmentation of the different national tax regimes, the variance in tax mechanisms, and the diversity in definitions applied by the various systems combine to provide tax planners with the necessary flexibility to minimize their tax liability. At the same time, states are also struggling with inter-state competition, each trying to undercut the other in an effort to attract residents and economic activity that can optimally use domestic resources and create positive externalities. Finally, the third challenge states face is how to engage on these two fronts and still hold on to their sovereign powers, both internally (by maintaining their legitimacy to rule by treating their constituents justly and ensuring their voice as well as exit options) and externally (by protecting their sovereign powers against supranational powers and MNEs).

The multilateral efforts do not offer a systemic solution for the problems with the international tax system. Thus, although they attempt to provide tools to combat tax planning and tax evasion, they do not attend to the inherent structural problems at the root of international taxation's problems. This may be understandable given the complexity of the issues as well as the number of parties involved. The substantive normative dilemmas and multiplicity of fronts with which actors must contend, as well as the variety of interests involved, tend to blur the picture and, as a consequence, confuse the solutions being pursued. The perspective advocated in this book – construing international taxation as a market where states compete by using tax strategically – is both appropriate and helpful for abstracting the challenges and clarifying the structural issues. It is appropriate since tax is the currency of the actual competition among states for resources and for residents. It is helpful since it helps in aligning the different solutions proposed for the actual problems at hand.

The market metaphor highlights three objections typically raised against markets. Parallel objections exist in the context of the international tax regime. The first objection takes the vantage point of an internal critique of the market, showing that many of the current problems with international taxation are in fact classic market failures that lead to a less-than-optimal functioning of the market. The other two objections are external critiques. One relates to the distributive results of the market and is clearly valid in the international tax context: namely, that in the absence of mechanisms that counter their "natural" operation, economic markets tend to broaden the gaps between the rich and poor. The second external critique refers to the commodification by the market, the claim being that when the market sphere infiltrates other spheres, it tends to crowd out norms that could be essential for the operation of the latter. In the tax context, this has manifested in the commodification of the state-constituent interaction due to the competition for residents and investments.

One way to summarize the problems raised throughout the book and to consider possible solutions is by reframing those problems in the terms of these market critiques. In what follows, I will elaborate on each of these critiques and demonstrate the ways in which they manifest in the international tax market. I do not, in this chapter, purport to offer a detailed roadmap for resolving the problems of international taxation. However, its articulation of the challenges of international tax as correlating with the concerns raised in the market critiques may guide us in evaluating those challenges and help us to consider some broad directions for appropriate policy responses.

7.1 Market Failures

Given the competitive nature of international taxation, it seems hardly surprising that the most acute problems of international taxation correspond with the classic market failures: transaction costs, free-riding, information asymmetries, and anticompetitive collusion.

a. Transaction Costs: To begin with, the decentralized structure of the international tax regime has produced significant conflicts between jurisdictions, creating, in turn, loopholes and double taxation, both of which imposing excessive transaction costs.[2] The discrepancies between jurisdictions compel taxpayers to invest considerable resources in studying the rules of the various jurisdictions in which they operate. Moreover, as Chapters 1 and 4 explained, the gaps and frictions between jurisdictions are prominently abused by tax planners seeking to avoid taxes through what has been termed "tax arbitrage."[3] Tax planning also creates excessive transaction costs for taxpayers, as well as for governments. Taxpayers pay for tax planners' fees in order to maximize their tax benefits. Governments, for their part, often pay enforcement costs when they challenge taxpayers' planning, as well as costs of legislation to close the loopholes. But even in cases where the eventual transactions these loopholes facilitate are desirable for governments, and even when they actively encourage them (e.g., when they attract taxpayers, thus providing their domestic markets with spillover benefits), the costs paid to tax advisors are pure transaction costs, which are net losses for both governments and their taxpayers. Double taxation, in turn, generates extra risks for the unwary, forcing taxpayers to invest resources in safe-proofing their cross-border activities. In welfarist terms, these are again pure transaction costs that reduce social welfare. Desirable solutions should focus on ways to decrease the costs and efforts invested in tax planning and tax advisement more generally; to reduce enforcement costs and the costs of proofing domestic legislation against the risks of unwanted tax planning; and to effectively prevent the costs of accidental cases of double taxation, so as to reduce transaction costs and increase efficiency.

---

[2] See Julie Roin, *Taxation Without Coordination*, 31 J. LEGAL. STUD. 61 (2002), describing the administrative benefits of an international tax-base harmonization: saving both taxpayers and government the administrative costs involved in filing, consulting, enforcing, and adjudicating multiple non-uniform bases of taxation. See also Ruth Mason, *Delegating Up: State Conformity With the Federal Tax Base*, 62 DUKE L.J. 1267, 88–1279 (2013) (explaining how tax-base conformity among states in the federal systems reduces various transaction costs); Steven A. Dean, *More Cooperation, Less Uniformity: Tax Deharmonization and the Future of the International Tax Regime*, 84 TUL. L. REV. 125, 152 (2009–2010) (describing the costs involved in figuring out the various rules and the interaction among them and then complying with them, as well as the transaction fees involved in the pursuit of tax benefits).

[3] See DIANE M. RING, *One Nation among Many: Policy Implications of Cross-Border Tax Arbitrage*, 44 BOSTON COLLEGE L. REV. 79 (2005) (comparing and distinguishing international tax arbitrage from the competition-harmonization debate and considering different ways to curtail arbitrage by pursuing both national and multinational instruments); Adam Rosenzweig, Harnessing the Costs of International Tax Arbitrage, 26 Va. Tax Rev. 555 (2007) (explaining and demonstrating the phenomenon of tax arbitrage and supporting a unilateral policy that will harness tax arbitrage to benefit developing countries).

B. Information Asymmetries: Another notorious market failure that states face in the international tax market is the problem of information asymmetry. As rightly emphasized by scholars and initiators of multilateral efforts (described in Chapter 5), the secrecy rules and opaque tax administrative procedures[4] in place in the various tax haven (and other) countries offer (or at least did so in the past) taxpayers the opportunity to hide their fortunes from their own governments and evade paying taxes. Since states lack the information they need to enforce their taxation, they operate half-blindly. Thus, their public benefits are often paid for by those who do not manage to conceal their fortune well enough.[5] Moreover, instead of directing their enforcement efforts at evaders and avoiders, states are forced to cast a wide net and over-invest in auditing law-abiding taxpayers. The outcome is that states inefficiently spend their resources on providing public benefits to and collecting taxes from evaders, making both their costs of enforcement and tax rates inefficiently high. Were states able to efficiently tax all their constituents, they might be able to better target their public goods and lower their costs (and hence their tax rates) without reducing the level of public services they provide.

However, even with regard to non-tax-evading taxpayers, who strictly adhere to the black-letter of tax laws, their state's lack of information plays a key role in the tax burden they bear, as many are able to creatively tax plan their economic activities. It is conceivable that were states fully aware of these schemes, they could better target avoiders and fine-tune their regulation to accord with the revenue needs of supplying the public services they wish to offer and taxing the group of taxpayers they wish to tax. Certainly, sometimes states purposefully offer loopholes, thus making tax planning an effective platform for states to price discriminate in favor of their mobile taxpayers. In the absence of perfect information, however, the taxpayers who are the most creative tax planners and tax evaders pay the least taxes, rather than the most valuable taxpayers or those with the most elastic demand for what the state has to offer.

---

[4] Omri Marian, *The State Administration of International Tax Avoidance*, 7 HARV. BUS. L. REV (forthcoming 2017), https://ssrn.com/abstract=2685642 or http://dx.doi.org/10.2139/ssrn .2685642 (describing the rogue behavior of tax-haven countries in facilitating tax-planning opportunities and exemplifying it with the Luxemburg leaked ATAs).

[5] Since the goods provided by governments are public goods – they have no actual knowledge, only estimations as to the level of their consumption by taxpayers. In domestic contexts taxes are meant to overcome this lack of information. However, absent transparency, not only the information regarding the level of consumption of public goods but also the information regarding the tax base (and particularly the income tax base) is lacking. Hence the need to obtain information from alternative sources.

Sharing information, however, suffers from a classic collective-action problem where each actor is interested in the other actors' cooperation but prefers not to share its own information (in order to attract investments from foreign taxpayers, for example). Like any classic collective-action problem, effective cooperation – if attainable – proves to be welfare-enhancing.

C. Free riding. Free riding is another market failure typical of international taxation. Since governments cannot exclude taxpayers from the use of public goods, they are traditionally financed through taxes. In the absence of functioning markets, public goods are best provided by governments who decide what public benefits to offer their constituents and impose taxes to pay for them.[6] Free riding undermines the efficiency of the provision of public goods by the state. It occurs when taxpayers manage to enjoy certain public goods provided by the government without paying their fair share in financing such services. As a result, states' capacity to provide (efficient) public goods is undermined.

Both the ability of taxpayers to evade taxes and the elaborate industry of tax planning facilitate free riding. When taxpayers are able to conceal their taxable income, they are free riding the public services they consume. Unfortunately, the absence of transparency in international taxation facilitates (even) more tax evasion than under domestic law. Tax planning also abounds in the international taxation sphere. While it is certainly not uncommon in the domestic law regime, the fragmentation and diversity of legal jurisdictions in the international sphere further exacerbates this phenomenon by providing taxpayers with increased opportunities to "game" the system. The variety of concepts, definitions, and rules in the varying jurisdictions enables taxpayers to present themselves, or the entities they operate under, differently in a number of jurisdictions, to characterize their activities under numerous sources, to set the timing and geographical source of their income differently across jurisdictions, and to creatively set the amount of their taxable income in different jurisdictions in ways that minimize their tax liability.

In ordinary market settings, diversity and fragmentation oftentimes improve market efficiency by better aligning consumers' preferences with

---

[6] Under the classic Tiebout model, bundling can help bridge the gap this mechanism produces between taxpayers' preferences and the provision of public goods, by having taxpayers select bundled packages of public services for a "price." Such a selection process is, admittedly, not perfect, but it does provide taxpayers with some choice and, therefore, better matches public goods with individual preferences.

producers' offerings. Hence, what exacerbates free riding is not diversity and fragmentation per se, but rather states' inability to attach a separate price tag to each fragmented feature of their domestic public goods. Under the current fragmented reality of international taxation, taxpayers do not have to "buy" the entire "package" of public goods. Instead, they can independently enjoy specific public goods and services from the great variety offered by different jurisdictions. States can neither exclude them from those goods and services, nor can they effectively tax them for that use due to the taxpayers' enhanced ability (due to the multiplicity of fragmented legal jurisdictions) – to tax plan their operations.[7] Since attaching price tags to non-excludible services is impossible, solutions should focus on ways to enable states to collect taxes by limiting the options for taxpayers to opt out of the taxing jurisdiction through tax planning and/or tax evasion.

    D. *Anticompetitive Collusion.* In Chapter 5, I described potential cartelistic tendencies on the part of certain (usually developed) countries, which cooperate with one another and are thereby able (if successful in their efforts) to promote initiatives that help them increase their market share of residents and investors and raise the "prices" they charge – that is, the taxes they collect. When such strategies create externalities either for other states or for taxpayers in general, they undercut market efficiency. Hence, one of the risks that international tax policymakers should keep in mind is (overly) successful coordination of policies among closed groups of states with corresponding interests.

The description of the classic problems of international taxation (tax planning, tax evasion, double taxation, and governmental collusion) as market failures helps clarify the issues at stake. The market depiction of

---

[7] Because they are not able to attach a price tag to public goods, the best states can do is use proxies. And because of the fierce competition among states, the proxies they can use effectively are not those that most accurately reflect the benefits the taxpayers consume but rather, the features that are in high demand, those with lower elasticity. (Taxes that states impose on other features, could be easily avoided by taxpayers, who free ride the public goods that the avoided taxes are meant to finance.) Thus, for example, a country with a desirable housing market could collect taxes from taxpayers who buy houses there; a country with a highly skilled labor force could impose taxes on those hiring domestic employees; a thriving consumption market could allow the state to collect taxes from sales within the country, and a superior corporate governance regime could facilitate a certain degree of increased corporate tax – all to the extent that the taxation does not completely undermine the attractiveness of the relevant features and assuming the tax will not be entirely rolled over to domestic taxpayers.

international taxation's concerns – in terms of transaction costs, free-riding opportunities, information asymmetries, and barriers to competition – explains why intervention in the market is necessary. But before I outline what I see as possible ways for such intervention, I will briefly discuss the two classic external objections to the market in the context of international taxation: namely, distributive-justice concerns and the problems that arise when the market encroaches on nonmarket spheres.

7.2   Distributive Justice

One of the most prominent critiques of the market – and where intervention is most required – is the regressive distributive results the market yields. When operating without disturbance, the free market has a tendency to increase and broaden economic gaps.[8] Not only is the market mechanism not constructed to reduce such gaps (as it is based on market actors doing what is best for themselves), but the currency of the market is inherently regressive due to the declining marginal utility of money. In other words, because the market responds not only to the intensity of satisfied preferences but also to one's ability to pay, it is inherently biased against those with lesser ability. Hence, markets alone do not resolve concerns of distributive justice. Quite the contrary: they are generally a source of distributive injustice. State regulation in general and, as stressed in Chapter 1, income taxation in particular, are often the answer for those pursuing justice.

Under tax competition, the state's ability to regulate distributive justice is compromised, since the state itself becomes, to a significant extent, a market actor, as illustrated in Chapters 1 and 4. The marketization of the state under tax competition in fact exemplifies the ineffectiveness of market mechanisms to promote distributive justice. When states become market actors, the pressure of competition makes adhering to principles of justice – both domestically and internationally – even more costly than usual. In their interactions with other jurisdictions, the rational move for states is to consider their own national welfare. This may be appropriate assuming no duty of justice exists between states. Chapter 6 elaborated on the complex question of whether justice imposes any duty beyond humanitarianism among states, and if it does, what form those duties would take.

[8] *See, e.g.*, Anthony T. Kronman, *Wealth Maximization as a Normative Principle*, 9 J. Legal Stud. 227 (1980).

But even proponents of inter-state distributive justice hold no hope of relying on the market as a facilitator of inter-state justice in the absence of supranational intervention in the market.

Moreover, as explained in Chapter 4, the market position of states in tax competition drives them to reduce their taxes, which undermines their ability to implement redistribution domestically. Since the taxpayers who fund the redistribution are usually not those who benefit from it, redistribution is not a marketable good and, therefore, cannot be effectively promoted by states under competition. As we have seen, the competitive-pricing mechanism (which, in international taxation, translates into tax competition) limits states' ability to redistribute wealth domestically through their tax system.

The bottom line is that in conditions of tax competition, income taxation cannot perform its traditional role as the remedy of choice for distributive gaps. Tax competition in fact only exacerbates the problem. Since under tax competition, the treatment (income taxation) is afflicted with the same disease (market competition), it only aggravates the problem. When taxes are subject to the rules of the market, they too cater to taxpayers' choice and are inherently regressive.

7.3   Undermining the Political Sphere

The third critique of the market applicable to the international tax realm is the claim that markets tend to crowd out nonmarket norms when they infiltrate other (e.g., social and political) spheres.[9] Allowing the conversion of resources, rights, and interactions into money enables the market to infiltrate different arenas of social and political influence. This convergence of formerly incommensurable arenas can potentially transform the dynamics of the nonmarket fields. When market norms enter nonmarket spheres, they tend to have a reductive effect on the underlying norms of the latter. Thus, for example, when money infiltrates the political sphere, it corrupts the ability of the political process to make decisions based on equal voice and empowers the rich with superior ability to influence the process. Hence, what Chapter 1 described as the commodifying effect of the market is a phenomenon that not only crowds out nonmarket norms but also has a coercive impact when it makes the lesser-offs vulnerable to the inequalities of the market in other spheres of life.

---

[9] *See* MICHAEL WALZER, SPHERES OF JUSTICE: A DEFENSE OF PLURALISM AND EQUALITY (1983).

In the context of international taxation, competition among states, as Chapter 1 illustrated, has the effect of introducing market norms into the relationship between the state and its constituents. When states compete for investments and residents, they have incentive to pursue attractive taxpayers based on how beneficial those taxpayers are to the state. When taxpayers are able to choose among taxing regimes, they often seek specific public goods and services that are instrumental to them. As explained in Chapters 1 and 6, the marketization and fragmentation of the state under tax competition undermines the political sphere. Under competition, the political sphere no longer controls the state-constituent relationship and states are no longer acting solely to implement the collective will of their constituents using their coercive powers. Instead, states are increasingly able to sell public services only to those taxpayers who are interested in and capable of buying them. In other words, instead of the political process determining the public services that will be provided to constituents and the level of taxation to finance these services, it is often the international tax market that does this. This erodes the power of the political process to decide autonomously a state's fate and subjects it to market norms and forces. Consequently, one of the key challenges in international taxation today is the decline of the state's political sphere. The state is losing its ability to independently mediate between exit and voice so as to preserve the political sphere's control over state fiscal choices in ways that ensure constituents effective participation in the political process and decision makers control of and, therefore, accountability for, the international tax policies in play.

7.4   A Possible Road Ahead?

As we see, then, the decentralized marketized nature of international taxation is responsible for many of its ailments. A shift in approach is vital to overcoming the persistent efficiency, distributive, and political challenges. The question, however, is which direction this change should take. As I have argued throughout, although many of the challenges of the current international tax regime derive from its decentralized structure, centralization is *not* necessarily the answer. Centralization and, particularly, constraining states' ability to effectively compete in the international tax market entail problems of their own, I have shown. Ignoring these problems in an attempt to neutralize the pitfalls of competition would be a mistake. Therefore, in contrast to the recent trend toward multilateral cooperation, which seeks more centralization in anticipation of the demise of the current competitive regime, the solutions I have supported in this book endorse competition as a vehicle for promoting the normative goals of international taxation.

It is important to note that the more competitive regime I support is not a first-best option. In a perfect world, states could possibly cooperate to optimize the combination of efficiency and distributive justice under a politically accountable international tax regime. They could, for example, work together to reinstall their legitimacy as a political entity by allowing each state to retain its redistributive functions through multilateral cooperation in enforcing national tax rules, on the one hand, and preserving global justice through transfer-payments between rich and poor countries, on the other. Such a world, however, is not only extremely complex to construct but also obviously utopic, if at all warranted. The magnitude of the collective normative choices it would require of states, along with the degree of commitment to and solidarity with other states and their constituents (most significantly in terms of inter-state distribution), makes this outcome unfeasible in the current state of international relations. Thus, we are left with two second-best options. One is to strive to approach the utopian world, employing cooperative strategies in order to achieve more (albeit not optimal) centralization. This would entail partial solutions: greater enforcement; increased tax rates that could support domestic distributive justice; and a diminishment of some of the free-riding opportunities. In the absence of inter-state transfer payments, however, this option also would yield likely, as we have seen, a regressive distribution of wealth in favor of rich countries. The second option – which I advocate – is to foster more competition by eliminating market failures. Both solutions, I should stress, mandate multilateral cooperation, and both present serious coordination challenges as well as limitations on political sovereignty and justice. They differ, however, in both their goals and the details of the cooperation they entail.

Rather than strive for a more comprehensive multilateral instrument that curtails tax competition, I maintain, a multilateral accord should seek to improve – indeed, perfect – competition. More precisely, in pursuing multilateral efforts, international tax policymakers should proceed with caution. Cooperative efforts should avoid focusing – in the name of efficiency, justice, or political sovereignty – on helping states sustain or perhaps increase their tax revenues by limiting tax competition, preventing a race to the bottom, or (even) requiring that states impose some minimum tax rate (so as to prevent such a race to the bottom). Instead, I suggest, these efforts should foster cooperation among states in setting and enforcing rules that support more, rather than less, competition among them (in other words, more efficient competition). This would require a number of improvements to the prevailing international tax system, including in particular: reducing transaction costs; increasing transparency; and assisting states in enforcing their domestic tax rules so as to decrease free riding. In addition, cartelistic behavior would have to be reduced, and the barriers to competition for (developing) states in the market for states would have to be lowered. The difference between this more competitive regime and a more centralized regime is not as dramatic as it may seem. Neither requires redistribution of wealth on a global scale (as may be prescribed by supporters of cosmopolitan global justice), and both require, as just noted, at least some cooperation among states and a certain degree of state deference to a supranational regime. However, the subtle distinction between what is currently on the table and what I propose is nonetheless significant: from the perspective I offer, competition, if properly calibrated and notwithstanding its dubious reputation, is conducive, rather than detrimental, to global welfare *and* justice.

This book does not purport to provide a comprehensive and detailed solution to the challenges of international taxation. And yet the dramatic developments in the field and the vast array of policy prescriptions raise a need for at least some consideration of the road that lies ahead. Thus, in what follows, I present, in very broad strokes, some of the mechanisms that may support the competitive solution I advocate. Before proceeding, however, I will consider two objections – that is, the two problems a market solution *cannot* be expected to solve: restoring distributive justice and reinforcing the political arena.

7.5   Two Possible Objections

The (improved) competitive regime I support does not resolve all of the problems that I have considered in this book. Naturally, even a market that is improved or even perfect is subject to the critiques of markets in general, which are difficult, perhaps impossible, to overcome. In the current global context, I claim, however, that multilateral efforts targeted at curtailing the market in the context of international taxation cannot resolve all of these problems either. In fact, such initiatives may create problems that surpass those that they target. The solutions for the problems of domestic justice and state sovereignty must, therefore, be sought elsewhere.

Redistribution is – allegedly – the key theoretical rationale in favor of a more centralized international tax regime. As discussed in Chapters 1 and 4, globalization has transformed the state-citizen relationship by turning states into market players competing for residents (individuals and businesses), factors of production, and tax revenues. Instead of powerful sovereigns with the capacity to make and enforce mandatory rules, impose taxes, and set redistribution, states are now actors in a competitive global market, where their ability to govern is shaped largely by supply and demand. With the growing mobility of residents and factors of production, the state no longer functions as a coercive regime that imposes whatever rules it deems necessary but, rather, increasingly, as a regime that is elective to a large extent. Consequently, (some) individuals and businesses have the ability to choose from a broad range of legal regimes, while states are pressured to offer competitive deals of desired public goods and services (including competitive regulation) at an attractive price. Redistribution has, accordingly, become a price that only some states can afford to impose on high-ability individuals and businesses. This competitive market reality has dramatically weakened states' ability to redistribute by pushing them to lower the prices they charge. Hence, one of the key concerns of sovereign states today is their increasing inability to sustain the welfare state, as they are forced to choose between being a more competitive state (i.e., one that attracts the most investments and the most valuable residents) and being a state that is capable of supporting the weaker segments of society.

The ultimate strategy for increasing domestic tax rates could, arguably, be for states to act together to curtail competition and raise taxes. But this book has demonstrated that in the international tax market, a more centralized international tax regime (assuming no inter-state transfer payments) tends to *undermine* global justice. While such a regime likely promotes domestic justice in wealthier states, it can at the same time impair justice in poorer states as well as undermine inter-state justice.

Unfortunately, increasing domestic redistribution *and* global justice is probably not a feasible goal for international cooperation to promote. For reasons explained in Chapter 6, the power gaps between rich and poor countries, as well as the lack of accountability of the existing international institutions, make the (clearly desirable) advancing of distributive justice on the domestic level without curtailing justice on the inter-nation level unlikely. There are two possible alternative avenues for restoring domestic justice, at least partially. Neither, however, falls within the parameters of international taxation. One route is for states to refocus on the commitment of their constituents to redistribution. States can try to – and if supported by multilateral assistance in enforcing their rules, may well be able to – bundle their community with their taxes. They can present their constituents with a true choice: to remain part of a certain group (e.g., Americans, French, etc.[10]) or to withdraw from that group. Assuming they choose the former option, there is a (distributive) price that comes with the package offered by their state. It is a delicate balance to be reached, as states have only limited wiggle room here. If they push too hard, they may lose the strongest segments of society; but appealing to taxpayers' sense of belonging could provide states with some leeway in collecting taxes for redistribution. Emphasizing domestic commitments might, however, also dangerously backlash at ideas of liberty – as states may be tempted to raise barriers between them and their neighbors, by raising the costs of exit and by increasing the requirements for entry. The income produced by MNEs could be an even more complex matter. Although constituent loyalty could translate – to some degree – into the reassuring mark of a strong state even for MNEs, its potential, in that context, is limited. Contending with the market failures I discuss in Section 6 below could further increase states' ability to collect more taxes from MNEs, at least to some extent. On the whole, however, states may be unable to effectively tax MNEs' income for redistributive purposes. And yet, multinational corporations may have an important role in balancing the power of governments in terms of liberty. Corporations' interests in preserving open, free, and global markets – although often condemned as providing MNEs with too much power of their own – may be the necessary counterforce to that of governments seeking refuge in short-sighted isolationism.

The other avenue for restoring some domestic justice may lie in areas of law that are less susceptible to inter-jurisdiction competition or planning than tax is. Despite the familiar advantages of income taxation as a venue for redistribution,[11] the decentralized structure of the international regime combined with the marketized, fragmentized nature of the competition between states could mean that other rules (such as property law, tort law, or other "nontax" laws) are a more effective vehicle for redistribution. The high electivity of income taxation – the fact that income taxation is highly prone to tax planning – relative to other areas of law

---

[10] Citizenship is an obvious way to implement such group belongingness. However, it entails significant drawbacks. See Ruth Mason, *Citizenship Taxation*, 89 S. CAL. L. REV. 169, 187–231 (2015).

[11] Louis Kaplow & Steven Shavell, *Why the Legal System Is Less Efficient than the Income Tax in Redistributing Income*, 23 J. LEGAL STUD. 667 (1994) have famously argued that income taxation is the most efficient way for redistribution and should therefore be preferred over redistribution within any other field of law (*e.g.*, private law).

makes income taxation an apparently less attractive locus for redistribution. Since regulatory competition occurs not only in income taxation but also in other legal areas governed by different choice of law rules, the best legal arena for redistribution is the area that is least susceptible to jurisdiction shopping. This means that tax laws and rules are not necessarily the best choice for redistribution,[12] for the wide range of planning opportunities and choice of alternative jurisdictions makes them highly elastic.

Furthermore, it is important to note that even though perfecting tax competition – the solution I propose – is not specifically designed to improve redistribution, it should nonetheless have a positive impact on redistributive efforts by diminishing tax-planning and free-riding opportunities. Since mobility and tax-planning capabilities are not equally allocated among taxpayers and since taxpayers with enhanced tax-planning capabilities are often the wealthiest and thus the prime targets of redistribution, limiting tax-planning opportunities is in itself progressive.

To be sure, none of this fully addresses distributive justice. But for justice to truly prevail, serious consideration of global justice must be part of any multilateral cooperation. The alternative, I am afraid, is worse: protecting domestic redistribution at the expense of the poor in poor countries, on the one hand, and curtailing exit and, thereby, the effective check on governmental waste and power, on the other. The bottom line is that short of securing justice for all states via an elaborate system of transfer payments to the poor in poor countries – which is both unlikely and not necessarily desirable in the absence of international political mechanisms – international tax cooperation might have to give up on the aspiration to collectively eliminate domestic injustice.

Another argument that allegedly supports greater centralization is the marketization of the political sphere due to competition. Here too, however, multilateral cooperation does not offer a good-enough answer. While competition might curtail voice, centralization might curtail exit. The former impedes voice by encouraging states to marketize their relationships with their constituents; the latter impedes exit by limiting the options available to taxpayers. Both undermine a healthy political process. As Albert Hirschman has noted, voice is not effective absent a real option to

---

[12] Tsilly Dagan, *The Global Market for Tax & Legal Rules*, 21 FLA. TAX REV. (forthcoming 2017), https://ssrn.com/abstract=2506051. For a similar idea in the local government context, *see* Brian Galle, *Is Local Consumer Protection Law a Better Redistributive Mechanism than the Tax System?*, 65 N.Y.U. ANN. SURV. AM. L. 525, 532–33 (2010).

exit, and exit without voice does not improve domestic policy.[13] However, perhaps more significant is the fact that while the market for states collapses the insulation of the political sphere from market values and norms, the multilateral arena does not necessarily provide an independent forum that can sustain such a political sphere. The problem is that the international arena is dominated by the holding out of (a select group of) influential states and powerful interest groups. Chapter 5 explained how such states often have the power to tilt the dynamics of the international arena in their favor. Hence, while the capacity of the domestic political arena has declined due to tax competition, using the international arena to reinforce it does not really improve political accountability, let alone civic coauthorship. If, indeed, the international arena is captured by strong players, this implies that it cannot provide the domestic political discourse with the necessary safeguards; it cannot be expected to act impartially when it comes to national independence. Hence, again, multilateral cooperation is probably no better than competition in terms of sustaining states' political sphere.

Again, this suggests that the solution to the erosion of the political sphere may lie elsewhere and not in international tax centralization. One option is to increase people's participation in the international political sphere by increasing the accountability of their representatives and providing them with more avenues to take active part in the international political process. Another option could be to increase the weight of more localized forums, to which people may feel more committed.

These questions are obviously beyond the scope of this book. For my purposes, it suffices to realize that multilateral cooperation is not necessarily the best response to the political critique of the market, and therefore, adopting competition as a path to improve international taxation should not be ruled out.

7.6   Perfecting Tax Competition

The market analogy to the challenges of the international tax regime could be helpful in identifying some directions for desirable solutions. The competitive solution I support has the advantage of building on existing competitive market mechanisms and improving them to enhance international tax policy, by fighting the market's failures. The challenge, of

---

[13] ALBERT HIRSCHMAN, EXIT VOICE AND LOYALTY: RESPONSES TO DECLINE IN FIRMS ORGANIZATIONS AND STATES (1972).

course, is how to reduce transaction costs; increase transparency; enhance enforcement and decrease free riding, while preventing cartelistic behavior as well as the barriers to competition for (developing) states. My purpose in this book is not to offer a specific solution, but rather to explain that in seeking solutions, we should pay attention to the costs of cooperation, and understand that cooperation alone cannot provide us with the complete answer. What follows should, therefore, be read as an illustration of a few alternative mechanisms that could be pursued to overcome these market failures – an agenda for further research if you may – rather than the end of a journey. They all require cooperation. But, importantly, this cooperation has to do with the rules of the competitive game rather than with the coordination of its results. These solutions range from quite experimental (and potentially unrealistic) components to elements that seem to already be in the process of being established. The most radical of these is the proposition to institute an inter-state antitrust agency to counter anticompetitive strategies by states; the more realistic suggested feature is an information-sharing system to counter asymmetrical information. A third possible mechanism would seek solutions for the structural question of rule-divergence among regimes, in an effort to prevent free riding and reduce transaction costs while, at the same time, preserving states' ability to offer a variety of taxing and spending regimes.

As we shall see, all of these solutions admittedly raise significant challenges of design, application and legitimacy. And yet, the solutions to some of the market failures seem more straightforward than others. Overcoming the collective action in sharing information – not to undermine the difficulties in achieving it – seems like an obviously necessary solution to information asymmetries, and could also help in reducing transaction costs and in preventing some types of free riding. Not surprisingly, this is also the area where most of the progress has been made in recent years. Other "fixes" are trickier. It is harder to identify the "gold standard" for tackling free riding and for countering anticompetitive strategies, and it is equally hard to present workable solutions to these problems.

a. Information Sharing

Information is, as described above, a crucial factor in the efficient operation of the international tax market; it is a prerequisite for a state to align the taxes it is paid with the public goods and services it provides. Since public goods are non-excludable, states cannot feasibly estimate their use by taxpayers. Taxes are traditionally being used as an alternative to the need to evaluate public-goods consumption. But absent information regarding their residents operating overseas, states are unable to properly enforce their international tax rules; thus, some taxpayers can free ride the public services the state provides without paying their fair share (however defined), while others are not offered the kind and amount of public goods that best fit their preferences. Increasing transparency is a solution because it allows states to better enforce their own taxes on their own taxpayers. With full information, states can better determine who "their" taxpayers are, what kind of resources they own, and how they wish to tax them, thus decreasing the ability of those taxpayers to free ride their public services; this enables states to offer more generous packages of public goods to their other constituents. Transparency, in other words, is the *sine qua non* of the efficiency of an international market for tax and public goods.

Since information is not easy to obtain, states need to secure the assistance of other states – where their residents' income is being produced. The host state in which the investment or activity actually takes place could more easily acquire the necessary information by forcing its own residents – most particularly, financial institutions – to provide this information. The process of collecting the information is expensive, however, with the administrative costs particularly steep. Moreover, host countries (particularly, but not necessarily, those that specialize in helping foreign investors conceal their overseas activities) can benefit from foreign investments as well as from the (lower) taxes those investors pay and therefore have little incentive to expose them. Thus, even though countries could generally benefit from obtaining information on their own residents, they each lack an incentive to collect and provide the information for other countries' use.[14] This is a classic collective-action problem, for which many have rightfully advocated the classic solution: cooperation. Information sharing is one context in which the textbook solution for a classic market failure may actually work.

As is often the case with collective-action problems, however, obtaining such cooperation is complex even for countries whose costs and

---

[14] *cf.* Philippe Bacchettaa & Maria Paz Espinosac, *Information Sharing and Tax Competition among Governments*, 39 J. INT'L ECON. 39, 103–21 (1995) (arguing that in a bilateral setting, hosts operating strategically may have an incentive to reveal information, an effect that disappears when many host states compete simultaneously for foreign investment); Michael Keen & Kai A. Konrad, *The Theory of International Tax Competition and Coordination* 59 (Max Planck Inst. for Tax Law & Pub. Fin. Working Paper 2012, July 6, 2012) (explaining that there can be a sharp divergence of interests, with high tax countries much more certain to gain from mutual information exchange).

benefits from information sharing are roughly symmetrical. The challenge for such cooperation is even greater for developing countries (for which the costs of collecting and providing the information may be prohibitive due to lack of technical capacities) and, obviously, for tax-haven countries (for which the losses from their reduced "tax haven business" may be considerable).[15] Thus, developing countries may legitimately require technical assistance as well as resources in order to establish a twenty-first–century collecting and reporting system of information. Tax-haven countries, in turn, although their reluctance to participate is less justified, might demand (explicitly or not) compensation for their self-harming cooperation.[16]

Overcoming this collective-action difficulty is indeed a significant challenge. But even if it can be overcome, the construction and operation of such an information-exchange system may be prohibitively costly. Exchanging information with multiple other states, each of which adheres to its own rules, is a daunting enterprise for the state as well as for its taxpayers. As usual, standardization can help. Standardizing the information collected and provided economizes on the costs of collecting and organizing the pertinent information. If all taxpayers in all jurisdictions are required to collect the same kind of information and arrange it and submit it in the same way, administrative costs would be significantly reduced. Again, a compatible standard would allow adopting states as well as complying taxpayers to benefit from the ability to use the same regulation and the same information in their dealings with other states.

As described in Chapter 5, considerable progress has been made in the pursuit of a global standard for information-sharing and standardized reporting.[17] The G-20 finance ministers, OECD member countries, and several nonmember countries have all endorsed a Common Reporting Standard for automatic exchange of tax information. The standard requires states to obtain specific financial account information from their financial institutions and automatically share it with other states on an

---

[15] *See* Itai Grinberg, *Taxing Capital Income in Emerging Countries: Will FATCA Open the Door?*, 5 WORLD TAX J. 325 (2013).

[16] Steven A. Dean, *The Incomplete Market for Tax Information*, 49 BOSTON COLL. L. REV. 1, 21 (2008); Adam Rosenzweig, *Thinking Outside the (Tax) Treaty*, 2012 WISC. L. REV. 717 (proposing to correct the assymentry in the incentives of small and large countries to cooperate by using mechanisms that would benefit small and uncooperative states and would serve as side payments).

[17] *See* Itai Grinberg, *The Battle Over Taxing Offshore Accounts*, 60 UCLA L. REV. 304 (2012) (arguing that we are witnessing the birth of a new international regime in which financial institutions act as cross-border tax intermediaries with respect to offshore accounts).

annual basis. More than 101 jurisdictions have publicly committed to implementing the standard.[18]

Remarkably, many developing countries as well as tax-haven states are among those who have committed to the standard. However, a successful exchange of information is yet to be achieved. As expected, developing countries struggle to adhere to the technical requirements of the standard, although other countries are encouraged to support them to achieve the necessary capabilities, which could be well worth their effort. Moreover, as states can select the countries with which they agree to exchange information, the Tax Justice Network recently complained that "the publication of the latest data shows that many countries, including some tax havens, are being very selective about who they are choosing to share information with. It seems that many OECD countries prefer to play this kind of 'dating' game among themselves...."[19] Consequently, it is still unclear if, and to what degree, the Common Reporting Standard will actually prevail.[20]

In addition, two further challenges threaten the ascendancy of this standard. First, while the current efforts seem hopeful, we may be witnessing a battle of standards; the United States, which was a pioneer with the FATCA rules that subsequently spread to many countries,[21] seems reluctant to join the multilateral efforts that followed its lead.[22] Second, the sequential nature of adopting the standard could be causing a problem in itself. The reason is that as more tax-haven countries adopt the standard, the remaining tax havens (those that avoid joining the network) are likely experiencing an increased demand for their tax-haven services. Hence, their costs of adopting the standard increase in tandem with the rise in their benefits from their haven business. The higher the costs of the standard, the lower the likelihood that they will join the network (but probably also the amount of international pressure on them to join it).

I do not want to understate these (and possibly further) intricate difficulties of resolving the collective-action problem and attaining a proper

---

[18] For a complete list, see http://www.oecd.org/tax/transparency/AEOI-commitments.pdf.

[19] See http://www.taxjustice.net/2016/10/25/oecd-information-exchange-dating-game/.

[20] Committing to international agreements without complying is not unique to the this context. See Steven A. Dean, *Philosopher Kings and International Tax*, 58 HASTINGS L. J. 911, 961 (2007) and references there.

[21] See Joshua D. Blank & Ruth Mason, Exporting FATCA, 142 TAX NOTES 1245 (Mar. 17, 2014).

[22] See William Hoke, *The Year in Review: Demands for Greater Tax Transparency Escalate in 2016*, 85 TAX NOTES INT'L 27 (JAN. 2, 2017).

standard, which are preconditions of a workable system of information sharing. But these efforts of cooperation – unlike many others I have criticized in these pages – are well worth our while, because such a system is a crucial element in a viable competitive market of international taxation.

b. Streamlining States' Tax Rules

The decentralized and fragmented nature of the international tax market allows for a great variety of taxing regimes. A variety in the products offered is ordinarily necessary to increase the market's ability to promote preference satisfaction. Taxing and spending regimes, as explained, however, are not ordinary products. They are mechanisms that are designed to provide for public goods that the market is unable to efficiently provide. In the global market these regimes are interconnected in the network of international taxing regimes. The variety in international taxing regimes, however, has led to incompatibilities among them. These gaps and frictions between the legal regimes produce – as mentioned above – significant transaction costs, double taxation and tax-planning opportunities that limit states' ability to effectively use their resources and collect taxes – that is, payments for the public goods they provide.

Working alone, states find it challenging to overcome these incompatibilities. In some cases, it may be possible: for example, a state can unilaterally prevent double taxation, impose certain GAAR rules, or collect taxes for its public goods by taxing the (rare) attributes that could be effectively linked to its jurisdiction and bundling the public goods and taxes it wishes to impose with such attributes.[23] However, cooperating with other states to create the necessary degree of compatibility between their jurisdictions could be more efficient in many cases. Complete harmonization of the international tax system, as I explained in much detail in Chapter 4, is both unfeasible and undesirable. Yet we can certainly think of more than one way to promote such compatibility.

The BEPS Project points in one direction: tackling specific cases in which incompatibility provides tax-planning opportunities. Thus, the BEPS Project sought to contend with tax-planning strategies, by, for

---

[23] The best candidates among the available attributes that could serve as such links would be those with the lowest elasticity – i.e., those that make taxpayers least inclined to shift to other (more appealing) jurisdictions. Hence, solutions could focus on attributes in high demand (in countries that are endowed with such features), on monitoring the techniques for opting out of certain jurisdictions (thereby increasing the costs of opting out), or on limiting the available options for opting out.

example, finding ways to overcome hybrid mismatches or by disallowing in one country deductions for payments that go untaxed in the other country. If successful, such an approach could certainly limit tax avoidance and help states align the taxes they collect with the services they wish to offer to certain taxpayers, thereby also limiting free-riding opportunities. And yet, this is a costly strategy, particularly when it requires that states monitor the rules of other states, as well as their taxpayers' strategies. Moreover, being mostly elective and limited to specific planning strategies, it does not eliminate the risk of serious mismatches among national tax regimes and carries the risk of pushing planning opportunities to different mechanisms – those that have not been specifically targeted by BEPS.

Another strategy to prevent mismatches among independent taxing regimes could be to de-link the tax collected from benefits provided. This could be effected by states' jointly setting a worldwide tax base (or even collecting taxes) and allocating parts of this tax base to the various states, according to some sort of formula.[24] Such a regime, obviously, would eliminate much of the initial incentive for taxpayers to artificially shift the tax bases between countries. Some have further suggested rethinking the entire international tax regime and adopting an alternative system, such as a destination-based or transaction-based mechanism.[25] If the benefits

---

[24] See e.g., Reuven Avi-Yoanh & Kimberly Clausing, *A Proposal to Adopt Formulary Apportionment for Corporate Income Taxation: The Hamilton Project* (Jun, 25th, 2007). Available at SSRN: https://ssrn.com/abstract=995202 or http://dx.doi.org/10.2139/ssrn.995202 (proposing unitary taxation of MNEs income, allocated among jurisdictions based on their domestic sales); Reuven S. Avi-Yonah & Ilan Benshalom, Formulary Apportionment–Myths and Prospects, 2011 WORLD TAX J. 371, 373, 378; Reuven S. Avi-Yonah, Kimberly A. Clausing & Michael C. Durst, Allocating Business Profits for Tax Purposes: A Proposal to Adopt a Formulary Profit Split, 9 FLA. TAX REV. 497, 500, 501–07, 510–13 (2009); Julie Roin, Can the Income Tax Be Saved? The Promises and Pitfalls of Adopting Worldwide Formulary Apportionment, 61 TAX L. REV. 169, 172–73 (2008). But see J. Clifton Fleming, Robert J. Peroni & Stephen E. Shay, Formulary Apportionment in the U.S. International Income Tax System: Putting Lipstick on a Pig?, 36 MICH. J. INT'L L. 1 (2014).

Peter Dietsch, CATCHING CAPITAL: THE ETHICS OF TAX COMPETITION (2015) Suggested an International tax organization that would provide a forum for governments to negotiate agreements on the rules of international taxation and would ensure those rules are enforced. Dietsch supports a unitary tax with formula apportionment system would first calculate the word-wide profits of MNEs, and then allocate claims to tax shares of these profits to states according to a formula that reflects the company's economic activity in each country. Each country would set its own rate as long as it does not undermine the fiscal autonomy of other states. See also Peter Dietsch & Thomas Rixen, *Tax Competition and Global Background Justice*, 22 J. POL. PHIL. 150 (2014).

[25] For a review of some examples of proposals for radically transforming international taxation, *see* Herzfeld, *supra* note 1; Alan J. Auerbach, Michael P. Devereux & Helen Simpson, "Taxing Corporate Income," in Stuart Adam et al., eds., Dimensions of Tax

a taxpayer consumes are de-linked from the taxes she pays (with taxes based on rather-easily determined features such as sales, employees, etc.), there is no tax price attached to specific public goods and services; and because avoiding tax under formulary apportionment requires real measures – such as reducing sales or shifting employees – it could be harder to plan around.

Setting the formula according to which states should be allocated what share of worldwide taxes is, of course, a serious challenge and – if the history of international tax cooperation has taught us anything – may raise significant issues concerning the allocation of the tax base, the exact elements that trigger taxation, and the costs of collection among states. Moreover, the degree of cooperation that would be required for decision making would likely generate resentment among states, as it would seriously undermine their tax sovereignty.

Another option to construct an international tax regime that would potentially reduce transaction costs and curtail planning opportunities and, thus, free riding, but without a need to allocate taxing rights among the various countries, could build on the network structure of international taxation. In a nutshell, such a regime would be based on a network of international taxation constructed of an improved – more transparent and more compatible – standard for international taxation.[26] If properly designed, such a standard would facilitate greater and more efficient competition and would better promote global (albeit not necessarily domestic) justice than both the current regime and the more centralized alternative.

Design: The Mirrlees Review (New York: Oxford University Press, 2010) 837; *Michael Devereux & Rita de la Feria, Designing and Implementing a Destination-Based Corporate Tax* (May 2014), available at http://eureka.sbs.ox.ac.uk/5081/1/WP1407.pdf (proposing a destination-based, cash-flow corporate tax); For a recent critique see Wei Cui, *Destination-Based Cash-Flow Taxation: A Critical Appraisal*, 67 U. Toronto L.J., 301 (2017). *See also* Dean, *supra* note 2 (suggesting a division of labor among taxing jurisdictions he entitles "deharmonization" as an alternative to harmonization).

26 Yariv Brauner, *An International Tax Regime in Crystallization – Realities, Experiences and Opportunities*, 56 TAX L. REV. 259, 262 (2003) has suggested a partial, gradual rule harmonization solution that would similarly aim at converging national tax bases. *See also* Roin, *supra* note 2, at 77 ("Indeed, only one solution [to the administrative costs and tax arbitrage] would be truly systemic: worldwide agreement on the definition of taxable income. International cooperation leading to the development of a common understanding of the tax base would simultaneously render obsolete the problems of multiple books, excess complexity, and arbitrage identified above."). For a comprehensive analysis of standardized tax base regime of states under the U.S. government see Ruth Mason, *Delegating Up: State Conformity with the Federal Tax Base*, 62 DUKE L.J. 1267 (2013) who considers the benefits and costs of base harmonization in the domestic U.S. federal context, and – given its stickiness – offers some improvements.

Establishing a winning standard, let alone an unbiased one, is far from a trivial matter, of course.[27] But once established and once a critical mass of countries has adopted it, it should be relatively easy to sustain the standard since other countries will be incentivized to join and then remain in the network due to the network externalities it produces.

Because international taxation is a network, taxpayers and states – the network users – could benefit from a standardization of international tax terms, concepts, and rules even if the details of the standard are not their best option. If all states were to adhere to a common standard for international taxation, taxpayers could save the costs of mastering the rules and terms of the foreign jurisdictions in which they operate. States would also save, and not only the costs of domestically designing an international tax system that is synchronized with both the complexities of the current international market and the laws of other states. Indeed, a unified standard could provide states with administrative, enforcement, and dispute-resolution benefits, quite similar to (or hopefully even better than) the benefits currently offered by tax treaties, only without the costly bilateral negotiations the latter entail. Moreover, like the tax treaty regime standard, an international unified standard would not only achieve greater coordination between countries' tax rules; it would also bolster investors' certainty, provide them with reassuring signals, and facilitate easier information gathering and cooperation in tax enforcement among states.

An international tax standard, furthermore, could (indeed, to promote efficiency it should) cover more ground than tax treaties. An effective standard should serve as a comprehensive manual for the operation of the international tax system in each of the cooperating countries. This manual would provide compatible definitions of states' tax bases as well as their operation. If, for example, the current source-residence system is to be preserved, the standard should set definitions and categorizations of taxable income; it should probably include an agreed-upon list of entities, timing and residency criteria, geographical sources of income, tie-breaking rules, interpretation, and modes of dispute resolution.[28] Such a standard could

---

[27] See Roin, *supra* note 2, describing the considerable (even prohibitive) political costs entailed in pursuing such a unified tax base.

[28] The key challenge here is to identify the areas where the benefits in preserving a variety of potential definitions exceed the costs of potential arbitrage opportunities. Thus, for example, while there may be costs to a unified definition for what is considered a corporation versus a partnership, and while some states would prefer form over substance and some otherwise, if the benefits of such variety are lower than the costs of tax-planning opportunities inconsistencies allow, uniformity should prevail.

also regulate the provision of information by taxpayers and its collection and sharing by states, and it could make the enforcement of foreign tax rules a manageable task for domestic enforcement agencies. By setting a standard with a more comprehensive scope, an international tax regime could emerge as a stable solution that simultaneously limits the potential for tax planning and reduces enforcement costs. At the same time, it would allow states to compete by offering differing combinations of the same "ingredients" and varying tax rates.

The beauty of the network structure of such a standard is that it could be self-enforcing. States would have incentive to abide by its rules due to the positive network-externalities they gain from being part of the system. Hence, instead of an enforcement system obligating members to monitor other members' systems and punish its defectors, which requires active collaboration among the cooperating states, such a standard would require only verification by an independent agency that a state is obeying the rules – approval that states would be incentivized to gain.

With an efficient standard in place, taxpayers would have very limited potential to game the rules of one jurisdiction using the rules of another jurisdiction. Arguably, the more expansive and detailed the standard, the less opportunities it would leave for tax planning (although greater planning efforts may be invested in exploiting the surviving loopholes). In addition, tax authorities would be able to focus their enforcement efforts on tax evasion rather than tax planning. They would also find it easier to collect information, as the categories required for this would be more comprehensible across national borders and, thus, their costs of enforcement reduced. At the same time, the risk involved in evading taxes would increase, due to more efficient and more targeted enforcement.

Designing the specifics of this standard is, of course, a (huge challange and well beyond my scope here), and its feasibility is – no doubt – highly questionable. Standard entrepreneurs would have to first decide whether to build on the source-residence paradigm underlying the current international regime or to devise a completely new model. The existing principles of international taxation – based on the familiar source and residence principles and double-taxation mechanisms – might be a comforting alternative, based on years of experience and practical trial and error. The existing regime also benefits from being the prevailing system and, consequently, from the stability of being the locked-in solution.[29]

---

[29] Wolfgang Schoen, *International Tax Coordination for a Second-Best World (Part I)*, 1 WORLD TAX J., 83 (2009) has predicted that "any proposal to simply wait for the extinction of source taxation in order to build a new and harmonious international tax

Of course, even if selected as the basis for an international standard, the existing principles would still require much fine-tuning and streamlining across jurisdictions, not to mention complicated transition arrangements. Definitions of residency and source would presumably have to be unified (e.g., regarding who is considered a resident where and the source and characterization of certain types of income); different types of entities and transactions would have to be standardized; determinations would have to be made regarding, for example, whether deductions should be unified. By no means will this be an easy task. Like the other coordinated mechanisms, the details of this arrangement could have significant distributive results (as determining source and residency rules tend to allocate taxing rights as well as incentives for economic activity). Hence, again, the designers of the standard will gain considerable power to affect the distribution of tax revenues and resources among states as well as within them. Perhaps most disturbingly, such a standard – by transferring much of the decision-making power to supranational processes and institutions, may undermine states' political autonomy, and could significantly infringe on notions of political participation and accountability, as well as undermine the subtleties of a more localized decision-making process.[30]

It is important to note that in order to promote efficient competition among states, a standardized tax system should emphatically *not* include a unified tax rate. Rather, it should allow for – even facilitate – efficient price competition among the various jurisdictions for the different bundles of public services they offer. By preventing much of the cross-jurisdiction arbitrage opportunities, such standard-based competition should – as Chapter 4 explained – be better aligned with citizen's preferences and curb wasteful tax planning as well as the costs of navigating the complex variety of definitions and rules. Like any standard, however, such a network would face two major risks. The first would be the risk of being locked into a suboptimal standard. The second risk would be cartelization – that is, that some (strong) states would collude to create biases in their favor. Hence, despite the potential advantages of adopting a compatible standard, caution must be practiced both with regard to its initial design and its potential abuse as a cartel-building platform.[31]

order on its ruins is not a realistic option. Source taxation on business profits will be in place for a long time in the future."

[30] For a comprehensive analysis of a coordinated tax base standard in the parallel federal case see Mason, *see supra* note 26 at 1288–1306.

[31] If not enough countries adopt the same standard, however, the problems of transaction costs and free riding may not be resolved. If different groups of countries were to offer varying standards, another type of competition – among standards – could evolve. This

It is also likewise important not to disregard the effect of such a regime on tax-haven countries. Such countries could derive extra benefits from undercutting the network. They could offer taxpayers precisely those features that other countries fear the most: planning and arbitrage opportunities, concealment of information from other tax authorities, and weak tax-collection enforcement. A tax-haven state could, for example, enable foreign investors to reduce their tax burdens in their home countries[32] by using competing definitions in its tax laws,[33] by providing creative ways to pay back taxes that can be credited in the country of residence,[34] or by simply refusing to share information with other countries.[35] Such countries can benefit from either attracting more investments and more residents or simply by collecting greater "toll charges" for their tax-haven services. Indeed, the more countries that join the prevailing network, the greater the incentive for tax havens to refrain from joining, and the more rewarding competing *against*, rather than *within*, the standard becomes for them. This derives from the fact that as countries join the network, although the

situation typically creates a "winner takes all" scenario, where the dominant standard tends to "take over" the market. See Stanley M. Besen & Joseph Farrell, *Choosing How to Compete: Strategies and Tactics in Standardization*, 8 J. ECON. PERSP. 117 (1994). Hence, absent consensus, we could expect different groups of countries to adopt different types of standards, until one standard predominates. Which groups of countries will be in a position to offer such a winning standard – and what advantages and disadvantages it may present for different countries – is another interesting question but, again, beyond the scope of this book. The immediate suspects are the OECD and G20, but other options, such as the EU and developing countries, could be interesting alternatives. *See, e.g.,* the recent BRICS AND THE EMERGENCE OF INTERNATIONAL TAX COORDINATION (Yariv Brauner & Pasquale Pistone eds., 2015), which takes a serious look at BRICS countries as a rising power in the international tax arena.

[32] *See* Marian, *supra* note 4.

[33] Thus, for example, differing definitions of corporate residency could establish foreign residency; differing definitions of debt and equity could transform dividend income into interest and vice versa; differing definitions of what constitutes royalties and what are the products of a sale of intellectual property could convert regular income into capital gains; differences in definitions could lead to the treatment of a transaction as a sale of property in one country and a lease in another; and differing definitions as to what constitutes a corporation and a partnership could allow for the flow-through of income and deductions.

[34] For some examples, *see* Charles I. Kingson, *The David Tillinghast Lecture: Taxing the Future*, 51 TAX L. REV. 641 (1996).

[35] For more detailed examples of tax-planning opportunities, *see, e.g.,* David H. Rosenbloom, *The David R. Tilinghast Lecture: International Tax Arbitrage and the "International Tax System,"* 53 TAX L. REV. 137 (2000); Edward D. Kleinbard, *Stateless Income*, 11 FLA. TAX REV. 699, 706 (2011); Dagan, *supra* note 12; Marian, *supra* note 4; IMF, SPILLOVERS IN INTERNATIONAL CORPORATE TAXATION 11 (2014); OECD, ADDRESSING BASE EROSION AND PROFIT SHIFTING (2013), http://dx.doi.org/10.1787/9789264192744-en.

network externalities increase, the pool of competitors for tax-avoiding taxpayers shrinks and – assuming that the mass of tax-avoiders does not decrease proportionally – the potential gains from tax-haven services increase.[36] Thus, some countries could certainly benefit from adopting an anti-standard tax system, resulting in the emergence of a parallel regime of non-network countries that thrive on assisting tax avoiders.

Whether a standard or anti-standard norm ultimately prevails is a big question. But what is also evident is that this dynamic sharpens the dichotomy between "legitimate" network members and "illegitimate" haven countries. Assuming a critical mass of countries adopt the network standard, they could use the fact that other countries have not adopted it to their advantage: the fact that a taxpayer resides or invests in a nonstandard country could help them flush out potential tax avoiders and identify "lemons." An effective network would ideally be able to distinguish between "good" and "bad" regimes based simply on whether or not they apply the standard. Presumably, countries operating outside the network are more likely to be tax havens. Thus, an effective network could inhibit free riding and arbitrage opportunities simply by punishing residents and investors in non-network countries. This could include imposing harsher tax rates on them, disallowing their taxes for credit purposes, blacklisting them, or subjecting their tax returns to more stringent scrutiny. At least theoretically (and, again, assuming a critical mass of countries that adopt the network standard), this could significantly improve the prospects of the standard's expansion and sustainability. Ideally, the BEPS Project could pursue this very end: namely, to ensure that as many countries as possible join the network of "legitimate" countries, thereby isolating non-network countries and enabling better targeted enforcement.[37]

To conclude, overcoming the gaps and frictions among the various jurisdictions and curtailing free-riding opportunities and transaction

---

[36] May Elsayyad & Kai A. Konrad, *Fighting Multiple Tax Havens*, 86 J. INT'L ECON. 295 (2012) (using this rationale to argue in favor of a "big bang" multilateral agreement over a sequential process of limiting tax havens one by one).

[37] Yariv Brauner, *BEPS: An Interim Evaluation*, 6 WORLD TAX J. 31 (Feb. 4, 2014), http://online .ibfd.org/kbase/#topic=doc&url=/collections/wtj/html/wtj_2014_01_int_3.html&WT.z_ nav=Navigation&colid=4948. Brauner argues that a paradigm shift in the norms of the current OECD-model based regime is necessary and that the BEPS's soft-law anti-abuse domestic laws are insufficient. In their stead, he suggests "more sophisticated allocation rules, active collaboration between tax authorities, departure from the bilateral-only structure of the international tax regime, and some form of implementation assuring mechanisms, to name a few. The introduction of such paradigm shift would be the primary test for the success of the BEPS project." *Id.* at 13.

costs are, indeed, the most acute challenge of the decentralized, competitive international tax regime, as current efforts in the international taxation arena indicate. As noted above, there are a few ways to think about potential solutions. Solutions could focus on the planning mechanisms, similar to the approach taken in the relevant parts of the BEPS Project. They could also think outside the current box and initiate a multilateral regime that allocates revenues or taxing rights among the relevant countries, opt for a different tax base altogether, or they could implement an elaborate standard for the operation of national taxing systems. Needless to say, all of these solutions entail a significant degree of cooperation among states; they all entail substantial political efforts and staggering amounts of detail coordination. Without any intention of minimizing these costs, what I have tried to stress throughout this book is that such cooperation, albeit undeniably necessary for increasing the efficiency of tax competition, should be limited to setting the rules of the game – so as to control transaction costs and limit free riding but at the same time prevent the undercutting of productive competition among states.

c.   An Antitrust Agency for States?

One crucial threat for the efficiency as well as the distributive results of the market – and the international tax market is no exception – is market dominance of a single market actor or the collusion of a number of market-actors that might tilt the market to their benefit by excluding their competitors or directly exploiting consumers. These threats are particularly formidable where some cooperation among market actors already exists, and even more so in a network structured market, where network products increase the risk of cartelistic behavior. Thus, an inherent danger of a cooperative regime – particularly one that includes a cooperative mechanism for constant updating, such as the multilateral instrument – is that cooperation might trigger cartelistic behavior among its initiators. As explained in Chapter 5, cooperating states may find it easy and helpful to use the shared framework as a platform for coordinating their taxes and thereby increasing their tax rates or promoting other self-interests (e.g., favorable allocation of tax bases) at the expense of some (e.g., smaller, less organized or late-comer) states or of taxpayers in general.

This challenge implies that competitive tax regime should strive to prevent anti-competitive behavior. To expand our institutional imagination, we could consider an antitrust agency for states. This agency would focus on preventing market actors from colluding in ways that impede competition and impose costs on other states as well as on taxpayers-consumers. The challenge, of course, is how to distinguish pro-competition cooperation from anticompetitive collusion. The end point of the spectrum of cases is quite clear: Coordination of increased tax rates or increased market-shares (e.g., cooperation by countries of residence to reduce source base taxation) would curtail competition under this regime. But coordination that would improve market access by providing more information would not. Similarly, coordination to reduce transaction costs and make use of economies of scale or scope in the design and enforcement of tax laws could facilitate more efficient competition. And yet, certain requirements could constitute barriers to competition (for example, pricey compliance with information-sharing requirements would bar certain poor countries from joining the club), while the bundling of certain benefits with resources that only some of the countries obtain could be anticompetitive (for example, the bundling of IP tax rates with actual research and development that benefits countries with superior R&D capacities could be an abuse of market dominance).

The challenge, therefore, is how to preserve or even increase cooperation that protects state sovereignty and sustains states' ability to independently design their tax systems in line with their preferences and thus allow for a variety of available jurisdictions, while preventing cooperative efforts from imposing excessive costs on certain jurisdictions and taxpayers in general.

In setting the guidelines for such an agency, one could draw on the expertise and experience of national antitrust agencies, in particular their regulations of joint ventures, trade associations and other network industries. I make no pretense of having the necessary expertise to offer concrete guidelines, nor the exact institutional safeguards (e.g., to prevent the abuse of such antitrust regulatory power). And yet, I would expect that, ideally, such an agency would ban any coordination that affects the autonomous setting of tax rates (prices) as well as public goods and services, and prevent any abuse of market-dominance and of barriers to taxpayers' ability to shift their residency or economic activities between jurisdictions. At the same time, the agency should support mechanisms that enhance transparency and the creation of legislative "manuals" so as to reduce transaction costs and the costs of resource and taxpayers' mobility between jurisdictions. Another challenge that could arise for such an agency would be whether it, in itself, could be insulated from political involvement (particularly of strong states). If the agency itself is biased in favor of stronger countries, it may (even) cynically serve to limit the capacity of weaker states to cooperate.

7.7 Conclusion

The normative challenges of income taxation under the current decentralized international tax regime are undoubtedly reason for concern. States – once the sole rulers of income taxation – are currently in a fragile position, facing competition by their peers and the pressure of MNEs. Under competition, states can no longer independently set and enforce the tax policies they (or, rather, their constituents) endorse. Instead, they find themselves subject to market forces – retaining only an impoverished version of tax sovereignty: one that is fragmented and determined by the relative market power of the states and their constituents. This marketized, fragmentized, and decentralized setting of contemporary international tax undermines efficiency, distributive justice, and ideals of political participation.

Instead of the almost instinctive reaction to the challenges of competition – that is, to advocate its curtailment – I have suggested in this book embracing competition and, rather than working against it (which I argued may be both impractical and bring about unwarranted efficiency *and* distributive results), capitalizing on its strengths. Thus, I suggested, the sense of urgency that "something needs to be done" on the international tax front will be better served if channeled towards a pro-competition initiative, as a vehicle for promoting greater efficiency as well as global justice. The main problem, I have argued, is not the very existence of the decentralized market for international taxation, but the fact that this market suffers from serious market failures that should be attended to in order to improve its operation.

The purpose of this book is not to provide solutions but to explore the problems of international taxation, to rearticulate its goals, and to shed a new (and critical) light on the calls for international cooperation on tax matters. These are times of change for international taxation. The public and political interest in this matter, alongside the calls for much-needed change, seem to be rallying support for increased cooperation among states in an effort to save their ability to tax. But not every form of cooperation is beneficial for all of the cooperating actors: cooperative initiatives also entail costs, some of which are too often imposed on developing countries and particularly on the underprivileged groups within them. These costs justify a serious consideration of the competitive alternative.

The ideas I have put forward to contend with the international tax market failures are admittedly imperfect and provisional; none of these suggestions is ready for use. My goal, however, is not to advocate for specific mechanisms or struggle with their highly complex details, but rather to set an agenda for a well functioning competitive international tax market that would enlist cooperative efforts to increase the global welfare pie, but would be cautious not to allow cooperative efforts to increase global injustice.

Many of the challenges of the current international tax regime derive from its decentralized competitive structure, but centralization is *not* necessarily the answer. Rather than strive for a more comprehensive multilateral regime that curtails tax competition a multilateral accord should seek to improve – indeed, perfect – competition. A coordinated international effort, despite its acknowledged difficulties, can – and I believe should – support an efficient *and* justice-enhancing competition.

INDEX

agenda-setting, 177–180
allocation of jurisdiction to tax, 44–50
antitrust agency, for states, 242–244
arbitrage (tax), 128, 198–199, 216–217,
  234–242
authority allocation, 44–50
Avi-Yonah, R., 36, 46–47, 121–122, 130,
  147–148
avoidance (tax), 127–128

Baistrocchi, E., 167–168
benefit taxation, 39
BEPS initiative, 157–165, 234–235
bilateral cooperation. *See also* tax
  treaties
  distributive ramifications of, 49–50
  effect on foreign direct investment,
    108–109
  game theory application to, 4
  in double taxation prevention,
    73–74
  in information sharing, 152–155
  in tax treaties, 81, 86–87, 143–144,
    146–149, 152–154, 166–168,
    177–178, 183, 237
  instruments of, 152–155
  interests served by, 7
  Tax Information Exchange
    Agreements (TIEAs), 152–154
  tax treaties history, 146–149
Blake, M., 190
Brauner, Y., 181
BRICS countries, 181

Caney, S., 190
capital export neutrality (CEN), 54–55,
  58–59

capital import neutrality (CIN), 55–58
capital ownership neutrality (CON),
  56–57
cartelization of states policies, 143,
  173–174, 242–244
coercive power of state
  and legitimacy, 199–202
  as rationale in cooperation, 144
  in distributive justice, 191–195, 201,
    206–211
Cohen, J., 191–195
collection, from foreign residents, 106,
  113
Commodification Critique of the
  Market, 216
  and identity, 22–23
Common Reporting Standard
  (Standard for Automatic Exchange
  of Financial Account Information
  in Tax Matters), 155–157, 232–233
competition/tax competition. *See also*
  bilateral cooperation; multilateral
  cooperation
  alteration of state's role by, 6
  and arbitrage, 128, 198–199,
    216–217, 234–242
  as solution, 223–225
  attempts to curtail, 149–152
  costs, benefits of, 121–128
  distributive justice effects of, 35–37,
    121–125, 227–228
  efficiency effects of, 31–35, 125–128
  foreign investment taxation, 31–32
  for residents, 33–34
  fragmentation, 26–30, 33–34
  harmful, 75, 146–154, 165–166,
    180–183, 213–214

location-specific rents, 36–37
  personal, collective identities, 38–41
  political participation and, 40, 48–49
  public services provision, 125–127
  state as recruiter of investors and
    businesses, 24–26, 31, 33,
    122–124, 197–198
  state-citizen relationship and, 12–14,
    23, 124–125
  state power inequality in, 228–229
  tax avoidance and, 127–128
  tax incentives, 39
  vs. cooperation as solution, 4–5, 10,
    120–121
  wealth/mobility connection, 36,
    38–40
  wealth redistribution and, 122–124,
    227–228
competitive neutrality, 56–57
Convention on Mutual Administrative
    Assistance in Tax Matters,
    155–156
cooperation. See also bilateral
    cooperation; multilateral
    cooperation
  inequality, distributive disparity
    among states/individuals, 206–211
  vs. competition as solution, 4–5, 10,
    120–121
credits. See also double taxation
    prevention

deductions. See also double taxation
    prevention
developing countries. See also BEPS
    initiative; multilateral
    cooperation; tax treaties
  asymmetrical tax treaties, 111–113
  barriers to competition, removal of,
    224–225, 229–230
  benefit-maximizing strategies,
    113–118
  biases against labor in, 143
  cartelization against, 143, 173–174,
    242–244
  desirability of tax treaties, 100
  distributive consequences of tax
    treaties to, 102–104, 119

distributive justice as duty to, 192,
    204–205, 207
  foreign direct investment in,
    115–116, 134, 210
  information sharing, transparency,
    152, 165, 230–234
  lock-in effect and, 174–176
  multilateral coordination
    disadvantages to, 137, 183–184
  relative bargaining power of,
    132–137, 168–170, 181–183
  revenue disparity in tax treaties, 7, 73
  strategies regarding tax treaties,
    113–114
  tax revenue allocation, 44–50, 135
  tax treaties, cooperation, motivations
    for involvement in, 8–9, 102, 110,
    113, 144, 167–168
  tax treaties, effects on, 77–78,
    100–104
  tax treaties rejection by, 116–118
  UN model, 101, 114–115, 148
distributive justice
  competition, effects on, 35–37
  cooperation as solution, 203–206
  critique, 221–222
  inequality, distributive disparity
    states within, 206–211
  multilateral cooperation in, 130,
    132–137, 140–141, 188–189
  political justice, 191
  redistribution as duty, 185–187, 191,
    211
  state legitimacy, sovereignty and, 10,
    187–188, 196–199, 206–211
  state's roles, coercive powers in,
    193–196, 225–227
  taxation goals, 17–19
distributive justice critique, 221–222
double taxation. See international
    taxation
double taxation prevention. See also tax
    treaties
  bilateral cooperation in, 73–74
  credits, 53–54, 65–66, 91–93, 98–99,
    105–106
  deductions, 53–54, 65–66, 86–91
  deferral, 66

double taxation prevention (*cont.*)
  economic allegiance, 45–49
  exemptions, 53–54, 65–66, 96–98,
    105–106
  foreign tax credit limitation, 66–67

efficiency
  as taxation goal, 15–17
  competition, effects on, 31–35,
    125–128
  multilateral cooperation costs to,
    137–140
emerging countries. *See* BRICS
    countries; developing countries
equal distribution, 18–19
equal sacrifice, 18–19
exemptions. *See* double taxation
    prevention

FATCA, 155
foreign direct investment
  bilateral cooperation and, 108–109
  in developing countries, 115–116,
    134, 210
  labor and, 62–65
  multilateral cooperation and,
    135–136
  tax treaties and, 82–83, 106–110,
    115–116, 169
  taxation of, 31–32
formulary apportionment, 176,
    235–236
fragmentation
  and tax planning, 27–30
  competition/tax competition, 33
  of sovereignty, 198–199
  of taxing and spending regimes,
    26–30
free riding, 219, 239

game theory, 4, 7, 60–62, 80–81
  analysis of tax treaties, 82–98
Global Forum, 152–154
global justice
  coercion, 191–195, 201, 206–211
  coercion and legitimacy, 199–202
  cosmopolitan, conception of, 190,
    211

left institutionalism, 191–193,
    195–196, 211
political justice, conceptions of,
    188–189, 191, 214
statist conception of, 9–10, 185–189,
    191–196, 199–211
global-normative approach
  applicability, 6–7

havens (tax), 27–30, 131–132, 150–151,
    198–199, 240–241
Hirschman, A., 228–229

identity
  community as tax policy
    consideration, 20–23
  personal, collective identities,
    38–41
IMF, 78–79, 116–118
incorporation, taxation and, 24–26
individual relocation, taxation and,
    24–26
information
  asymmetry, 218–219
  automatic exchange of, 156–159
  sharing, transparency, 152, 165,
    230–234
Instrument to Modify Bilateral Tax
    Treaties, 170–171
international taxation
  allocation of jurisdiction to tax,
    44–50
  anticompetitive collusion in, 220
  as decentralized competitive market,
    1–2
  cooperation as strategy, 68–70
  current regime, 4, 6–7, 159–165,
    168–170, 236–237
  deferral, 66
  domestic tax policy and, 2
  foreign investment, 62–65
  free riding in, 219, 239
  information asymmetry in,
    218–219
  market failures in, 216–217, 239
  national interests as focus of, 44,
    65–68
  national preferences in, 62–65

strategic taxation, 60–62
taxation authority allocation,
    44–50
undermining political sphere
    critique, 222–223

Kingson, C., 67–68
Knoll, M., 56–57

League of Nations report, 44–50
lock-in effect, 174–176

market failures critique of international
    taxation, 216–220
marketization
    and tax planning, 27–30
    capital markets as leverage, 31–33
    and competition for residents, 33
    international taxation and, 24–26
market valuation in coercive
    legitimacy, 196–199
Mason, R., 56–57
mobility
    of capital, 2–3, 8, 31–32, 64–65,
        124–127, 130, 135–136, 139–140,
        177–178, 242–244
    of residents, 5–6, 14, 24–26, 33,
        122–124, 139–140, 196–202, 213,
        218–219, 225–227, 242–244
Moellendorf, D., 191–193
multilateral cooperation. See also
    competition/tax competition
    achievement, sustainability of,
        130–132, 215–216
    agenda-setting, 177–180
    asymmetric capabilities, 168–170
    cartelization, 143, 173–174,
        242–244
    challenges in, 214–215
    collective good as rationale,
        144–145
    competition, attempts to curtail,
        149–152
    Convention on Mutual
        Administrative Assistance in Tax
        Matters, 155–156
    costs, outcomes of generally, 7–8
    defections, 131–132, 152

distributive justice in, 130, 132–137,
    140, 203–206
efficiency costs, benefits of,
    137–140
FATCA and, 155
foreign investment effects, 135–136
Global Forum, 152–154
governmental waste, incentives to
    reduce, 138–139
harmonization of rates, policies,
    128–130
inequality, distributive disparity
    among states/individuals,
    206–211
information, automatic exchange of,
    156–159
information sharing, transparency,
    152, 165, 230–234
lock-in effect, 174–176
network effects, 170–173, 176,
    235–239
OECD's role in power structure
    remodeling, 180–183
participation, rationales for,
    142–143, 166
participation, strategic rationales for,
    166–168
revenue allocation, 135
revenue vs. financial market
    orientations in, 132–133
special interests, effects on, 139
state sovereignty as rationale, 144
strategic consideration, 7–8, 58–59,
    70–71, 146–149, 166–168
tax evasion, 150–151
tax havens, 27–30, 131–132,
    150–151, 198–199, 240–241
Tax Information Exchange
    Agreements (TIEAs), 152–154
vs. competition as solution, 4–5, 10,
    120–121
multilateral instrument, 159–165,
    170–171, 224–225

Nagel, T., 191–196, 199–202, 208
network effects, 170–173, 176,
    235–239
    lock-in effect, 174–176

neutrality
  capital export neutrality (CEN), 54–55, 58–59
  capital import neutrality (CIN), 55–58
  capital ownership neutrality (CON), 56–57
  competitive neutrality, 56–57
  efficiency and, 15–17
  flaws of, 57–60, 68–69
  in promotion of welfare, 50–53
  national neutrality, 56
  partial, 53–57, 69

OECD Model Tax Convention, 78–79, 101, 113–114, 147–148, 232–233
OECD's role in regime design, 180–183
optimal taxation, 16–17

partial neutrality, 53–57, 69
personal, collective identities, 38–41
planning (tax), 26–30, 198–199
political participation, political sphere, 40, 48–49, 191, 222–223

Race to the Bottom, 7–8, 35–36, 120–121, 123–124, 128–130, 143, 224–225
redistribution as duty, 185–187, 191, 211
Report on Harmful Tax Competition (OECD), 149–154
residency
  competition/tax competition for, 33–34
  state as recruiter, 24–26, 31, 33, 122–124, 197–198
  state-citizen relationship and, 12–14, 23, 124–125
Richman-Musgrave, P., 50–51
Roin, J., 137–138
Ronzoni, M., 203–204

Sabel, C., 191–195
Sangiovanni, A., 191–193
Shaviro, D., 59, 70

Smith, P., 190
source (basis of taxation)
  transaction classification, 27–30
source rules, 105–106, 198–199
  withholding taxes, 175–176
Standard for Automatic Exchange of Financial Account Information in Tax Matters (Common Reporting Standard), 155–157, 232–233
state as recruiter of investors and businesses, 24–26, 31, 33, 122–124, 197–198
strategic taxation, 60–62

tax arbitrage, 128, 198–199, 216–217, 234–242
taxation
  allocation of jurisdiction to tax, 44–50
  collection, from foreign residents, 106, 113
  distributive justice goals of, 17–19
  efficiency goals of, 15–17
  fragmentation, 26–30
  identity, community and, 20–23
  labor, foreign investment and, 62–65
  marketization and, 24–26
  ring fenced activities, 31–32
tax avoidance, 127–128. See also tax planning
tax havens, 27–30, 131–132, 150–151, 198–199, 240–241
Tax Information Exchange Agreements (TIEAs), 152–154
tax planning, 26–30, 198–199
tax rules, streamlining, 234–242
tax treaties. See also double taxation prevention
  advantages, benefits of, 105–107
  agenda-setting, 177–180
  as regressive redistribution mechanism, 7, 77–78, 102–104
  asymmetrical, 111–113
  bilateral cooperation in, 81, 86–87, 143–144, 146–149, 152–154, 166–168, 177–178, 183, 237
  credits, 91–93, 98–99, 105–106

deductions, 86–91
developing/emerging countries,
    benefit maximizing strategies,
    113–118
developing/emerging countries,
    effects on, 77–78, 100–104
double, 27–30
double taxation alleviation by,
    72–80, 100–102
exemptions, 96–98, 105–106
foreign direct investment and,
    82–83, 106–110, 115–116, 169
game theory analysis of, 82–98
history of, 146–149
host country national interests,
    82–84
host country policy preferences, 84
jurisdiction, revenue allocation,
    99–100, 102–104
lock-in effect, 174–176

network effects, 170–173, 176,
    235–239
OECD Model Tax Convention,
    78–79, 101, 113–114, 147–148,
    232–233
participation, strategic rationales for,
    166–168
relief granted by, 76–77
residence country national interests,
    84–86
residence-host country interactions,
    74–76, 80–82, 100
revenue allocation disparity, 73
single tax ideal, 101
subsidies, 82–84
symmetrical, 111
tax-sparing arrangements, 115–116
    UN model, 101, 114–115, 148
Tiebout, C. M., 122–123
transaction costs, 216–217, 239